The publisher and the University of California Press Foundation gratefully acknowledge the generous support of the Atkinson Family Foundation Imprint in Higher Education.

THE ATKINSON FAMILY 

IMPRINT IN HIGHER EDUCATION

The Atkinson Family Foundation has endowed this imprint to illuminate the role of higher education in contemporary society.

Justice Lessons

Justice Lessons

System-Affected Scholars and the Future of Criminal Justice Transformation

Grant E. Tietjen

UNIVERSITY OF CALIFORNIA PRESS

University of California Press
Oakland, California

Library of Congress Cataloging-in-Publication Data

Names: Tietjen, Grant E., 1975– author.
Title: Justice lessons : system-affected scholars and the future of criminal justice transformation / Grant E. Tietjen.
Description: Oakland, California : University of California Press, [2025] | Includes bibliographical references and index.
Identifiers: LCCN 2024026867 (print) | LCCN 2024026868 (ebook) | ISBN 9780520394070 (cloth) | ISBN 9780520394087 (paperback) | ISBN 9780520394094 (ebook)
Subjects: LCSH: Ex-convicts—Education (Higher)—United States. | Prisoners—Education—United States. | Social justice—United States.
Classification: LCC HV8883.3.U5 T54 2025 (print) | LCC HV8883.3.U5 (ebook) | DDC 365/.6660973—dc23/eng/20240821
LC record available at https://lccn.loc.gov/2024026867
LC ebook record available at https://lccn.loc.gov/2024026868

33 32 31 30 29 28 27 26 25 24
10 9 8 7 6 5 4 3 2 1

Contents

Acknowledgments

I now realize that it takes a whole village and several years to write a book, including the support, participation, and advice of many wonderful individuals. First off, I would like to thank the legal system–affected people who allowed their voices to be heard in this book; without them, this book would not exist. I can only hope that I have done your stories justice and thank you for all of your selfless efforts in the struggle for inclusion, transformation of carceral systems and higher education, and social equality. Next, I would like to express gratitude for the endless patience, direction, and even emotional support from one of my best friends, who is also an English professor and award-winning poet, Dr. Emily Kingery. Your assistance throughout the writing process, helping me conceptualize ideas, and guidance on how to tell a story were invaluable. When I was lost in the writing process and felt hopeless, you helped me find my way out. I would also like to thank Professor Emeritus of English Dr. Carl Herzig for reading through parts of my book proposal and providing useful feedback that helped to establish the foundation of this process. Also, I would like to thank my University of California Press editor, Maura Roessner, for her infinite patience with me throughout the writing and publication process. I greatly appreciate your supportive advice and always positive encouragement. It makes a difference. Finally, I would like to thank the many other people, too numerous to mention, including my always reassuring family, several close friends, and many awesome academic colleagues (including but not limited to Professor Jeffrey Ian Ross, Associate Professor Jennifer Ortiz, and Dr. Nicholas Park) for listening to my concerns during the research and writing process, for your advice, and for offering encouragement.

List of Abbreviations

ASC	American Society of Criminology
BIPOC	Black, Indigenous, and People of Color
CC	Convict Criminology
CLS	criminal legal system
DCC	Division of Convict Criminology
FBI	Federal Bureau of Investigation
FBOP	Federal Bureau of Prisons
FI	formerly incarcerated
FICGN	Formerly Incarcerated College Graduates Network
FIST	Formerly Incarcerated Stronger Together (Northeastern Illinois University)
HP3	Huskies Post Prison Pathways (University of Washington–Tacoma)
JPP	*Journal of Prisoners on Prisons*
P2P	From Prison Cells to Ph.D.
PO	parole/probation officer
PTSD	post-traumatic stress disorder
SAA	system-affected academic
TRAC	Transforming Renewing Achieving Connecting (University of Nebraska–Omaha)
USI	Underground Scholars Initiative

Introduction

The Just World Hypothesis Becomes an Unbalanced Equation

As I write this chapter, massive crowds of protesters across the U.S. (and many cities around the world) are marching against social injustices perpetrated by segments of America's criminal legal system (CLS) against oppressed and marginalized communities of color. The perpetuation of racial bias and social inequality against the poor and/or historically marginalized minorities by the U.S. CLS is certainly not a new phenomenon. The advent of the American phenomenon of mass incarceration, brought about over forty years ago by the "tough-on-crime" policies of the 1980s and 1990s, has produced a system of carceral subjugation, suffering, and tyranny that is globally unmatched. While incarcerated population numbers have dropped slightly in recent years, the U.S. still has the highest rates of incarceration of any country in the world, and the impacts of mass incarceration are still wreaking havoc on disadvantaged communities across the nation.

Nearly twenty years ago, I was part of that massive archipelago of endless prisons, state/federal/private confinement facilities, and jails, serving a sentence for a drug conviction in the Federal Bureau of Prisons (FBOP). As a new occupant of this giant system of cells, dormitory-style cellblocks, and endless drably painted steel and concrete structures, I began to experience the "pains of imprisonment" described by Sykes (1958/1974) in *Society of Captives* (which I would not read until years later) with overwhelming intensity. I struggled to make sense of all the insanity I saw around me. My incarcerated peers were ground down by the despair, the banal, never-ending routines, the mindless tedium, and the continual threat of violence that comprises some segments of prison life. Certain events stand out to me as stark reminders of the impact this environment had on the people with whom I was confined.

When incarcerated, I would walk laps around the cellblock tiers to pass the time. During one of these strolls I encountered a young Black man sitting on a stairway, and he said something to me that I will never forget. The tier I was walking around was located in a cellblock of the Federal Transfer Center, an FBOP facility in Oklahoma City where I was an inmate serving time for a drug crime.[1] The other man reached out to make conversation, asking me where I was from, and when I asked where he was from, he responded with a blank, catatonic stare that purveyed despair, "Nowhere, man." There was nothing left to say, as he seemed uninterested in continuing the conversation after that point. As I considered this brief conversation almost twenty years later, I thought about the degenerative effect that incarceration had on the people I encountered in prison, many of whom would return to broader society in a traumatized state (Hochstetler et al.; Liem & Kunst, 2013): frustrated, further marginalized, socially hobbled, and angry. Many incarcerated people come from oppressed Black, Indigenous, and People of Color (BIPOC) and low-income communities (Alexander, 2010; Wilkerson, 2020), having already endured lifelong exposure to the intersectional social inequalities of racism and classism (Collins, 2000; Crenshaw, 1991, 2017; Desmond & Emirbayer, 2009; Emirbayer & Desmond, 2015). In areas where social inequality is more severe (as evidenced by research I would later encounter in college) and per capita rates of incarceration are much higher (Gray, 2018; Pettit & Gutierrez, 2018; Sampson, 2019), BIPOC and low-income communities have been weakened to a point where they are rendered socially and economically incapable of survival. Yet more and more of us (system-affected people) are finding our way to higher education (Ross et al., 2010) and learning how to harness the potential that activist and critically focused scholarship has to speak to and reform systems of power and sociostructural inequality. The CLS produces a sense of hopelessness and despair in those who pass through its institutions, which can result in a defeated and frustrated worldview. The actions of system-affected activists and critical scholars can exert a positive influence on impacted individuals and communities, subsequently creating spaces for empowerment, opportunity, and transformative change.

As for myself, I grew up in homogeneously white Nebraska as a middle-class farm kid; from birth I was inculcated with a sense that society was fair and justice was blind. Lacking the formal education from which I would later learn about multiple forms of social inequality, I struggled to answer the questions of why Black and Hispanic men, and poor people in general, seemed to receive longer sentences than individuals like me. Furthermore, I saw that many of these individuals did not have good legal defenses in court, were often sent to harsher prisons than mine, and frequently seemed to be very angry and full of despair. I quickly realized that the differential treatment of my fellow BIPOC and low-income incarcerated peers within the criminal legal system was the norm, not the exception. I was witnessing what I would learn years later in college is the institutionalized and blatant racism and classism perpetuated by the criminal legal system.

As if awakening from a bad dream that one desperately tries to remember and interpret before it slips away, I still struggle to this day to make sense of the carceral dystopia that I witnessed. I continually attempt to reconcile myself with the blatant inequalities, suffering, and oppression that resided behind the walls of which I was, in some instances, also a victim. While still in prison, I tried to console myself with the "just-world" hypothesis (Lerner & Montada, 1998). I told myself that we prisoners all deserved this treatment, and in my ignorance, I believed that this was how justice was supposed to be served. While sitting in my cell, I was frequently overcome with a feeling of powerlessness. I was just a single person among millions of women and men hidden away in isolated prisons that society had chosen to forget. Yet no matter how many times I repeated to myself these trite rationalizations in an effort to make sense of my dissonant reality, I could never fully balance the equation in my head. When the concept of "equality under the law" was revealed to be a chimera, my sense of fairness and justice was shattered. Consequently, I bring to this book that weight of the internalized inequality and disharmony I have grappled with every day for the last twenty years.

The traumatic events and inequalities experienced by the system-affected people speaking within this book share the common thread of contact with the criminal legal system. Nonetheless, the drive to help others with similar experiences and to search for ways to make this situation right varies due to factors such as individual, social, racial, economic, and demographic differences. Another common thread exists in the fact that at some point during and/or after their direct exposure to the carceral system, these system-affected people accessed the opportunity to engage with higher education, scholarship, and activism (as individuals and in organized groups). In this framework, they began the work of balancing the equation of justice for their directly contacted peers and for themselves.

INTRODUCING AN EMERGENT LIVED-EXPERIENCE MOVEMENT TO THE CLS

The criminal justice and criminological disciplines have filled libraries with scholarship on subjects such as statistical analysis of crime data, crime theory, and ethnographies of crime-related subcultures. Thousands of books, reports, and peer-reviewed articles span decades. Yet despite all of this study and work, the CLS track record is generally regarded as an abysmal failure. The U.S. has the world's largest prison system (Weiss & MacKenzie, 2010), has high rates of recidivism (Alper et al., 2018), and performs very poorly in comparison to other developed countries on many criminal justice performance metrics (Richardson & Hemenway, 2011). Yet I do not intend to repeat a bunch of crime statistics that you have likely already heard. I want to present to you a largely unexplored facet of the CLS and the criminological academy. The carcerally impacted population has for years been in direct contact with the CLS, been incarcerated in prisons, endured the denigrating collateral consequences of criminal convictions, and/or lost family members to the justice system.[2] Yet while continuing to endure the damaging effects of carceral contact, this expanding and diverse population has become proactive in social justice measures. Among many other things, formerly incarcerated (FI) individuals are earning college diplomas (Binnall et al., 2022; Copenhaver et al., 2007; Murillo, 2021; Ross & Vianello, 2021), organizing impactful activist-scholar networks, attaining academic and professional positions, and mentoring other lived-experience students. They are also now a growing presence at the research and policy tables that may shape the future of criminal justice in the U.S.

I assert that an effective means to build support for both (1) elimination of the social need for prisons and (2) humanistic transformation of higher education's knowledge and perceptions of carcerally impacted people and mass incarceration itself is through the growing activist scholarship movement of system-affected academics. Their lived-experience perspectives can provide missing insights needed to assist with this process. The use of the insider viewpoints within system-affected academic (SAA) research and literature carries on this high-impact social science tradition. An example is the classic sociological book by W. E. B. Du Bois, *The Souls of Black Folk* (Du Bois, 1953), in which the author used examples from his own life to elucidate and provide valuable context for concepts (e.g., discrimination, racism, racial inequality). This book will seek to use the lived experiences of the author and the scholars he interviewed in the same capacity.

Further, contained within this growing activist scholarship movement is a dynamic that could provide vital structural support for the reciprocal changes that occur between the individual SAA and their affiliated institutions of higher education. From 2020 to 2021, SAAs were interviewed about how they experienced higher education, their relationship to the SAA movement, and their interpretation of this growing social justice action. Then, representative examples of SAA written scholarship and media are interpreted, to present the academic and social justice messages/themes contained within.[3]

This book presents a movement that harnesses the worth and meaning of surviving oppression and struggle. For example, recent literature such as Miller's (2021) exploration of living through the struggles of reentry for FI people in Chicago, *Halfway Home*, presented an example of the value of carceral lived experience. This book is about a growing movement of system-affected people who, having engaged with formal education, are determined to use their lived experience to help their oppressed peers. Within their struggles for social equity within higher education, a reciprocal transformative process between SAA members and the university has been identified. Having found agency through educational credentials, people within what I identify as the SAA movement are attempting to play a part in focusing the missions of higher education and the CLS toward engaging with humanistic social justice. This endeavor includes a strong representation of engagement in the process of prison abolition among the ranks of many newer SAA members, as a means of disassembling systems of oppression. A framing of the systemic injustice problems within the U.S. CLS and the early efforts of SAAs is necessary to understand the historical underpinnings of the SAA movement.

OUT OF THE CHAOS OF A BROKEN CLS AND THE EARLY PHASE OF SAAs

Out of the chaos and social upheaval of the tough-on-crime era, oppressive and draconian criminal justice polices emerged in both the U.S. and abroad. Members of the SAA population, often working together with like-minded justice-free scholars (those without carceral system contact), are attempting to work toward greater justice and equality for those impacted by the justice system. This movement's increasing sphere of influence is generated from the actions of both individuals and organized groups. Previous literature (Richards & Ross, 2001; Ross & Richards, 2003; Earle, 2016; Tietjen, 2019) has argued that the impetus behind the organization of groups of justice-impacted activist and critical criminology scholars was the vexation and anger that incarcerated people, FI people, and their allies experienced when the wider framework formed by academia, prison administrations, society at large, and politicians ignored and/or marginalized their voices, experiential wisdom, and concerns.

Formerly incarcerated, acquaintance-contacted (incarcerated family and loved ones), and conviction-only (legal conviction without incarceration) members of these groups directly experienced the oppression, structural bias, and discrimination (in varying capacities) that the nineteen million people who have been convicted of felonies in the U.S. (Shannon et al., 2017) endure every day. Further, many scholars without a criminal conviction may have had indirect experience with the socially destructive and oppressive impacts of mass incarceration, such as having an incarcerated acquaintance. During their arduous journeys from prison to higher education and academia, many early SAA members, who survived the difficult journey from the justice system to scholarship, discovered that institutions of higher education could serve as a powerful and legitimate conduit through which to deliver their critical scholarship and knowledge to society while also providing assistance in bringing social equality to the millions oppressed by the CLS. In addition, it must be noted that SAA groups have been working alongside a recent powerful social movement of system-affected activists and advocates who are working outside of academia at the community and carceral system levels (from within and outside of the CLS) to bring about reform and progressive change within the U.S. and international justice systems (Berger, 2013; LeBel, 2009; Maruna, 2017; Smith, 2021).

Within this book, the population of focus, which I am part of, is referred to as *system-affected academics* (SAAs), the respective organized networks of activist and critical scholars are referred to as SAA groups, and the entire movement of all groups is referred to as the SAA movement. The adjective *affected*, meaning "acted upon; influenced," was not chosen out of convenience, but out of a sense of the breadth of variation in regard to the experiences carcerally impacted individuals describe and how they interpret the manner in which the CLS intersects with their lives. The CLS effect described by many people with direct system contact is quite varied and multifaceted. Some people with direct system contact describe prison as a terrible place from which they received no benefit and through which they suffered a great deal of trauma (Murphy, 2012). They left prison in worse shape than when they went in. Within another segment of research, FI people describe the suffering experienced in prison as generating the personal motivation to positively change their lives (Richards, 2004; Tietjen, 2013; Bint Faisal et al., 2018). Others point to experiencing a degree of relative stability in the often tedious yet rigidly structured hours and days that predominantly make up prison schedules (Tietjen et al., 2019; Honeywell, 2021), when compared to the often chaotic and/or problematic life circumstances many people in prison found themselves in prior to incarceration. Yet I must strongly emphasize that virtually none of these perspectives professed that the institution of prison was intrinsically beneficial in and of itself, although they did describe the survival and adaptation reactions to the harsh conditions of incarceration as altering individual behaviors in capacities that were of benefit to their educational journeys.

For example, I describe my own experience with incarceration as multifaceted, since it felt as if I had been living in multiple realities at the same time. First and foremost, I would describe my encounter with the carceral system as quite damaging in many regards. I still bear the psychological scars of its trauma to this day (nearly twenty years later). Through another lens, the harsh shock of prison provided space for latent positive developments to take hold within my life, such as the reestablishment of my love for learning and education. For example, as a result of the hopeful encouragement I received during my dark hours of incarceration from the many mentors (e.g., friends outside of prison, past professors, many fellow incarcerated people) who took an interest in my well-being, I was influenced to engage in certain positive changes (such as education).

Yet I want to firmly establish that prison did not intentionally "do" this *for* me. In other words, I am *not* arguing that prisons as an institution benefit those who are housed there, which would wrongly encourage the use of incarceration as good policy and practice. On the contrary, I take the stance that prisons have a very destructive impact on the people confined there, such as amplifying and creating mental health problems (Collier, 2014), eroding supportive social networks (Murray, 2005), diminishing opportunities for life-course success (Ewald & Uggen, 2012), and functioning as an agent of traumatization (Murphy, 2012). The system, through its tradition of referring to prison residents in institutional nomenclature as numbers or "inmates," stripped us of our humanity. In addition, we, as incarcerated men, were continually subjected to verbal degradation from certain members of the prison staff. For many people behind the walls, prison is a constant battle with anxiety and depression. When incarcerated, my mental health declined, and I began taking medication as a means of grappling with the overwhelming strains of incarceration. In regard to trauma, Battle et al. (2003) found that the demographics of prison populations, which include a greater likelihood of previous substance addiction, poverty, and childhood abuse, place the incarcerated at a far higher risk for post-traumatic stress disorder (PTSD). In their meta-analysis, Baranyi et al. (2018) discovered that rates of PTSD in incarcerated populations around the globe were much higher than in the general population. Many FI people experienced the long-lasting effects of prison traumatization for years after their release back into society (Bloom & Bradshaw, 2021; Morash et al., 2020; Murphy, 2012). Another factor possibly associated with PTSD in prisons is the fear of violent victimization (Murphy, 2004). In the majority of the fourteen or more facilities I was housed in while under the supervision of the FBOP, I was frequently exposed to and lived in constant fear of violence. I witnessed men under severe duress in often heavily overcrowded facilities struggling to confront the strain of the carceral environment. Schmid and Jones (1991) argued that FI people who return to society have had their identities permanently altered by incarceration. They cannot separate the prison personality from their former personality. Consequently, returning to society as a "normally" functioning individual after enduring such strain was very difficult for me. I often experienced increased difficulty with engaging comfortably in everyday social interactions. Navigating public engagements was frequently clouded by my institutionalized mentality, in alignment with Clemmer's (1940) concept of prisonization. I had internalized many behaviors that were necessary to successfully navigate the daily interactions of prison, including the adoption of a new set of cultural norms. I was prone to overanalyzing, distrusting, and/or misinterpreting others' remarks to me and was often offended by only slight forms of disrespect. Referring to the hypervigilance I developed in the carceral landscape, I was constantly looking over my shoulder and would grow nervous if I was not facing the door in a room.

SAA members' pathways to academic and activist positions and careers, as well as the actions they engage in while working in those positions, have been influenced by a complex mix of interactions and experiences within the CLS. While certain events that occurred during incarceration and CLS interactions may have worked in some incarcerated individuals' favor, spurring them toward educational attainment and self-improvement, other dynamics of the carceral environment have hindered potential life-course success, creating health and structural impediments/hurdles that are difficult to overcome. The dynamics created by the summation and contrasts of these difficult and traumatic experiences may explain what has motivated many SAA individuals to engage in critical and activist scholarship, while also shaping transformative attitudes (including decarceration) toward the CLS.

Transformative SAAs: We Have Always Been Here

Within the totality of the concept of higher education, history has produced many examples of renowned and/or infamous great thinkers, advocates for justice, and scholars who were system affected. Of course I would not classify all of the worldviews of this diverse grouping of individuals as aligned with the values and goals of the SAA movement. Nonetheless, these individual lives and actions reflect the fact that various people who came into contact with the justice system were able to go on to access, utilize, and work within higher education and to change the world in various positive capacities. For example, Dr. Martin Luther King Jr., wrote his famous *Letter from Birmingham Jail* (King, 1992) while being held in that Alabama jail after his arrest for participation in various civil rights protests in 1963. King, one of the most influential activists for human rights in the history of humanity, had received his doctorate in theology before his short stint in jail for civil disobedience. Another towering figure in the fight for civil rights and freedom, in this case from British imperial tyranny in India, was Mahatma Gandhi. Gandhi studied law at University College at London and was called to the bar in 1891, before returning to India to practice law. In 1922 Gandhi was convicted of sedition, and he was imprisoned for three years by the colonial government for his role in mass-organized peaceful protests against the British oppression of the Indian people. Gandhi, like King, went on to become a world-renowned figure and symbol of peaceful resistance against oppression.

In regard to academia, Antonio Negri, a professor of philosophy who garnered acclaim for empire (Negri & Hardt, 2000), served prison time in Italy for involvement (still contested) in left-wing extremist political actions. His book received international attention for its bold explanation of a world that has moved beyond nation-based imperialism to a new postmodern vision of globalization, in which racism and inequality still exist. The book includes solutions to make global society more egalitarian, and Negri was directly involved in political activism that focused on these goals. Back across the ocean in the U.S., we find Bill Ayers, a professor of education known for his activist scholarship work on urban education reform. As a former leader of the Weathermen Underground, a communist political activist group during the 1960s, Ayers was charged with weapons and bomb crimes by the Federal Bureau of Investigation (FBI) for his involvement in politically motivated bombings, yet these charges were later dropped. He eventually retired as a distinguished and award-winning professor from the University of Illinois at Chicago. Thus, the meaningful efforts and prosocial work of independent SAAs is certainly not new as a phenomenon. Yet in the next section I explain that the early phase of SAA activity, which developed into a broader movement, came about as a response to widespread state-sponsored social inequality and oppression.

Facing Oppression on Two Fronts

Out of frustration with the seemingly hopeless scenario that living life with a felony conviction presented, a small number of system-affected people turned to academic pursuits within the criminology and criminal justice fields as a means of improving their life chances. Thus, in 1997, the early Convict Criminology SAA network was formed. Many CC members had hoped to find acceptance within social science fields such as criminology, criminal justice, and sociology, which presented themselves as "progressive," but instead quickly found themselves excluded and/or marginalized. Thus, they faced oppression on two fronts, in the (1) criminal legal and (2) educational systems. During this era of harsh social and political rhetoric and policy toward crime and people convicted of crimes, the knowledge, presence, and scholarship of SAA individuals within the academy were not always welcomed (Richards & Ross, 2001). Several people faced open scorn and/or bias from fellow criminology and criminal justice academics and perceived that their scholarship was often ignored and denigrated. Other CC members described how their colleagues did not want to associate with them due to the perceived-stigma-by-association effect (Tietjen, 2013). Yet CC moved forward, mentoring other members of the SAA population (several of whom went on to become active members of this SAA group), producing scholarship, and advocating for equality for system-affected people within higher education.

At the same time that the nascent CC group was organizing in 1997, another group comprising numerous SAA people was also forming. Critical Resistance was founded in large part by Professor Angela Y. Davis, a well-known scholar with direct carceral system contact, in California, as an organization focused on the elimination of the prison industrial complex and prison abolition. Viewing the CLS as an oppressive institution that furthers race, class, and gender social inequalities, Critical Resistance continues to organize and take action in multiple chapters in major cities from coast to coast. This group has a broad membership comprising of carcerally impacted and many concerned justice-free activist members from various backgrounds. While Critical Resistance is not entirely an SAA group, it is a grassroots, community-based movement founded by a FI activist academic, which has many academic members, collaborates with universities, and shares similar visions in regard to critical perspectives and activist initiatives against the CLS.

These early members (before the early 2000s, dating back into the early twentieth-century work of FI criminologist Frank Tannenbaum) of the SAA population and closely aligned groups began the difficult work of clearing the path from the CLS to institutions of higher education for carcerally impacted people, resulting in an academic means of critiquing and organizing against this system. On their own, without mentorship or guidance from previously established SAA group members, the initial individuals fought their way to advanced degrees in higher education and even faculty and leadership positions in universities. They helped build foundational support networks for subsequent generations of similar scholars. Yet during the tough-on-crime punitive era of the 1980s and 1990s, SAA groups fought a different battle against more overt social stigma, open bias and discrimination, and harsher policies. In the 2010s and early 2020s, a shift in societal and political attitudes toward criminal justice in the U.S. has led to the acceptance of more progressive policy (Williams & Kaplan, 2019). While mass incarceration still exists, the American prison population has begun to (very) gradually decrease. Ross (2021) points out that in recent years, a greater emphasis has been placed on successful prisoner reentry with the passage of federal criminal justice bills, such as the Second Chance Act (2007) and the First Step Act (2018). Subsequently, the criminal justice narrative has gradually shifted toward a more progressive stance. Within this environment of increased acceptance of people with criminal justice–impacted backgrounds, a space has been created for more SAA groups to organize. The advent of the contemporary phase of SAA groups, their development, and their powerful social impact is the topic of this book.

In order to further explore the dynamics of CLS failure and the societal inequality that generated the current proliferation of the SAA movement, the research reported in this book seeks to answer various broader, general questions: How were group members impacted by the CLS, and how did this experience influence their educational pathways and innovative use of academic learning within transformative justice work? Next, what motivated the various SAA groups of organized activist-scholars to engage in their unique brands of critical and activist perspectives pertaining to the CLS? Further, the book explores how SAA members find their place (in groups and as independent SAA individuals) and how various SAA groups are structured; and then explores SAA group missions, stances toward the CLS and higher education, and visions for the future.

Yet before launching into these important research questions and theoretical discussions, it is important to map out the history and organization of SAAs, as a means to establish a frame of reference for the development of this movement.

HISTORY AND ORGANIZATION OF SAAs

To establish a comprehensive understanding of the SAA movement, it must be noted that this process could be conceptualized as occurring in early and later phases. The earlier founding individuals with direct system contact entered the scene as early as the 1960s and included Professor John Irwin's *Project Rebound* in 1967 (Sheehan, 2012), Professor Angela Y. Davis's *Critical Resistance* in 1997 (Shaw, 2009), and the early CC discipline/network in 1997 (Richards & Ross, 2001). This book is focused on the more recent phase of SAA development, which encompasses the proliferation of multiple sets of SAA scholars organized since the mid-2010s. Regardless of this concentration, the initial period from the late 1960s to the 1990s played an important role in demonstrating that system-affected people could organize to enact prosocial change within both society and the CLS through the framework of higher education.

In the tumultuous years of the 1960s and early 1970s, an era of resistance to oppression and authority set the world on fire. A movement comprising individuals and organized groups fighting for justice against institutions they no longer believed in was occurring across the U.S. and around the world. Actions—such as African American, Hispanic, and Native American people organizing to fight for their civil rights; the Vietnam War protests; and women fighting for an equal rights amendment—were catching the world's attention. Further, the CLS was not immune to these world-changing developments; subsequently, incarcerated and FI people started standing up for their right to be heard as well (Berger, 2014). Several social movements of the 1960s focused on working with and supporting the causes of incarcerated and FI people in their struggles to overcome inequality and oppression within the CLS. Speaking of these specific movements of the 1960s, Ross (2021) stated: "Many efforts focused at least in part, on assisting convicts or ex-convicts re-enter society" (p. 14).

In 1967 the well-known criminologist John Irwin, a FI professor at San Francisco State University and mentee and coauthor of Donald Cressey (Irwin & Cressey, 1962), began *Project Rebound* to help FI people gain access to higher education.[4] The director and student staff of this program were often FI themselves, many of them volunteers. Since its founding, Project Rebound has expanded to several California universities, collaborating with these respective institutions. The program has even expanded to offer counseling services, health care, traveling assistance, academic advising, and mentoring for FI students. Irwin also lent his support to the formation of other SAA groups, such as CC in the 1990s (Richards, 2013; Ross, 2021). Irwin offered moral support to new members and sat in on the early CC panels at the American Society of Criminology (ASC) conference.

The political activism of George Jackson in Soledad Prison in California fell within the parameters of these activities (Jackson, 1970). Jackson, incarcerated in the California prison system in the 1960s until his untimely death in 1971, was mentored by several revolutionary thinkers while incarcerated, and he educated himself on the political writings of Marx, Trotsky, Lenin, and Mao. Jackson was revolutionized while in prison and became a charismatic and well-liked thought leader and organizer among his fellow incarcerated people. As a prolific and powerful letter writer (Jackson, 1970, 1972), he attracted global support from left-leaning global academics and activists.

Another example of protest-era prison activism is the 1971 Attica prison riot in the Attica Correctional Facility in New York (Thompson, 2017). The incident was catalyzed when the men incarcerated in Attica attempted to ask for more humanistic treatment and political rights from the prison administration. Thirty-three incarcerated men, mostly African American, and ten prison guards and civilian employees were killed when the state attempted to quell the situation with extreme violence. Another such action involving the justice system was the highly publicized trial of Professor Angela Y. Davis in 1970, following unproven accusations of her involvement in an armed takeover of a Marin County, California, courtroom (Aptheker, 1975). Davis was accused of supplying the weapons for the armed courtroom takeover yet was acquitted of all charges in federal court. As a Black scholar, she was also deeply involved in supporting the activism of imprisoned Black men in standing up against racism and human rights violations taking place in U.S. prisons, including the prison protests of George Jackson and his fellow Soledad inmates, "The Soledad Brothers."

While the actions already presented in this brief history of the SAA movement have provided much-needed resources and support for FI people from the late 1960s until the present, the tough-on-crime era of the 1980s and 1990s introduced a new type of bias, discrimination, and fear into American society (Jones, 1995). The harsh narrative of punishment-centered criminal justice legislation led to draconian sentencing, mass incarceration, and politically and socially reinforced fear of the groups whom society perceived as committing crime, while also encouraging unchecked bias toward those convicted of crimes. The nation's incarcerated population began to expand rapidly. Already established prisons were quickly filled to overcrowding levels, and new prisons were built at a furious pace. Additionally, because 95 percent of incarcerated people return home from prison at some point (James, 2014; Travis, 2005), a massive population of people with felony convictions was created. This ever-increasing and rapidly expanding segment of the population was faced with the brutal realities of living life with a criminal conviction in the U.S. The collateral consequences of a criminal conviction in the U.S. diminish opportunities for life-course success and increase the probability of recidivism (Love et al., 2013; Mauer & Chesney-Lind, 2002; Pinard, 2010; Uggen & Stewart, 2014).

Structure of the Current SAA Movement

In my exploration of the SAA movement, the actions of which have taken root in the U.S. and internationally, I frame this movement by explaining the three major branches of the SAA movement, then provide examples

TABLE 1 REPRESENTATION OF ORGANIZATION OF SYSTEM-AFFECTED ACADEMICS

System-Affected Academics	Year Established
Unaffiliated SAA Groups	
1. Convict Criminology (early phase)*	1997
2. Convict Criminology in U.K.	2011–12
3. Division of Convict Criminology in American Society of Criminology	2020
Formerly Incarcerated College Graduates Network	2014
From Prison Cells to Ph.D.	2017
University-Affiliated SAA Groups	
University SAA Groups	
Formerly Incarcerated Stronger Together at Northeastern Illinois University	2014
Transforming Renewing Achieving Connecting (TRAC) at the University of Nebraska–Omaha	2017
Convict Criminology at the University of Westminster in London	2016–18
The California School	
Project Rebound (early phase)*	1967
Underground Scholars – University of California	2013
Rising Scholars, California State University Long Beach**	2016
Independent SAA Individuals	
Numerous	Various

*Early phase is described elsewhere in this chapter. Such groups provide the foundation of the SAA movement, and this can play an important part in establishing how the more recent proliferation of SAA groups (the focus of this book) came to be.

**A separate organization called the Rising Scholars Network, with educational programs for incarcerated and formerly incarcerated students, was founded in 2020 in the California Community College system.

of SAA groups and individuals within each branch (see table 1). Also, the reason for my categorization of SAA movement is to reflect, as best I can, the thoughts and voices of the SAA members whom I interviewed for this book; consequently this framework reflects their perceptions of this issue. While it must be noted that there are many organizations within the U.S. and internationally that are comprised of incarcerated and carcerally impacted people outside of the specific groups listed within this book, it should be emphasized that I focused on members of the SAA population who were critical and activist-scholars involved in higher education and research, mostly in fields that focus on the CLS and criminology, yet in other fields as well. The representation of the SAA movement presented in this book is not meant to be comprehensive, since due to its rapid growth, there is much more material than could have been included in the breadth of this book. Even during the writing and publication of this book, SAA groups were quickly sprouting up at colleges and universities across the United States and in many international locations. For example, a carceral lived experience conference titled "Convict and Lived Experience Criminology Symposium," involving a growing group of Australian SAA members, was held in March 2024 at the University of Southern Queensland in Australia and featured SAA presenters from Italy, South America, the United Kingdom, and the United States.

Further, the diversity of locations from which the international sample of system-contacted participants included in this book hails demonstrates the extensiveness of the SAA movement, while also using the snowball sampling method to extend the reach of this discussion.[5] While the number of people in this sample may be viewed by some as small, I want to emphasize that this research is focused on presenting unique and rich examples of people involved in the SAA movement, not a thin representation of hundreds or thousands of people. In addition, many SAA people, for very personal and relevant reasons, choose not to talk to researchers. While the engine behind the buildup of mass incarceration and the social harms it has inflicted on humanity is centered within the CLS, the U.S. is certainly not the only country to endure the outcomes of oppressive CLS practices and policies. Thus, a very relevant emphasis within this book is the importance of international SAA involvement, including but not limited to international members of the SAA group CC and SAA individuals who are not affiliated with groups (independent SAA individuals). Once again, it should be noted that this book is not meant to be a comprehensive description of the entire SAA movement, but is a qualitatively premised exploration of the major groups that the author determined would most broadly and impactfully represent the major branches and phenomena presented in these chapters.[6]

The Major Branches of the SAA Movement

I divide the SAA movement up into three major branches based on group membership or lack thereof and group affiliation or nonaffiliation with educational institutions (see table 1). The individuals in the first branch, *unaffiliated SAA groups*, are not affiliated with any specific educational institutions. The second, *university-affiliated SAA group* branch, is composed of organizations formed with the support of a specific university or university system. The third branch is made up of the numerous independent SAA individuals who are not attached to any specific organized group.

Unaffiliated SAA Groups. Unaffiliated SAA groups operate without direct affiliations to institutions of higher education. These groups come in various, often overlapping forms, such as nonprofits, informal networks of scholars and activists, and academic society divisions. Such organizations, while having some variation in the focus of their missions, can mobilize their members and carry out their work anywhere nationally and internationally. The groups I include in my research from this branch are Convict Criminology (in the U.S. and the U.K.), Formerly Incarcerated College Graduates Network (FICGN), and From Prison Cells to Ph.D. It must be noted that membership in groups that are unaffiliated with institutions of higher education is more diverse. They are not entirely composed of academics and scholars. There is strong representation of system-impacted professionals, dedicated activists, and allies within these organizations working both together with SAAs and on their separate initiatives in regard to advocacy. Yet much of their work and actions align with SAA values.

CC in the U.S. and U.K. The CC group first formed as a loosely associated network of SAA individuals not affiliated with any specific academic institution, in the tough-on-crime era of the 1990s, with the support of such scholars as the late John Irwin (Ross & Richards, 2003). CC scholars and academics hail from around the globe. The early CC members were dissatisfied with the exclusion and/or marginalization of the inside perspectives of FI scholars within the academies of criminology and criminal justice and wanted to speak out against the openly encouraged bias and discrimination faced by FI scholars and academics. The CC group of affiliated scholars, academics, and activists focuses on bringing the insights of the incarcerated, FI, and acquaintance contacted to the academic fields of criminology and criminal justice. CC literature (Richards, 2013; Tietjen, 2019) states that the group focuses on three primary issues: (1) producing rigorous scholarly research; (2) mentoring of FI scholars, and (3) advocating for progressive justice reform. Also, many CC-affiliated scholars and justice advocates work outside of academia in organizations and with causes that seek to rectify systematic carceral inequality. CC strives to both bring relevance to the carcerally impacted perspective in criminology and inform progressive justice reforms in CLS policy and practice.

In 2020 CC formally became the Division of Convict Criminology (DCC) within the ASC. The DCC continues the inclusive vision of the informal CC network that existed from 1997 to 2020, yet it now has an ASC-sanctioned constitution, administrative officers, standing committees, and benefits from the support of an internationally recognized criminological society. Further, CC's international presence and diversity (Ross et al., 2016) has continued to expand, as discussed in the recently published *Convict Criminology for the Future* (Ross & Vianello, 2021). While CC and the DCC are not affiliated with specific universities, they still have a powerful impact on higher education through the collective efforts of their organization, the actions of their individual members who are often influential at their own respective universities, and the mentorship action and scholarship engaged in by their members.

CC in Great Britain. Roughly modeled on the CC group formed in the U.S., CC was established in Great Britain in 2012. Aresti and Darke (2016) pointed out that about one hundred people in Britain affiliate with CC, comprising FI scholars, traditional criminology scholars without CLS contact, and incarcerated people. Since its formation, the group's academic and public impact has increased, and the members have developed a growing body of scholarship.

There is some divergence of perspective in regard to how CC members in the U.K. perceive their place in the larger group of CC, which has taken on a more international presence in the last decade or so (Ekunwe & Jones, 2011; Ross & Vianello, 2021). Some U.K. members perceive CC within Britain as a separate contingent of CC, with characteristics that are unique from those of the wider network. In some recent conversations with certain members of CC from the U.K., there was some consensus that they wish to be part of the larger unified international CC group and to not function as a separate faction. In interviews for this study with various U.K. scholars of CC affiliation, it was indicated that the University of Westminster in London has a strong focus on CC scholarship. Several CC academics instruct at this educational institution, where they produce CC scholarship, advocate for SAA people, mentor carcerally impacted individuals, and teach CC scholarship. This group would fit into the "university-affiliated SSA group" categorization presented in the next section.

Formerly Incarcerated College Graduates Network. Formed in 2014, the FICGN, originally started by Assistant Professor Chris Beasley, became a nonprofit organization in 2019. FICGN has built up a substantial following of around one thousand members in forty-three states (Gewin, 2019). This group has successfully used social media (Facebook and X, formerly Twitter) and social events, such as cookouts, to promote its mission and attract membership. Operating without a specific university or institutional affiliation, FICGN functions as a network of FI students and college graduates, and its members work in multiple fields, including as professors, administrators, staff members, and attorneys. Through creating a supportive space for FI college graduates, FICGN seeks (among many other goals) to break through the negative stigmatization of this population and to demonstrate the value of the justice-lived experience to society. Among its many initiatives, FICGN advocates and promotes prison and postprison educational opportunities for FI college graduates, attempts to change social perceptions of FI people, advocates for CLS policy changes, and provides employment resources for system-contacted people.

From Prison Cells to Ph.D. Established in 2017, From Prison Cells to Ph.D., also referred to as P2P, is an organization focused on helping people who are system affected overcome barriers they encounter upon societal reentry through accessing higher education. Its mission states, "To help inspire others with similar backgrounds to excel beyond what society and life circumstances have set to be the norm" (From Prison Cells to Ph.D., n.d.). Members provide mentorship, counseling, training, and resources to assist in facilitating a more successful reentry process. P2P also helps members of the SAA population with navigating college, student loan, and employment processes. Through its consulting services, trauma-informed care and equity diversity inclusion training services (with a focus on system-affected people) are available to employers and educational institutions. One of the group's cofounders, Stanley Andrisse (2021), author of *From Prison to PhD: It Is Never Too Late to Do Good*, overcame a ten-year prison sentence to become an endocrinologist at Johns Hopkins Medicine. In addition to his successful career as a highly published diabetes researcher (Andrisse et al.,

2018), Dr. Andrisse has also become a powerful education advocate for the FI. As an unaffiliated SAA group, P2P provides educational assistance and resources to the people it serves across the country.

University-Affiliated SAA Groups

Within the SAA movement, many members of the population and their allies have formed organized groups within universities and colleges across the country. Such entities often receive resources, mentorship, and academic support from their respective schools. Their group members are frequently students of the affiliated university. This branch (University-Affiliated SAA Groups) is composed of two segments, (1) university SAA groups, and the (2) the California school. I have included the California-specific segment of this branch because certain SAA participants within my research have referred to a unique SAA movement/phenomenon occurring in that state and also because of the strong public presence of such groups there. Potentially due to California's more progressive political environment as well as the strong support from many of their major university systems, the California SAA groups have become very successful organizers. They have been effective at creating programs, providing funding, and securing resources for system-affected academics. This is not to say that the organizations outside of California are not effective or impactful. Factors such as the political, economic, and social environments that universities are located in, along with the type of educational institution (e.g., small private liberal arts college, large state research university, regional university), may also influence the relative success of university-affiliated SAA groups. Less progressive political environments may limit potential SAA support in some colleges and universities.

University SAA Groups

TRAC (Transforming Renewing Achieving Connecting) at University of Nebraska–Omaha. TRAC was founded in 2017 at the University of Nebraska–Omaha (UNO) as the Nebraska Post-Secondary Prison Education Project, before being renamed TRAC in 2018. This SAA group, founded and partially staffed by system-affected academics, serves several purposes. TRAC recruits academics to teach college courses in classrooms within the Nebraska State Correctional system. Further, TRAC holds meetings at UNO for students with system contact, providing a sense of community for students. Also, TRAC is involved in community and political advocacy for equal rights for the system-affected in Nebraska. TRAC is privately funded by donors who are directly involved with system-affected justice work.

Formerly Incarcerated Stronger Together (FIST) at Northeastern Illinois University. FIST was started by FI students in 2014 at Northeastern Illinois University (NEIU). English professor Timothy Barnett acts as the group's faculty adviser and liaison to NEIU's administration. The group has organized numerous events to draw awareness to issues surrounding mass incarceration and social injustices that exist within the CLS, such as NEIU's Day of Reflection on Mass Incarceration in 2018 (Rodriguez, 2018). Rodriguez explained that group members refer to FIST as a club and speak to the desire to create a place where FI people and individuals with family members in prison can feel safe, welcomed, and unstigmatized.

CC at the University of Westminster in London. The CC group at the University of Westminster in London has built a program of study within its college. It comprises both system-affected senior professors and graduate students. Yet it is worth noting that while this group is affiliated with a specific institution of higher education, members view themselves as unified in solidarity with the larger network of CC members in the U.S., Italy, South America, New Zealand, and Australia, and do not wish to be defined as separate from the larger whole. This belief comes from the sentiment that they are stronger together, supporting their fellow lived-experience SAA peers. This group has produced many impactful SAA scholars in recent years and continues to expand.

The California School

Project Rebound. A California State University–based organization, Project Rebound was founded in 1967 by John Irwin, a renowned scholar and FI criminologist at San Francisco State University, whose goal was to help FI people complete college degrees. Those who staff and administer this program are often FI themselves, many of them volunteers. Since its founding, *Project Rebound* has expanded to several California universities, collaborating with these respective institutions. This program has even diversified its services to offer counseling, health care, traveling assistance, academic advising, and mentoring for FI students. Many involved with this organization are also affiliated with other aspects of the

SAA movement, such as Rising Scholars or Convict Criminology, or as independent SAA individuals.

Underground Scholars Initiative (USI). Founded in 2013 by University of California–Berkeley students Danny Murillo and Steven Czifra, who both shared the experience of incarceration in their pasts, USI was developed as an organization focused on supporting system-affected University of California Berkeley students (MacFarquhar, 2016). USI's website states that the organization is working toward "developing a prison-to-school pipeline within the University of California educational system."[7] Since its inception, USI has gained interest from both FI and system-impacted California students and from the wider public, and has been involved in major CLS reform initiatives at the national level, with many members being awarded prestigious grants and fellowships.

Rising Scholars CSULB. Founded in 2016 by a group of students at California State University–Long Beach (CSULB), Rising Scholars CSULB is intentional in being inclusive of all system-affected students. While Rising Scholars does not have an official university web page, a page is in the process of being constructed.[8] The group's X page describes Rising Scholars as "connecting students affected by the CJ system, directly or indirectly, with resources that help increase success." Criminal justice associate professor and lawyer James Binnall, who also has carceral lived experience, serves as Rising Scholars's academic adviser (Williams, 2018). Rising Scholars, which claims approximately twenty-five members, was formed to meet the needs of SAA students on the CSULB campus. It must also be noted that in addition to this group, there is a Rising Scholars Network in the California Community College system, not to be confused with this similarly named SAA group.[9]

Independent SAA Individuals

Around the globe, there are individual SAA-oriented scholars who are not part of any specific organized group yet are still aligned with the goals of the SAA movement from their professional, scholarly, and ideological perspectives. These individuals are independent actors and often publish research and media informed by their respective criminal justice experiences (if located outside the U.S.). Such individuals can also be involved with professional and nonprofit organizations (non-SAA organizations) and both activist and critical scholarship. Internationally, these individuals hail from regions and countries such as Scandinavia, New Zealand, Australia, Italy, and South America (Ekunwe & Jones, 2011; Newbold et al., 2014; Vianello, 2015; Ross & Darke, 2018; Weis, 2020). In addition to producing academic literature and media, some of these individuals are working toward organizing their own distinct groups of people with carceral lived experience, spreading awareness about the plight of system-affected people in the educational system, and/or working with more established SAA groups from afar. Further, not everyone in this camp with formal system contact chooses to disclose their CLS experiences (similar to people within SAA groups), yet they still engage in work, such as community justice and research, that advocates for the carcerally impacted.

SAAs AND UNIVERSITIES: A RECIPROCAL TRANSFORMATION

The concept of a reciprocal transformative dynamic between system-affected academics and the institution of academia underlies and reinforces the SAA movement's growing support and impact. The relationship formed between system-affected academics individually, or within the organized groups and the university systems that they may be affiliated with, can have the potential to influence transformative change within each entity at the macro (entire justice system), meso (university institution), and micro (individuals and SAA groups) societal levels.[10]

Influence of the SAA Movement on Universities

From the perspective of establishing the conceptualization of the SAA movement's influence on the institution of higher education, there are several factors that deserve attention. Initially, SAA individuals perceived universities as a means to attain a college degree, a well-respected and highly regarded symbol of accomplishment that serves as a socially desirable and legitimate means of advancement toward life-course success. Yet the SAA movement changes the university through such processes as students becoming SAA group members, the collective actions of SAA groups as a whole, the individual actions of independent SAA individuals, and the varying levels of involvement students have in SAA actions. The commonplace journey of attaining educational credentials functions as a powerful process for this group of people. Through awareness campaigns organized by SAA groups, coupled with activist and critical scholarship and media produced by system-affected students and faculty, the institution of higher education ends up being educated about the gravity and scope of the struggles that such students and faculty face. Support for the establishment of funded and dedicated SAA spaces can be fostered through advocacy efforts (on the part of system-contacted students and faculty), which exemplify the opportunities that such groups can generate. The SAA movement is proactively attempting to carve out supportive spaces within higher education for populations with justice system contact (direct and indirect contact). This process of garnering SAA legitimation on college campuses can be an uphill battle within the modern-day neoliberal university (Moody, 2022; Slaughter & Rhoades, 2000), where support for the system-affected population is certainly not guaranteed. Within supportive college campus spaces, many SAA groups and individuals are provided the opportunity to more effectively and actively engage in actions such as social justice work and activist scholarship, which may function to strengthen the social justice reach and potential of institutions of higher education.

Influence of Universities on the SAA Movement

Framing the conceptualization of the institution of higher education's influence on the SAA movement involves denoting several important factors. I would be remiss not to begin this discussion with the basic benefits of learning. Yet because universities are far from perfect institutions, this study also discusses how some of the institutional flaws that perpetuate inequality and oppression may uniquely impact SAA people.

In regard to educational benefits, SAA students acquire knowledge and skills vital to understanding the concepts of social equality, human rights, critical criminological theories, and transformative criminal justice practices. Their newfound insights are added to the SAA population's collective human capital pool. Yet in addition to providing knowledge gained from completing college courses, educational institutions can give the SAA population the resources and institutional support needed to effectively organize, while also serving a socially respected platform. Universities can also be a source of funding for activist and advocacy initiatives, adding to the legitimacy of SAA group efforts. Another primary and high-impact function of the university system, in addition to recognized educational credentials, is the production of rigorous scholarship and research. Such scholarship can be a cornerstone for social movements (Bevington & Dixon, 2005). Access to this transformative mechanism gives the SAA movement a powerful and well-respected instrument for disseminating its insights, lived experiences, and insider perspectives to critical criminology, sociology, the CLS, and society at large. Examples of SAA-related scholarship cover multiple perspectives, such as reentry struggles after incarceration (Soto, 2016), perceptions of stigma (LeBel, 2012), issues of race (Walker, 2016), and incarceration's impact on family members (Arditti, 2002).

Regarding how universities can potentially function to hinder the educational and academic process for marginalized groups, universities act as a powerful locus for constructing, reinforcing, and reproducing status quo societal systems of power. For example, critical SAA faculty in the tenure and promotion process may have to dilute or sterilize their research focus in order to align with the conventional values of mainstream scholarship. Also, SAA professors who are open about their carceral lived experiences are asked to stifle their voice to avoid potential bias from faculty peers on tenure committees; thus they are not able to fully express the truths of their work. The modern neoliberal university can function to stifle the ideas of the oppressed while also exacerbating class and racial divides (Connell, 2019; Slaughter & Rhoades, 2000). In discussing the social equity impacts of those times when academic departments are shuttered due to failing to meet business model expectations commonly used in the modern-day neoliberal university, Haiven (2014a, 2014b) stated, "These often have the effect of quenching or obstructing the most dynamic and important insights and tendencies to have emerged from marginalized approaches, such as Indigenous epistemologies, feminist and queer analyses and methods, ethnic studies approaches, and anti-racist and anti-colonial theories" (Haiven, 2014b, para. 4).

Such marginalized groups are often disproportionately represented in SAA populations, in comparison to the often more affluent and middle-class demographics of university student populations, even though these demographics have been shifting recently (slowly) toward more socio-demographic diversity (Fry & Cilluffo, 2019). Thus, the positive potential of SAA populations within modern profit-centered university models (Connell, 2019) can be compromised without dedicated support from within these institutions.

A human-focused progressive education can provide a stable structure for building networks of like-minded students and academics who possess shared life experiences, while also supplying exposure to the potential knowledge, mentorship, and assistance contained within the larger population of students and academics. Subsequently, education focused on social good, not solely on expanding capitalist profit margins, gives SAA group members and individuals access to a large pool of social capital that can aid in not only expanding individual opportunity structures but also increasing the transformative reach of advocacy and activist campaigns.

ADDITIONAL COMPONENTS OF THE SAA MOVEMENT

In addition to the proliferation of independent SAA individuals and groups that have organized since the mid-2010s, the movement has additional components that are vital to perpetuating humanistic transformation within the correctional system. Such factors include expanding international influence, high-impact research, literature, and various forms of print and digital media produced by SAA members.

An Expanding International Presence in Need of Support

SAA presence has begun expanding around the world. The scope of this book includes independent SAA individuals (operating outside of SAA group affiliation) and the international work of the CC SAA group. Because the international U.K. presence of CC is more long-standing and developed, this book has highlighted its work. Also, this book frames and discusses the significant presence of independent SAA individuals, specifically in the U.K. and Australia. Yet it must be mentioned that there is further SAA work going on around the world that could not be included in this book due to time, resource, and logistical constraints. For example, there is more SAA action in Australia, where other directly impacted people are working toward acceptance within higher education, such as the Incarcerated Students Education Initiative (Nyland, 2023) at the University of Southern Queensland. Also, because of a need expressed by Australian scholars, the DCC in the ASC and faculty from the University of Southern Queensland are currently working together to build SAA links to Australia, through discussions, academic collaborations, and mentorship efforts. Further, in additional emergent SAA movement efforts on the international front, scholars and students in Italy and South America are also struggling for admittance to the halls of academia (Ross & Vianello, 2021). Only recently has light begun to be shed on their struggles, and exposure of their plight (and actions to empower them) is in need of being further developed, along with a need for organized support from more resourced and established sections of the SAA movement.

SAA Group Academic and Media Content

In another vein, the SAA population creates substantial amounts of written content and media. This is a growing library of work that is continuing to expand even as this book is published. Arguably, a central means of dispersing the broad array of lived-experience perspectives and unique insights of these activist/critical academics is through a topic-diverse body of scholarly literature (Beasley & Jason, 2015; Binnall, 2021b; Binnall et al., 2022; Kavish et al., 2016; Ross & Vianello, 2021; Warr, 2016) and academic media content produced by and about issues relevant to this movement. Such content can be found online, in newspapers, on television news, in libraries, and in bookstores. Through these mediums, the SAA movement's transformative message is given a conduit for transmission to the academy, the CLS, and ultimately the public. Another important facet of media content that heavily contributes to this movement is literature produced about SAA groups by nonacademic sources, such as feature articles in major periodicals and newspapers, including the *New Yorker* (MacFarquhar, 2016) and the *New York Times* (St. John, 2003). Thus the scholarly, activist, and public media imprints produced by and about these groups are wide ranging, including a full spectrum of scholarly research, thought pieces, issue and policy statements, websites (Berkeley Underground Scholars, n.d.; Project Rebound CSULB, n.d.; Division of Convict Criminology, n.d.; Formerly Incarcerated College Graduates Network, 2024; Transforming, Renewing, Achieving, and Connecting, n.d.), podcasts (e.g., *The Criminology Academy*, episode 36, January 17, 2022), social media (CSULB Rising Scholars, n.d. [on Facebook]), and periodical pieces.

OVERVIEW OF THE BOOK

I have designed this book to present the varied and complex human experiences of SAA group members, while also discussing the theoretical implications, policy potential, and social dynamics of the perceptions and scholarship exhibited in these chapters. I begin each chapter with an anecdote from my personal experience as an FI scholar and SAA group member, often recalling events that have happened throughout my life that are pertinent to each respective chapter's focus. Following is a brief overview of the content of each chapter.

Work on this book began in 2020, during a very troubled time in U.S. history. The global COVID-19 pandemic was raging unchecked from coast to coast, and because state and federal legislatures and their respective

CLSs refused to respond in a humane capacity and release incarcerated people (or released insignificant/insufficient numbers of people from correctional facilities), thousands of incarcerated people were forced to stay in their correctional facilities. This situation essentially forced a deadly contagious virus upon an extremely vulnerable population, as thousands of incarcerated people lay sick and/or dying in crowded prisons and jails across the country. As preposterous and unimaginable as this sounds, this event is just one of innumerable injustices that the CLS has foisted on incarcerated and system-impacted people, a population that disproportionately hails from marginalized and disadvantaged communities. Often such demographics lack the social, economic, and political resources with which to legally challenge such illegal violations of their human, constitutional, and civil rights. The purpose of highlighting these points is not an attempt to sneak a rageful diatribe against the CLS and systemically reinforced inequalities into my book (not to discount the seriousness of these issues or the anger that oppressed people may have toward their oppressors). The purpose is to demonstrate to you, the reader, that the suffering of people in correctional systems is quite real. Prison is not an imaginary fictional story plot, such as in a Hollywood movie, where you can dismiss the struggles of incarcerated people as an imaginary reality. Their struggles are our struggles, we are all interconnected, and if society fails them, it harms us all. We are at risk of losing our humanity.

Chapter 1 conceptually sets the stage for the book's argument that the work of SAA groups can assist in transforming dysfunctional CLS policy through the establishment of how and why the correctional system is failing. I then present the diverse body of CLS lived experiences collected from the people who participated in this research. In the next sections I begin building the framework to support my argument. After pointing out the harm that tough-on-crime policies have inflicted on lived-experience populations, I briefly establish how group formation processes interact with social movements. Next, I frame the activist and critical scholarship and explain how the SAA movement has harnessed these instruments to transform conventional criminological scholarship. This is followed by a section presenting how the SAA insider perspective (Baca Zinn, 1979) benefits the criminological academy and criminal justice policy. Chapter 1 concludes with a brief mention of the qualitative research methods fully explained in appendix B.

Chapter 2 establishes the first half of the reciprocal transformative effect between SAA individuals and institutions of higher education, specifically the effect of academic institutions on the SAA individual. The initial sections contain an exploration of how and why SAA members engage with higher education, explore the value of educational mentorship, explain how the social stigma of direct carceral contact interacts with these individuals' academic journeys, and present the obstacles they may have encountered in their educational careers. The final sections highlight how SAA members grapple with social inequality, and parse out how the bias and/or discrimination they may have experienced within the criminal legal system or higher education, or as the result of SAA group involvement, has influenced their perceptions of institutions of education and justice.

Chapter 3 delves into the second half of the reciprocal transformative effect within the SAA movement that exists between SAAs and institutions of higher learning: the SAA population's social justice transformative influence on the university. Analyzing how SAA group members and independent SAA individuals frame the dynamics of their initial encounters with SAA groups or their own experiences, and how they found their place within their respective organizations while navigating academia, presents valuable insights into their influence on the educational institutions with which they interact. Additionally, the respective branches of the SAA movement have varying influences on their affiliated institutions, which further clarifies the SAA groups' diverse transformative impact on higher education. This is demonstrated by examining SAA members' perceptions of their group roles and group structures (which vary by branch).

Chapter 4 explains that SAA branches function as an effective vehicle for advancing high-impact critical and activist measures against a biased and dysfunctional punitive correctional system. Further, these branches concurrently assist in creating a more humanistic correctional system while also advocating for the rights of SAA people. In this chapter I establish that members of the SAA population often view themselves as activist and critical scholars working to transform the broken and oppressive system of mass incarceration, while also working toward dismantling the old system and creating more functional institutions. To wrap up chapter 4, a discussion of the varying visions for the future points to hope, such as greater SAA diversity, further work toward justice system transformation, and various actions to ensure the long-term viability of the SAA movement.

Chapter 5, demonstrates that SAA activist/critical scholarship is a concrete transformative mechanism. Through the spoken and written words of SAA members, I seek to capture the wider human experience of writing within the SAA movement and the meaning of writing to SAA scholars. This scholarship and research, coupled with literary, news, and digital media, is a product of activist/critical thought. Our writing evolves over time, as we grow and advance as scholars and as a movement. This is one of the primary mediums through which the insider perspective reaches and influences academia and the CLS. Works such as critical and activist scholarship, research reports, policy recommendations, and issue statements function not only to transfer the unique insights of the SAA movement to the academic and carceral institutional communities but also to lend their message scientific legitimacy. Further, SAA media in news and literature periodicals spread public awareness about the movement's ability to progressively reshape the CLS and higher education. The scholarly works, news, digital media, and literature produced by the SAA movement can function as the intersection at which the reciprocal transformative processes of the SAA movement and higher education meet, further expanding their impact on the wider sphere of criminal justice policy and practice. Yet at the same time, our writing is a personal experience, in which we as system-affected people can tell the world what the carceral system is really like through our perceptions.

The concluding chapter, 6, provides a synopsis of the major takeaways from each chapter and pulls them together to support the main argument that one means of assisting in the transformation of the broken, punitive CLS can be through the activist work of SAAs. Their lived experiences and insights can provide useful humanistic perspectives on the problems inherent in the justice system. SAA members are both the teachers and the subjects of their own lessons, even if they do not always refer to themselves (outing themselves) directly in their lectures and research (Mobley, 2003; Tietjen, 2019). The growing societal footprint generated by the insider-informed perspectives contained within SAA activist/critical scholarship, mentorship, and media demonstrates that the movement's transformative impact is dispersive, subsequently radiating out to the justice system. SAA branches bring lived experiences coupled with rigorous academic/professional training to CLS scientific and policy tables. Their work frames the insights of those who have faced discrimination and been shut out of carceral policy and criminological academic discourses.[11] This is a missing component that could support creating effective humanistic transformation within the CLS.

CONCLUSION

This book will demonstrate that even though a precariously small group of carcerally impacted critical and activist-scholars and academics has managed to successfully navigate the halls of academia and address some of the systematic injustices of the criminal legal system, the issues of repression within the correctional systems of the U.S. and other countries are far from resolved. This is the reality that incarcerated, FI, and acquaintance-contacted people face every day. This book presents the argument that a means to assist in transforming our broken punishment-centered CLS is through the growing activist scholarship movement of system-affected academics. Their lived-experience perspectives can provide the missing insights needed to help create humanistic transformation within the correctional system. This is their story.

CHAPTER I

Finding Out That the Door Is Open

In the spring of 2005 I was an FI, twenty-nine-year-old undergraduate college student, wrapping up my final year of my bachelor's degree in sociology. One of my professors, who was one of my first academic mentors, had arranged for me to present a roundtable paper on my experiences within the prison-industrial complex at a regional sociology conference. I was exceptionally nervous and feeling overwhelmed by impostor syndrome. Surely, I thought, a senior faculty member was going to sit down at my roundtable and inform me that my work was terrible and that a convicted felon like myself had no place in academia. Defeated, my academic career over, I would return home in shame and live out my days at a dead-end job, continually wondering what could have been.

As it turned out, only one person showed up for my discussion, a critical criminologist who advocated for the FI and studied how mass incarceration perpetuated inequality. He'd seen my topic, he told me, and was intrigued. When I told him my story of lived correctional experiences, he excitedly said that he knew just the people for me and told me about a group called Convict Criminology. He believed that CC might be able to function as a support network for me and help me further my academic pursuits/aspirations. I found out that CC, comprising carcerally impacted people and justice-free allies, used scholarship to advocate for social equality for the incarcerated and FI. Shortly thereafter I reached out and introduced myself to Professor Stephen Richards, one of the cofounders of CC.

Gaining connection to an SAA group as a system-contacted college student opened up a world of support, opportunity, and guidance for me. Before that point, I had been somewhat directionless, drifting through the world of higher education. I had no idea what opportunities existed in academia for people with felony convictions. I knew I wanted to further my education, but I had no notion of how to navigate academia effectively or how to focus my course of studies in a manner that would increase my likelihood of professional success. Further, in addition to both the social and human capital accessed in my SAA group, I was informed that "the door was open" (Tietjen, 2013) to people in academia with criminal convictions. Yet CC also pointed out that socially marginalized groups and historically oppressed people of color face even more bias and structural barriers within higher education. Also, after speaking to several formally incarcerated CC members, I found out that self-doubt and lack of knowledge about opportunities in academia for carcerally impacted people was a common issue with which nearly all of them struggled. I also learned that when given proper mentorship and support, SAA members, working together to support one another, were able to obtain educational credentials, attain faculty positions in universities, and even publish scholarship. This knowledge provided me with hope that there was a chance for me to use academia as a means of building a career, while at the same time using scholarship to address progressive justice reform for people with CLS contact.

Over the years I would learn through my own experiences in higher education, in addition to the shared insights of my SAA group, that the process was neither easy nor equally accessible to all system-affected people. Some scholars were denied entrance into certain parts of academia, such as graduate programs, prestigious institutions, tenure, and faculty positions, based on reasons such as the types of crimes they had been convicted of and their felony convictions in general. Others were accused by their academic peers of committing petty acts or subjected to bias and hostility in their university departments. Further, as mentioned in the previous paragraph, many SAA group members from marginalized/underrepresented groups were fighting against significant social-structural obstacles of intersectional oppression such as racism, classism, homophobia, and sexism. Thus, the transition from a college student still reeling from the trauma I had internalized from the chaos of prison to a member of an SAA group taking part in a burgeoning movement was enlightening and empowering, if at times also overwhelming. In a general sense, my journey was similar to those of many of the

SAA members presented in this book. We learned about the often unjust nature of the criminal justice system and academic institutions in two phases, initially from our firsthand experiences and then from our academic training.

FROM OUR EXPERIENCE, IT'S NOT WORKING

From the growing ranks of SAAs, a massive storehouse of carceral lived experience is speaking. Through the medium of the SAA movement (including activist and critical scholarship, formal statements on social justice issues, and awareness campaigns), this multifaceted and diverse message frames a narrative that punitive criminal justice policy and societal stigmatization of system-affected people is oppressive. These broken CLS policies and practices produce destructive and counterproductive societal outcomes.

The damaging reach of punitive policies and practices, along with the ethos of tough-on-crime culture, extends beyond correctional facilities to the streets, interfering with successful societal reintegration of the FI (NeSmith, 2015). Kaylee, an SAA member and college student, frames how the punishment of the carceral system reached far beyond the completion of her formal legal sanctions: "I couldn't get a, I couldn't rent an apartment. I couldn't, you know, at one point. At one point, I couldn't even be like a chaperone for my kids' field trips." Returning to society with a conviction includes thousands of temporary and permanent postincarceration collateral consequences of criminal convictions, which further penalize, diminish opportunities, and hinder freedom of movement for the rest of their lives (Ewald & Uggen, 2012; Love, Roberts, & Klingele, 2013). For system-contacted people, including SAA scholars and students, such collateral consequences, coupled with social bias against them, can impede life-course success (Jones, 2015; Tietjen et al., 2019; Uggen & Stewart, 2014). Such impacts are fueled by negative public perceptions of people who possess criminal records (Denver et al., 2017; Lageson, 2020; Uggen & Blahnik, 2016). Further, another recent body of literature discusses how perceptions of the redeemability of people with legal convictions are formed (Maruna & King, 2009; Reich, 2019). To initially frame this discussion, when addressing the topic of "redeemability" of people convicted of a crime, the framework is already problematic, as it sets the stage for the deficit model of the individual, not the massive sociosystemic problems that have often already failed them long before they arrive at the doors of a prison. Yet large segments of the general public tend to view system-contacted people from the perspective of individual redeemability and freewill decision-making. They base their beliefs on such factors as political viewpoints and type of crime someone was convicted of, and form opinions about whether or not system-impacted people can "change their ways" based on this.

The shared carceral lived experience within the SAA demographic speaks to a narrative of a failed legal system and may help to shed light on the often unseen structural and systemic obstacles that impact the lives of people with system contact. SAA members have *lived* the unsuccessful outcomes of such broken policies and practices, which perpetuated failure among and discrimination against the system affected. With academic training, SAAs can provide unique scholarly insights into the societal and systemic dysfunction that occurs in a legal system framed around criminological research dependent on state/federal grants, practitioner opinion, and uninformed public/political preferences.[1] The message of the lived-experience activist-scholar population provides a direct witness to the brokenness of legal system policies/practices. Thus, through our stories we are better equipped to shift the cultural ethos/public sentiment toward helping system-affected people, which can have greater positive impact on generating support for eliminating the social need for prisons and creating more supportive educational environments for the system affected. Yet before I delve into more experientially based SAA concepts later in this chapter, I want to present an SAA theoretical model of action, then discuss how mass incarceration, tough-on-crime polices, and various other biased and dysfunctional practices have functioned to create a system of marginalization and intersectionality with harmful social outcomes for the SAA population.

SETTING THE STAGE

Many academic books on justice movements start with framing the history and trajectory leading up to the current state of the movement, and I certainly respect the utility of that practice. But in addition to that, I am going set the stage of this book in the direction of theory, praxis, and action, with the focus on empowerment in order to more accurately capture the action-focused energy of the movement. The SAA movement is more than just scholarship; it is a diverse group of carcerally impacted people engaged in attempting to advocate for equal rights their population and to transform society, the CLS, and higher education in humanistic directions.

The reader will quickly notice that I place myself within this research. I am a subject within my research and am directly part of this movement. This is important to framing SAA as an inclusive and accessible group of real people (not hiding away in the abstract heights of elite academic castles) who are at the same time impactful and rigorous scholars.

Advancing a Useful SAA Theory

From the multiple theories (already established theories) I present later in this chapter 2 as foundational to framing the SAA phenomenon, coupled with my suggestions for advancing a theoretical model of an SAA organization (Tietjen, 2019), I offer the beginning of a unified SAA theory that can be used to advance our movement.[2] I begin the process by emphasizing three major components that need to be addressed in building this theory. The SAA theoretical model advances the academic reach of the field beyond vague notions of "me-search" or redemption narratives, often criticized as too biased or lacking scholarly rigor, to a more impactful social science phenomenon. In the first section I explain how insider perspectives have strong potential for confronting and questioning status quo criminological knowledge and revealing new developments at the organic level within findings being examined by the academy. In the second section I explain how mentoring and collaboration within the SAA movement acts to bridge disjointed areas of individual experiences and knowledge, generating new ideas and concepts to form into the creation of new understandings of criminological phenomena. In the third section I emphasize that enduring the traumas and rigors of the total institution of prisons, coupled with the stigmatization that FI people face after incarceration, can function to generate improved reflexivity in system-contacted scholars. This process challenges the notion that their subjective experiences somehow nullify completely the findings of FI scholars in analyzing their own backgrounds.

This preliminary theoretical model attempts to assert that the strengths and dynamics of the SAA movement work together to accomplish several tasks. For example, SAA scholars could create a more organically sound criminological scholarship, function as a continually evolving storehouse of lived-experience knowledge, develop their own networks of empowerment, and access thought processes developed to cope with the traumatic journey through incarceration to engage in more clear and critical reflexivity within the study of criminology.

Part 1 of SAA Theory: Inside the Machine

What makes the SAA movement unique is that it treats the system-contacted academic as both a subject of the scholarship and the scholar. In other words, this group is simultaneously what is being studied, who is conducting the study, and the people teaching and researching both (Jones et al., 2009; Mobley, 2003). Most certainly there are potential complexities when one is so directly familiar with a research topic, but open acknowledgment of one's position can help contextualize these issues. I am not trying to state that we as SAA scholars have an absolute lock on expertise within the domain of critical corrections and criminology. Our knowledge is subjective in nature. But I am arguing against critics who would say otherwise, that our subjective knowledge can have important value in regard to informing effective criminal justice policies and practices and building programs that create equality for system-contacted populations. Much of SAA scholarship tends to break from and challenge conventional prosystem criminological doctrine and aligns more closely with critical perspectives (Young, 2002).

SAA members and scholarship often question systems of control and power (Foucault, 1977a, 1977b) that influence the CLS. When attempting to understand how being inside the carceral machine influences the SAA worldview as a whole, it must be noted that there is a spectrum of critical stance. Some members choose to work within the system to change it, while others have decided to have no contact with the institutions of corrections and law enforcement. The latter group does not align with conventional criminology and asserts that mainstream scholarship often perpetuates and upholds the systems of oppression that operate within the American CLS.

An example of the oppressive systems adopted by mainstream criminology is the open use of prosystem and stigmatizing terms such as *felon* or *offender* in academic literature. In a 2018 report from the Urban Institute, Okeke and La Vigne (2018) pointed out that when society uses such dehumanizing language, "we define them by the worst act of their lives, creating a stigma that lingers long after they've paid their dept to society." Thus, among the more critical ranks of the SAA movement there are many discussions about the meaning and importance of language usage.

Several SAA groups have produced statements or guides that attempt to more clearly define humanizing language usage according to their visions of appropriate verbal expression in regard to the system contacted. It must be noted that there is variation in opinions on what type of speech is appropriate to use, both within and between SAA groups. Some of these language discussions shift with the gradual temporal changing of cultural norms, and other revisions occur with turnovers in SAA group leadership. Yet these ongoing discussions have the potential to reshape SAAs' impact on justice transformation and to reach a wider spectrum of justice-impacted people.

Part 2 of SAA Theory: Mentoring and Collaborating

Throughout this book I frame the process of mentorship as a primary focus of the SAA movement, yet here I want to advance this discussion and propose that mentorship be framed as a key component of SAA theoretical development. Taylor (2008) described *bridging* as attempting to traverse cultural disparities between the mentors and mentees, and I submit that a bridging culture is formed within the SAA mentorship process. This dynamic forms a knowledge conduit through which the shared insights and knowledge of multiple cohorts and cultures of the SAA movement can evolve (Tietjen et al., 2019).

The specific directions that the SAA movement could evolve through the mentorship-generated bridging culture will require further study to determine. Yet the mentorship findings within this book could support looking at certain areas. For example, mentoring relationships could lead to cultivating more diverse types of research methodologies. Mentoring could also direct the general focus of the SAA member toward such important yet different areas as activism, leadership roles, research, teaching, and scholarship. Many people have multiple mentors, each specializing in specific areas such as faculty career development, writing skills, and publication. Yet other mentors fill more of an all-purpose position, guiding their mentees as role models.

Another strength of the SAA movement emphasized throughout this book is our collaborative efforts. We often attempt to work with each other to produce papers and initiatives, so we are building with others who have similar life experiences. These cooperative efforts can also function as an extension of SAA bridging culture, pulling together stores of knowledge to create greater comprehension of SAA issues and increased advocacy for our causes. The mentorship process can also work in tandem with collaboration, as more experienced scholars work together with newer SAA members.

Much of SAA scholarly work captures fragments or incidents of the SAA experience. While this is important, we have yet to fully collect, categorize, and interpret the perspectives that we define and the knowledge we have collected. The next step for us is to synthesize the collected direct institutional knowledge, incarceration cultural capital, and experiential information archived within the collective group of system-contacted academics into a functional theory of SAA. The quality of and degree to which we take part in mentorship and collaboration will impact the scope and breadth of SAA theory formation.

Part 3 of SAA Theory: Trauma and Stigma in the Total Institution

After incarceration, the people who return home take on a double life (Tietjen, 2019) when considering their intellectual and personal worldviews: one life shaped by the total institution (Abbott, 1982; Goffman, 1963) of prison and the other shaped by social forces of the world outside of prison. While some point out that this could be an obstacle to objective study, Jones et al. (2009) argued for the contrary. They can be supported somewhat by Goffman's (1959, 1961, 1963) work on total institutions and stigma, but the issue becomes far more complex and even beyond Goffman's work when the theorists themselves are the people being stigmatized within total institutions.

The FI SAA member follows an ongoing pathway of struggling to overcome the stigmatization attached to the "ex-convict" label, while struggling with the collateral consequences of a legal conviction (Brisman, 2004, 2007; Pinard, 2010). SAA members who work in academia and research may often work with colleagues who, while well intentioned, may not fully comprehend the obstacles and structural oppression that system-contacted people face. The stigma of a criminal conviction carries with it the further weight of manufactured public fear (Simon, 2007). Additionally, we currently live in an age of digital surveillance and access to unprecedented amounts of online information about legal backgrounds, leading to suspicions and exclusion (Earle, 2016; Lageson, 2020) merely based on the results of an online search. Another dynamic to consider is how the process of overcoming and coping with the traumas of legal system contact influence the scholarly actions of SAA members (Green, 2018).

Even though prisons are often overcrowded and noisy places, for many incarcerated people there is also a sense of isolation from society.

Many prisons are located in remote rural places, while the majority of people confined there are from urban centers. Additionally, the very nature of prison is a closed total institution surrounded by walls and fences. This transmits a powerful statement to incarcerated people that they are cut off from society. Further, the sensory overload of the carceral environment forces many to withdraw in order to grapple with the intense strain of prison life.

What happens after incarceration and other forms of system contact is also important to this narrative. When returning to society, the stigma and collateral consequences of a legal record in one's background can be an isolating experience in itself. Being socially labeled as an "ex-convict" or "criminal," being denied access to employment opportunities, and even being blocked from renting a place to live, all while struggling to make ends meet in an ever more expensive world, can place the potential SAA scholar in a position of being rejected and unwanted by society. The self-awareness and introspection developed by FI SAA members are traits required to survive during imprisonment and upon reentry.

These traumatic experiences are not something that most would choose to endure for the sole purpose of accessing unique traits. The outcome of this forced conglomeration of events can lead to directly contacted SAA members developing characteristics or abilities through their forced exposure to a crucible of difficult experiences. Thus, many FI scholars may possess the ability to think more reflexively and critically in their criminological analysis. Contrary to the protests of critics who believe our lived experiences introduce excessive biases, this can become more relevant to the SAA member when studying populations that they are part of and perhaps improve the rigor of our work.

Theory into Action: Joining the Three Parts of SAA Theory Together

This is still a developing theoretical model, yet I want to attempt to provide a coherent pathway for moving these concepts from abstraction to meaningful social action, which is one of the underlying purposes of the SAA movement. Of the three components mentioned directly before this section—(1) the unique impact of being an insider, (2) SAA mentorship as a warehouse of collective knowledge and generator of useful scholarship, and (3) perspectives legitimating the value of our trauma and stigma-forged carceral experiences—SAA scholars generally encounter carceral trauma first, then move through an ongoing dynamic

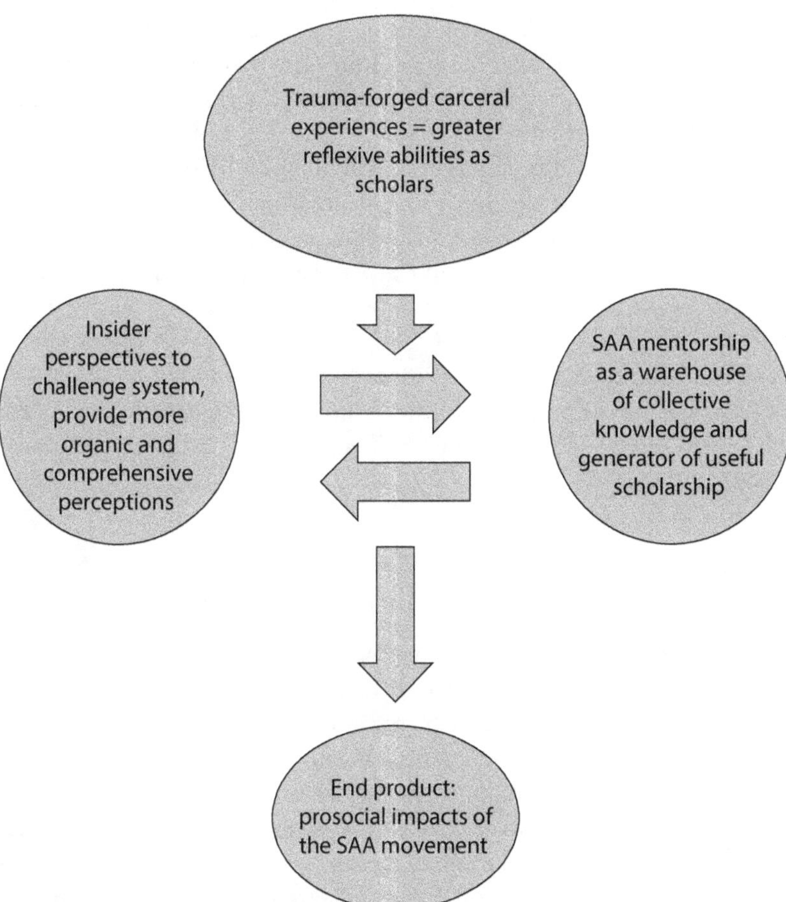

FIGURE 1. Components of SAA movement theory, including trauma-forged carceral experiences, carceral insider perspectives, cumulative scholarship producing stored knowledge of SAA mentorship, and collective positive social impacts of the SAA movement

interaction of the next two process over the course of their academic pathways (see figure 1).

For most SAA members, the various types of carceral contacts (incarceration, probation, electronic monitoring, institutions of the legal system, incarcerated family members) are likely to have resulted in life-altering, traumatic experiences that powerfully shifted their worldviews. Subsequently, they now view social realities through an altered, post-carceral lens. This new frame of perception interacts with both the insider perspective and mentoring/collective knowledge components of this theoretical model, which in turn reciprocally interact between themselves within the SAA universe. I propose that this dynamic, when functioning in a productive capacity, can lead to a gradual and continual process of progress marked by increasing equality and opportunities for system-contacted people alongside expanded powers to influence criminal legal policy. Of course, key components would have to be in place to increase the likelihood of success, such as motivated and reliable members, with access to adequate and proper resources. While much more research needs to be done to determine how this process would operate, I postulate that the three major theoretical premises already proposed could function to generate the prosocial impacts of the SAA movement. Let us now consider the difficulties that system-impacted people face when reentering society and the benefits that higher education can provide them.

THE QUAGMIRE OF COLLATERAL CONSEQUENCES AND THE POTENTIAL OF HIGHER EDUCATION

The monumental institution of mass incarceration in the United States has been in operation for over four decades, since the tough-on-crime era of the 1980s and 1990s. Each year more than 650,000 people are released from correctional facilities back onto the streets (Wagner, 2014), and over those decades, millions of people have been processed through the world's largest criminal justice system. Approximately 19 million American citizens (Shannon et al., 2017) have felony convictions on their records, and 6.7 million Americans are under the supervision of the CLS, including those in correctional facilities, on probation, in community corrections, and on parole (Jones, 2018). During the tough-on-crime era of the 1980s and 1990s, sensationalized media representations of crime and people who commit crime fueled dehumanizing stereotypes (often thinly veiled code language for racist themes) of the dangerous and animalistic "superpredators." During this era, young African American men and young men of color from historically oppressed minority groups were often targeted by politicians and the media as being prone to criminality, such as the wrongfully convicted Central Park Five (Cohen & Spinak, 2018; Duru, 2004). This process influenced public opinion, motivating further tough-on-crime sentiment, and society became more hostile to and suspicious of people with legal convictions.

Hundreds of thousands of people are released from prison every year, and these newly released people quickly encounter the next phase of punishment: the debilitating and often unexpected impacts of a felony conviction, referred to as "collateral consequences" (Ewald & Uggen, 2012; Love et al., 2013). This phase of punishment can last for the duration of their lives, as FI people find out that they are blocked from access to public assistance, housing, voting rights, and multiple forms of employment. Such destructive carceral system, civil, and private sector policies were implemented nationwide. While their impact was felt throughout American society, they had a particularly pernicious effect on marginalized and disadvantaged groups. Families were destroyed and entire neighborhoods decimated as millions of American citizens were processed into the U.S. CLS due to the tough-on-crime justice initiatives that began in the 1980s.

Draconian legislation and criminal justice policies criminalized more behaviors and actions, mandated long-term incarceration, eliminated parole, and forced the courts to use mandatory minimum sentencing guidelines. Clear (2008, p. 5) pointed to the impact of mass incarceration on American communities: "The growth in imprisonment has been concentrated among poor, minority males who live in impoverished neighborhoods." Criminal justice statistics are often tossed around in casual conversations, but I want to emphasize that these statistics represent human beings. In a society continually bombarded with twenty-four-hour news cycles, members of the public have a tendency to dehumanize the people data represents, and to perceive them as banal abstract concepts. They do not see the actual carcerally impacted individuals who are trying to survive, reintegrate themselves back into society, and pull their lives together after enduring the often damaging and long-lasting effects of contact with the correctional system.

The Impacts of Collateral Consequences

As a large body of criminological scholarship indicates, one of the more insidious ramifications of a criminal conviction in the U.S. is the ubiquitous phenomenon of collateral consequences (Love et al., 2013; Mauer & Chesney-Lind, 2002) for people with criminal convictions, which includes thousands of civil regulations, rules, and institutional guidelines. Such consequences were greatly expanded in the tough-on-crime 1980s–1990s, and Pinard (2010) pointed out that policymakers and legislators failed to anticipate the long-term negative impact that such actions would have on minority and marginalized communities.[3] Yet several decades later, the damage caused by collateral consequences, amplified by the magnitude of mass incarceration, is limiting the life chances of millions of people in the U.S., and the reach of these events extends into higher education.

To further articulate the effects of a criminal conviction, Miller and Alexander (2016) presented the concept of the "carceral citizen," describing how this status alters the course of the individual from the moment they receive their new legal status. Further, Loyd (2015) discussed how carceral citizenship, used to support international apartheid practices, has become a global phenomenon. The people affected by these practices are subject to new rules and regulations, must follow laws that others do not have to follow, can be excluded from many social benefits, are stigmatized, and are singled out as subjects of bias and derision. This phenomenon creates a completely new type of existence for the convicted person, a reality that affects all facets of their life. Economically, socially, and historically oppressed demographics (e.g., BIPOC, low-income populations), who are disproportionately represented in the justice-contacted population, are more likely to be the victims of such destructive impacts. Further, carceral citizenship severely hinders civic participation, limiting or restricting such actions as voting rights and jury duty, allowing criminal legal institutions to reinforce harmful carceral stereotypes under the cover of procedural rules (Binnall, 2018). This phenomenon functions in an intersectional capacity to reinforce inequality within educational attainment, which includes excluding millions from experiencing the full benefits/privileges of higher education.

Intersectionality (Collins, 2000; Crenshaw, 1991, 2017; Desmond & Emirbayer, 2009; Emirbayer & Desmond, 2015), a key framing concept within this book, is a powerful theoretical paradigm based on the work of Black feminist scholars to explain how the various factors of a person's sociopolitical identity (e.g., race, class, gender, age, physical abilities, sexual orientation) function together to reproduce and create inequality, oppression, and/or privileges. This book's research participants are also often forced to grapple with the additional intersectional component of being labeled by society as system-affected individuals (even if they may not personally identify themselves by this label).

Miller and Stuart (2017) further explained how the impacts of carceral citizenship interact with higher education: "The bureaucrat, employer or school administrator may issue a license or lease to a well-qualified applicant, or admit a straight-A student into a prestigious university. It is, however, in the power of these actors to delay the process, reject the application or require additional steps solely because the applicant has as criminal record. This is despite their qualifications. In almost any other circumstance these actions would be considered a form of illegal discrimination because most other vulnerable groups have the rights and protections of conventional citizenship" (p. 537).

Thus, having encountered this system, and/or having been informed of the consequences to which they would soon be subjected, future SAA people began working within and organizing in institutions of higher education. Yet before pursuing this topic further, the logical next question is: What does previous scholarship and research say about why people with lived justice-system experience choose to pursue higher education? More specifically, what does the literature say about why SAA group members choose higher education?

Higher Education Is a Way Out, but Only If You Can Access It

From the decimation of entire segments of American society and the widespread damage resulting from the massive scope of a runaway-train punitive justice system that disproportionately impacts marginalized and disadvantaged populations (while also reaching into all segments of American society), a precious few (but growing) FI women and men have accessed higher education, harnessing its social justice potential by engaging in various forms of activist and critical scholarship.

As captured in the hopeful narrative of this book, a growing number of system-impacted people are accessing and successfully utilizing higher education (Dholakia, 2023). There is still a struggle ahead, as illustrated in a report by Cornwall in 2023, demonstrating that while 70 percent of incarcerated people want to obtain postsecondary credentials, only 4 percent of this population are able to receive college degrees, compared to 29 percent of the general population. This places system-impacted people at a distinct disadvantage in a job market in which over 66 percent of jobs will require at least a bachelor's degree by 2031 (Cornwall, 2023). Yet in 2016 around forty thousand people who were incarcerated participated in an experimental Pell Grant program. Further, in 2020 Congress reinstated widespread prison access to Pell Grants, with Pell funding available to universities that develop prison education programs. As a result, the number of incarcerated and FI people poised to engage with higher education is set to drastically expand. In regard to expanding university-affiliated SAA programs, Project Rebound, a program within the California State University system (the largest university system in the world), published a report (Project Rebound Consortium, 2022) that indicated increased state funding and drastic increases in rates of graduation for its college programs, growing graduation rates by 150 percent from 2019 to 2021.

Mukamal et al. (2015) reported that much of what holds FI people back from using higher education is structural, citing lack of financial resources to pay for the hefty price tag of college, including the costs of tuition and external costs of childcare and reliable transportation. Further, BIPOC and low-income populations, both groups composed of people who are often more susceptible to sociostructural barriers within education, are heavily overrepresented within the U.S. CLS and subsequently are less able to access higher education due to the collateral consequences of a legal conviction (Pryor & Thompkins, 2013). Jared, an FI faculty and SAA group member, frames how he perceived the likelihood of his accessing academia before he engaged with higher education: "I remember always like, looking up to professors as if like that was something that was like kind of cool, what they did. And like, you could do a lot with that. But it was like somebody like me didn't get to be something like that, right?" Even though he admires professors, he has been socialized to believe that achieving such a goal was denied to people with criminal convictions. He views the door as shut to people like himself.

Many studies have also pointed to college application attrition due to criminal history screening on college applications as denying access to institutions of higher education for many students (Custer, 2018; Halkovic & Greene, 2015; Johnson et al., 2021; Rosenthal et al., 2015). Another major factor of exclusion on the pathway to educational credentials is racially biased standardized tests, which have a long history of denying People of Color access to universities (Karabel, 2006; Knoester & Au, 2017; Rosales & Walker, 2021). The skyrocketing costs of attending college also heavily contribute to the exclusion of carcerally impacted populations (Elliott & Lewis, 2015; Jackson & Reynolds, 2013). Additionally, a study by Couloute (2018) indicated that after prison, opportunities for (and levels of) further education are lower than in the general population. Certainly not least of all, experiencing stigma on the college campus (Alvarado, 2020; Binnall et al., 2022) can impede the educational success of carcerally impacted students.

Another structural blockage that discourages system-contacted people from pursuing higher education is exclusion from licensure in many professional fields such as medicine, financial planning, law enforcement, certain types of transportation jobs, and primary education (Ajunwa & Onwuachi-Willig, 2018; McCann et al., 2021). If there is no chance of working in a professional field that requires professional college credentials because of a criminal conviction, it follows that system-affected people will not take the risk of investing in a costly education that is basically certain to not provide gainful employment.

Thus, many of us with criminal convictions began to search for ways to overcome the structural barriers that system contact placed in our pathways. A small contingent of system-affected people arrived at a potential solution: engagement with higher education and the attainment of academic credentials. Their pathways to education varied, perhaps having encountered an encouraging mentor, possessing social capital and/or access to privilege, having heard anecdotal accounts of previous successes, or having stumbled across research on the topic. Whether individuals arrived at the doors of higher education through random chance or because of an informed decision, evidence supports the potential positive outcomes of this action. In fact, education is one of the top predictors of reduced rates of recidivism after incarceration (Bozick et al., 2018; Davis et al. 2013).

From the perspective of educational research in prisons, Manger et al. (2019) cited Cross (1981) in a study that discussed why more adults do not participate in educational programs within Norwegian prisons. Cross explained that one of the ways adults are denied access to education is through institutional barriers such as "policies, procedures or exclusion criteria that systematically disadvantage certain groups of people" (Manger et al., 2019, p. 713). Manger et al. (2019) found that incarcerated people who are serving longer sentences tend to be more likely to experience institutional barriers to education, as they have encountered more such roadblocks over time. Discussing that people engage with education due to major life transitions, Nuriddin-Little (2020) found that FI Black men, with support from an educational program, were motivated to engage with further college after prison.

In a 2015 report from the University of California–Berkeley and Stanford law schools, Mukamal et al., (2015) attempted to answer the question of why people with criminal convictions decide to go to college. Subjects reported (1) feeling like college education was their only option to improve their lives; (2) that a college education would help them contribute to society; (3) that education would help them overcome their obstacles, having been inspired by other FI people; and (4) wanting to help other people who were incarcerated. In Kallman (2020), FI people reported engaging with college education in prison for reasons such as wanting to make a good impression on the courts and to improve their chances of parole. They also explained that once they gained some education, they developed a hunger for more and then began to really like it. In another account, Kallman (2020) stated, "Janus, a man of color in his 30s who has served two prison terms and who reports having been a strong student in high school, explicitly connects the solitude and isolation of the prison environment to his desire to study" (p. 7). Thus, the prison environment can have the latent effect of creating a space in which incarcerated people may decide to interact with higher education, as in my experience with incarceration. Others reported that education allowed them to escape their negative surroundings and provided the opportunity to know themselves better.

While system-affected people struggled to access higher education, the policies and practices that constituted the tough-on-crime mentality of mass incarceration were being built on conventional scholarship and social discourse, which presented people convicted of criminal offenses as untrustworthy, unable to be rehabilitated, making decisions based purely on self-will, and purely "deviant" in mentality (Samenow, 1984). Other research, such as Martinson's (1974) infamous "What Works" article, suggested that rehabilitative programs do not work to correct criminal behavior and thus there is no point in trying to help them. Such poorly constructed studies fueled the fires of negative public sentiment toward system-affected people, while giving politicians the political inertia needed to pass draconian criminal and sentencing codes that shoved millions of people into U.S. prisons. The works of Martinson (1974) and Samenow (1984) functioned to "other" (Spivak, 1985; Stabile, 2015) system-affected people, placing them in a dehumanized group outside of "normal" or "good" people and giving credence to the notion that there was something intrinsically and irredeemably "wrong" with them. In another othering discussion, Garland's (2002) "criminology of the other" described use of a theoretical paradigm that views people who commit crime as a group apart, troublesome outsiders capable of deviance and treachery who are very much unlike us wholesome "normal people." Also, Spivak (2023), in her essay "Can the Subaltern Speak?," pointed out that marginalized groups, speaking to the struggles of the colonized Indian people during British rule (similar to FI populations in the U.S.), often lack a social platform from which to be heard and are without the means to politically advocate for themselves in areas such as economics and policy. However, much of the work of SAA members attempts to overcome, expose, and eliminate such stereotypes and oppressive policy, an immense task by any measure.

In the next section I explain how lived-experience insider perspectives can assist in humanizing system-affected people in the eyes of society (we have always been human beings), thus providing a means to see through the haze of negative societal opinions about this population. Through the actions of SAAs within activist scholarship, classroom instruction, policy/program development, and advocacy for the system contacted, the *insider* view that SAAs possess can assist in breaking through the hegemonic grip that status quo institutions of power (including conventional criminology) hold on interpretations of criminology and the CLS (Newbold et al., 2014). Further, they can develop agency in building their own empowered identities (Jensen, 2011), essentially rejecting dehumanizing labels.

INSIDER PERSPECTIVE

The use of insider perspective has played an important part in bringing forward the experiences of those who share direct life experiences and/or statuses with the population(s) and/or issue(s) they are studying. Further, insider perspective can function to allow marginalized and underrepresented people the opportunity to directly analyze their own experiences. In some cases insiders, because of their unique viewpoint, may possess a powerful bridge of understanding with those like themselves, especially in the context of scholarly work. Deb, a professor and system-affected SAA member, emphasizes the value of working with those with lived experience: "People who have been in the system; who better to say what we should do, or who better to think of research ideas and think of what we should be studying because they have that insider knowledge." When the researcher is studying groups/populations of which they are a member, they are engaging in *insider research* (Dwyer & Buckle, 2009; Kanuha, 2000). Thus, as Dwyer & Buckle (2009, p. 58) stated, "the researcher shares an identity, language, and experiential base with the study participants (Asselin, 2003)." Adler and Adler (1987) referred to the researcher with insider perspective as a scholar with a "complete membership role" in the research process, which can give the qualitative investigator a certain amount of acceptance among their research population.

When one attempts to fully parse out the nuances of insider perspective, it soon becomes clear that possessing a shared experience with the subject population of study does not guarantee the researcher a comprehensive understanding of the people they are examining. Conversely, not sharing a common status does not necessarily denote that the researcher is entirely detached from a group. Often, the researcher informed by lived experience may understand only a small slice of the topic. As Dwyer and Buckle (2009) stated, "Holding membership in a group does not denote complete sameness within that group. Likewise, not being a member of a group does not denote complete difference (p. 60).

To provide context for sharing group membership experience, although the author of this book has been incarcerated—a life event he shares with several other SAA group members—in many cases he shares only a small range of experiences with the people he interviewed for this book. For example, his incarceration experience was twenty years ago; thus, when talking to individuals who were recently incarcerated, he can relate only partially, because major components of the CLS have changed since then. If he is speaking to someone incarcerated in a state correctional facility, his experience differs due to the fact that he was housed in a federal correctional facility. If he is talking to a person who spent prison time in a maximum-security facility, his experience diverges again, as his prison was a minimum-security one, and there are significant policy and practice variations between the two security levels. To add another level of nuance, even individual institutions vary greatly in administrative policy, practices, and the subcultural norms of incarcerated people and prison staff. Therefore, it is not unlikely that the qualities he experienced within his facility would be unfamiliar to an individual who is or was incarcerated in a different facility, even if it is of the same security level and legal jurisdiction as his own.

The researcher without insider perspective may also share perspectives and have extensive interactions with multiple group members, and/or have a strong academic knowledge base of the topics/issues impacting the groups they are studying. Yet it must be noted that while the outsider generally cannot possess most of the insights possessed by those in the group they are studying, the knowledge they do have can provide some degree of common understanding and may increase researcher sensitivity toward the plight/struggles of those with whom they are interacting in the research process.

Critiques of and Responses to the Insider Perspective

The importance and use of SAA group members' insider perspective, in activist scholarship, the classroom, policy/program development, and advocacy for the system contacted, is a vital missing component needed to bring about humanistic and effective criminal justice transformation. The possession of insider perspective (Baca Zinn 1979) (also referred to as lived experience in this book) is infused not only into SAA groups' scholarship and actions, but also into the fabric of their identities. It must be noted that SAA people can use insider perspective in a wide range of research methods (Horowitz & Uggen, 2018; Tietjen, 2019; Newbold & Ross, 2013; Tietjen, 2013; Yeager, 2004), including statistical analysis (Tietjen et al., 2019), qualitative in-depth interviews (Custer et al., 2020), case studies (Abeyta et al., 2021), and theorization (Crewe et al., 2014).[4] Insider perspective was used by many early SAA scholars, such as in the CC group, and continues to be heavily valued in the vibrant SAA literature of today. It must be noted that insider perspective does not have to be directly stated or disclosed by the authors for it to inform their research. SAA lived experiences can function to influence how studies are framed, providing unique opportunities to illuminate perspectives and social dynamics that impact people with system contact.

Many group members have been directly impacted by the CLS through courts; incarceration (CLS lived experiences); criminal convictions; or family, friends, and loved ones who have been incarcerated, and this gives them a unique perspective on the justice system. The *insider* view within SAA groups can assist in breaking through the hegemonic grip that status quo institutions of power and the conventional academy have traditionally held on interpretations of criminology and the CLS (Newbold et al., 2014).

The insider perspective, central to the argument of this book, is one of the driving centerpieces of the SAA movement's ability to transform its members and their educational institutions, and it has the potential to transform the CLS (which oppressed them) in a humanistic capacity. Ramona, an FI independent SAA member, discusses the potential of insider perspective: "If you want to you can become a criminologist, you have this kind of insider perspective that you can use to help." She uses her insider perspective to help system-impacted people organize and advocate for themselves, often working with more formal SAA groups.

Smith (2021) pointed out that Alinsky (1946) emphasized the inclusion of "native leaders"—those who are closest to the situation—in social movements. This book builds on a body of scholarship from critical scholars who have studied system-affected populations over the past several decades. For example, previous criminological literature has referred to the recent mass mobilization of system-affected scholars who are demanding a place at the policy table of transformative criminal justice as a revolution. Maruna (2017), in his work on a growing desistance movement led by those with lived experience, stated that activists with insider perspective are advocating for "nothing about us, without us" (p. 16), in regard to the means by which criminology and criminal legal policies are researched, discussed, and enacted.

Richards et al. (2010) emphasized that FI academics who work within criminological fields bring a unique insight to their disciplines. The voices of carcerally impacted people were often not recognized in the academic study of crime. The inclusion of such perceptions can illuminate dynamics that would otherwise be disregarded or unnoticed by researchers and academics who have not had exposure to prison and postprison situations. The lived narratives of incarcerated and FI people and others under the supervision of the CLS (i.e., people on parole/probation, those on community supervision) are ironically and often not heard in the discourse of criminal justice research (Tietjen, 2019; Ross & Richards, 2003). Through the presence of carcerally impacted academic insiders in institutions of higher education—and the activist and critical research they espouse—more accurate representations of the structural inequalities endured by postcarceral populations (within and outside of higher education) can be illuminated and then be used alongside other forms of evidence to inform CLS policy and practice.

The usefulness and credibility of the insider perspective has been at the center of debate in several humanistic academic disciplines that focus on topics such as social equality. Tillman (2002) pointed to an ethnographic study by Foster (1997) of African American teachers, suggesting that perhaps an insider researcher from the same cultural background as the participants would be better equipped for this research topic. Within feminist studies, Acker (2000) noted that the use of the insider and outsider perspectives by feminist scholars has been a subject of contention, pointing to past studies and discussions she had had with her colleagues in which they debated whether or not the insider perspective introduces excessive bias into the qualitative research process or improves the research. Their findings led Acker to believe that the benefits of the insider perspective outweighed the potential flaws. Some critics question whether scholars who engage in criminological insider perspective research can maintain objectivity while discussing their own personal perspectives and experiences within the CLS (Bosworth, 2004; Lilly, 2009; Maghan, 2004). Defenders of the insider perspective within social sciences research point out that such research, which is often part of qualitative analysis, recognizes the reflexive use of subjectivity as an important part of the research process (Honeywell, 2021; Tietjen et al., 2019; Earle, 2014). In addition, some SAA members and groups emphasize that their inside experiences can, in many circumstances, further substantiate criminological research. This argument adds that these insights may not be illuminated by other research methodologies.

Multiple Pathways to Transformation

While the issue of how insider perspective should be used in scholarship (including research and classroom instruction) has been a topic of spirited debate and critique in some SAA groups, the powerful impact of insider perspective on scholarship is not disputed. Regardless of whether SAA members choose to self-disclose any past system contact or decide not to reveal their past, such lived experience has a powerful influence on their scholarship (e.g., academic publications, classroom instruction, conference presentations). In regard to differing positions on insider perspective, during anecdotal interactions with SAA members in recent years, I have gleaned that full agreement about how the issue should be framed does not exist. Some past members believed that the insider perspective was the primary viewpoint and should be more highly valued than other forms of research—stating that non-insider-perspective research (both qualitative and quantitative) was less relevant or irrelevant. Others have taken a more inclusive approach, believing that insider perspective is part of a more comprehensive understanding of correctionally focused criminological phenomena and should be included with non-insider-perspective forms of research, thus shedding light on issues/events that outside research perspectives might have missed. On the other end of the spectrum, a certain smaller group has expressed that insider perspective should not be used at all, stating that current ethnographic and qualitative research on system-affected people would suffice to provide the carceral human experience in place of the SAA member's personal perspective.

Although the following discussion covers the various insider viewpoints contained within the SAA movement, this book emphasizes the immense commonalities contained within their lived perspectives and argues that the SAA movement should focus on the power and meaning of these shared experiences for those who have been in the carceral system. While arguments against the use of or overemphasis on insider perspectives have been thrown at SAA groups over the years (some critiques being well-meaning and others representing prosystem processes of marginalization), our collective strength lies in demonstrating to the world that our insider perspective–informed research is valuable and rigorous in its own right. While being realistic about the realities of our perspectives, SAAs should not frame our insider perspective work in a diminished light in order to accommodate attempts to minimize our impact and negate the value of our experiences by those who would align themselves with conventional and prosystem arguments.

Some practitioners of insider perspective research methodologies state that the *insider* has nuanced knowledge of the personal experiences of other people with whom they share a group membership (e.g., fellow people who were incarcerated). Yet another viewpoint is that the researcher's lived experience of incarceration is the focused knowledge of their experiences coupled with their firsthand knowledge of the facilities, administrative practices, policies, and personal interpretations of the subcultures of incarcerated people (Earle, 2014). The process of serving time in prison is the experience of preserving the self—perhaps a necessarily self-centered endeavor of protecting the self from the rigors and pains of imprisonment (Sykes, 1958/1974). Thus, an incarcerated person's energies are not focused on observing or learning the personal behaviors and habits of fellow incarcerated people, except as necessary to successfully navigate the carceral landscape. To explain it another way, the insider perspective researcher knows their own lived experiences but not the direct personal experiences of others. The insider perspective–informed researcher can speak only to superficial/peripheral shared experience, such as the shared carceral environment or interactions with similar types of situations (Levinas, 1987). This is not to imply that the shared environments and experiences of the researcher and the researched are not significant to lived experience–infused analysis (they provide a great deal of valuable context), but is instead an attempt to establish a more comprehensive understanding of the dynamics, limits, and parameters of the insider perspective research process.

A significant portion of SAA members choose to continue to engage with insider perspective research throughout their careers because they value being able to harness their lived experiences. It potentially gives a sense of meaning and value to the carcerally impacted portions of their lives (often long periods under the supervision of the system, or having lost loved ones for many years, who may return home from incarceration traumatized and damaged). As Binnall (2021a) stated in regard to carceral lived experience, "What we saw, felt, and heard while part of the carceral system is invaluable knowledge—data—that certainly informs any discussion of criminal justice issues. We are insiders." Such experiences are life-defining milestones to carcerally impacted SAA members, providing them with a means to transform their previously stigmatized system contact into tools to enact prosocial change, similar to Maruna's (2001) "redemptive scripts." Further, there are some peer-reviewed scholarly periodicals that are inclusive of research using insider perspective. For example, the *Journal of Prisoners on Prisons* (*JPP*), published in Ontario, Canada, has served as a venue for critical-criminological academic discourse by incarcerated and FI people since 1987. While supporting all types of recognized research methodologies, the *JPP* is also open to research premised on and/or including direct experiences of incarcerated and FI people. Considering that the journal is focused on critical-criminological and criminal justice topics, and many of those who submit research have direct carceral system contact, it should not come as a surprise that insider perspective is commonly used by *JPP* authors.

While some past SAA literature discusses members of the SAA population claiming that insider perspective is the only research that truly captures the carceral experience and/or is the only type of research that can truly reform the CLS (Ross et al., 2016; Lilly, 2009; Bosworth, 2004; Maghan, 2004), a certain viewpoint in recent scholarship speaks to avoiding what Earle (2014), an FI criminologist, referred to as "identity essentialism" within SAA scholarship. This speaks to steering clear of placing the identity of the *insider* as the most central and consequential perspective within the research process, a critique that has been leveled at the CC SAA group since shortly after its formation. Further, many modern SAA group perspectives view insider perspective as vitally important, alongside many other components of research. Lived experience is accessed by members of the SAA population in various ways (through friends, loved ones, and/or family members who have direct carceral-system contact). They view insider perspective as necessary to creating a comprehensive and rich perspective on criminal legal and correctional systems and phenomena. As Earle (2014) stated about CC,

> I think it would be a mistake for Convict Criminology to claim definitive insights or credentials for researching prisoner's experiences, or that there is a single, authentic truth to incarceration. We cannot 'tell it like it is' but telling it like it was for us will enrich the field for all. (pp. 435–436)

Earle's explanation of the scholarly and social impact of the experiences of SAA people within the CC group provides a means to frame the usefulness of their lived experiences. This is accomplished by avoiding the overclaiming of insider perspective's reach while still acknowledging that lived experiences have an important meaning and purpose in society.

The insider perspective–suffused research process is not perfectly linear (Jewkes & Letherby, 2001). Inside perspective often informs the qualitative research process (Dwyer & Buckle, 2009), using such methodologies as autoethnography, ethnography, case studies, and various types of field research. Sometimes insiders and outsiders shift roles, as Tietjen (2013), speaking to system-affected academics in general, pointed out:

> The insider-outsider perspective is quite complex, and can be a constantly shifting position during the research process, with outsiders also acting as insiders and vice versa. A resolution to these extreme views is posed in the form of both insiders and outsiders uniting under the same banner in creating good research. (pp. 54–55).

It should also be noted that because of the traumatizing experiences they have endured as a result of the carceral system, some members of the SAA population choose not to utilize insider perspective within their scholarship. They do not want to relive these experiences (Tietjen, 2013), and thus they engage with the many other useful forms of research available to criminologists. However, for those who do choose to use their insider perspective, their often difficult experiences gathered through direct carceral system impact can serve as readily accessible sources of qualitative data for scholars who often do not initially have the resources to construct or fund large research studies (though some SAA group members have eventually gone on to work on well-funded, high-profile research projects).

CATALYSTS FOR THE SAA MOVEMENT

Group Formation

Forsyth (2019) explained that the main factor drawing together members of a social group is the sharing of some sort of social tie. SAA group members have two common social categories. First, they are affected by the CLS in some capacity, whether having been confined within the system during a period of incarceration; having been convicted of a crime (which may or may not include incarceration); or having an acquaintance, family member, or loved one come into contact with the justice system. Second, they are engaged with higher education in some manner, as a student and/or working within higher education as an academic.

In Tuckman's (1965) multistage model of group development, groups normally progress from formation and orienting to each other, to testing boundaries/internal conflicts, to cooperation, to making successful progress, to eventually dissolving. Although these concepts are not covered in the scope of this book, it is worth noting that the various groups presented in Tuckman's study exist in different stages of the developmental process and because of this may focus their energies in different capacities. Some of the earlier SAA groups, such as Project Rebound and CC, are now in their midstages, cooperating and engaging in accomplishment of goals. For example, CC accomplished the goal of becoming a division of the ASC in 2020.

One dynamic of long-standing SAA groups that speaks to the longevity of their productive activity phases is the seemingly impervious and virulent nature of the problems on which these groups are focused, such as the massive inequality and oppression generated by outcomes of nearly four decades of punitive justice and mass-incarceration policy in the U.S. Other, more recently formed (but quickly growing) SAA groups, such as Underground Scholars and FICGN are still in the early stages of development, orienting themselves to other members and to the academic and social environments in which they find themselves while beginning to accomplish goals. One such example would be FICGN becoming a formal nonprofit organization in 2018.

Regarding the binding nature of shared experience, the SAA movement might also be compared to the group commonalities that exist in twelve-step organizations for overcoming addiction, such as Alcoholics Anonymous and Narcotics Anonymous (Borkman, 2008). Members of these groups come together to support one another in overcoming struggles while also improving their own lives. Marie, an active SAA group member and productive scholar, captures this dynamic: "I'm very group oriented and, you know, kind of seek out people that are like-minded because I really feel that there is power in the collective." The strength of these shared carceral lived experiences should not be underestimated or minimalized. There is a bond here, a communal form of capital that needs to be further understood and utilized in the process of reconstructing a legal system that perpetuates social healing in place of social harm.

SAA as a Social Movement

While I acknowledge that there are different types of social movements, such as reform, revolutionary, redemptive, and alternative (Flynn, 2011),

I do not presume to label the SAA assemblies represented in this book uniformly based on my own ascription. Rather, this study respects that they each define themselves differently, based on their values, norms, and worldviews. To theoretically establish SAAs as a social movement, first there is a call to attention of the already established platform for transformative legal movements. To frame the topic of SAAs within social movements, the concepts of "skin in the game" (Leitz, 2014) and "standing" (Beckwith, 1996; Ferree, 2002; Meyer & Bourdon, 2020) are presented as a means to understand the place of the academic with carceral lived experience in this process. I then point out the emergent nature of this undertaking (Maruna, 2017; LeBel, 2009; Ferrell, 1999; Ferrell et al., 2015; Ferrell et al., 2016), as SAA is still a growing and developing movement.

The platform for social movements to change the legal system (such as SAA) has been established within the current social/political milieux of more rehabilitative and progressive criminal legal policy. These developments are assisted by the continued development and expansion of the retroflexive reformation (Cressey, 1955) and wounded healers phenomenon in criminological and criminal justice academic circles, policy, and practice. Maruna (2017) stated that during the time frame of the recent proliferation of SAA groups in the U.S. and the U.K., the means of reducing crime and criminal progressive justice reform is shifting away from large grant-funded studies and cold, quantitative program assessments, toward the actual communities themselves. This movement is especially powerful when system-affected people work with other system-affected people.

Traditionally, academia organizes panels and workshops and produces scholarship to advocate for issues impacting oppressed and/or marginalized groups, but those impacted by current social problems are now becoming actively involved in the movement, emphasizing the concept "nothing about us, without us."

A keystone to the SAA movement is our direct involvement in the issue: we emphasize that we have standing (Beckwith, 1996; Ferree, 2002; Meyer & Bourdon, 2020) and skin in the game (Leitz, 2009, 2014). This is a vital part of our movement, because similar to Leitz's (2009, 2014) work on the Iraq antiwar movement organized by families of veterans, SAA members in this study have skin in the game (Leitz, 2009, 2014). We, our friends, and members of our families are directly impacted by the brutality and trauma of the CLS, through the blunt physical incapacitation of incarceration and the removal of friends and loved ones from our lives, only to have them returned to us carrying the harmful social, physical, and mental health scars of the correctional system with them. Because we care about the people in our group, we feel compelled to fight for them and to protect them from harm, from the physical and psychological harms of prison to the social harms of the bias, exclusion, and discrimination they face up reentry into society.

Another vital component of the social movement is standing. Who speaks for the movement? Meyer and Bourdon (2020) broke down the concept of standing within their discussion of the gun debate and who is allowed to have the standing to speak for a social issue. Ferree (2002) discussed how standing as a movement is presented to the media, also pointing out that the key issue is having control of how the movement's message (and image) is presented to the public. These processes can be somewhat controversial, contested, and often political. For example, even if a person within the SAA movement were to speak publicly on the subject, that does not automatically translate to their being perceived as having standing by the public or by the movement itself. Also, just because the media covers a movement does not mean that the movement has control of what the media are saying about it. Thus, building favorable standing is important.

Beckwith (1996) discussed the standing of women who were family and loved ones of miners being involved in a miners' labor movement. By explaining how they are uniquely involved and presenting themselves as directly impacted by the movement, they construct a powerful standing within the movement. Within SAA efforts' attempts to construct supportive public standing, people with direct carceral contact such as incarceration or with incarcerated family members are using scholarship and the resources of higher education to present the public with how they are impacted by the traumas and oppression of mass incarceration and an unjust CLS. This book, through the unified voices of system-impacted scholars and academics, attempts to present the strength of their direct claims to witnessing and living through both the personal and social pains of mass incarceration.

The mining women (Beckwith, 1996) had more or less standing based on how close their perceived contact was to the movement (wives and mothers were given more standing than sisters and daughters). Within the SAA movement, those with direct system- contact, having served time in prisons or correctional facilities, may publicly be perceived as having more standing than those without such experiences, even though the actual movement comprises a far wider spectrum of carceral experience, including strong allies without system contact.

Within SAA groups working to build supportive public standing, there may be differences of opinion about who is best suited to be the public face of the organization, based on such issues as speaking ability, earnestness, and type of system contact and legal conviction. There has even been some debate over systems of inequality being perpetuated within some SAA groups, as they have been accused of marginalizing certain populations within their ranks based on existing systems of inequality, such as gender and race. Also, some people interviewed for this book discussed SAA group specific modes of exclusion such as type of legal conviction (e.g., excluding more stigmatized convictions such as sex and violent crimes) and length of time served (e.g., giving preference to longer sentences served as a sign of more credibility). These topics were discussed because of a common love for fellow SAA members and as a means of improving SAA movement solidarity and equality for all involved.

Maruna (2017) referred to the CC SAA group when discussing social movements and inclusion of the directly oppressed within social movements:

> Importantly, the "nothing about us without us" revolution is already starting to emerge in academic criminology in the form of a movement called Convict Criminology (Richards & Ross, 2001). Largely consisting of ex-prisoner academics, Convict Criminology has made important strides in changing the way in which crime and justice are researched in both the US (see Jones et al., 2009) and the UK (Earle, 2016). (p. 16)

This movement is presented as a revolution within critical criminological scholarship and policy development that recognizes and incorporates the expertise of those directly affected by the criminal justice system instead of excluding them from the solution-making process. To further this point, Maruna (2017) stated, "Inclusive social science is good social science" (p. 16).

Further, building on the criminology and criminal justice social movements literature of Maruna (2017) and Lebel (2009) and the literature of cultural criminology (Ferrell, 1999; Ferrell et al., 2015; Ferrell et al., 2016), I present SAA groups as an emerging social movement. Maruna (2017) argued that desistance from crime is in and of itself a developing social movement. When speaking to the potential unity of groups of FI people, LeBel (2009) explained a sense of unity, obligation, and support in working with others with a common bond, and Hamm (1997) wrote, "Providing a supportive community and a network of individuals with shared consequences, these groups can be interpreted as transforming an ostensibly individual process into a social movement of sorts" (p. 169). To illustrate, Tomás, a charismatic SAA group member and student, optimistically speaks to the potential expansion of this movement at his university: "So I think it's just gonna keep on moving forward and growing, for real. Long [*sic*] as people are planning to see that they can achieve a degree and see by examples of other people, there's going to be more people applying and being part of it." Maruna (2017) explained how social movements (e.g., SAA) often start out small in scope but have the potential to expand if they are supplied with enough mobilization and support, such as Rosa Parks refusing to move to the back of a bus in 1955, and then, only fifty-three years later, the country electing its first Black president. Such a movement is currently taking place in the United States, as SAA groups continue to organize alongside other community-based criminal justice reform groups (Berger, 2013). Several SAA group members spoke about perceiving that they were part of a movement to challenge the system. Deb, an acquaintance-contacted professor and engaged SAA group member, describes the increasing strength of the movement: "But if you have a group, if you have a, you know, a large group, a growing group of people who all share the same vision and goal, then that builds more momentum to challenge those norms." She is pointing to the expanding SAA movement's ability to take a stand against the oppressive practices and norms in the academy that exclude or marginalize system-involved people.

In regard to the benefits of system-affected people working with other system-affected people, LeBel (2007) referred to Cressey's (1955) concept of retroflexive reformation, in which FI people working to help other struggling FI people succeed in realizing positive benefits from their actions, exhibiting greater psychological well-being and reduced likelihood of relapsing into criminal behaviors and criminogenic attitudes. In this process, the struggling SAA person being assisted by another SAA person receives hope and experience from a comrade who *has been there* (LeBel et al., 2015), generating a feeling that something should be given back to pull the others behind them up. This creates a cycle of empowerment among system-impacted peers, while generating a sense of meaning and purpose in their lives. From recent discussions I have been involved in amongst directly impacted populations regarding solutions to criminal justice–related structural social inequalities (many such ideas originate from groups impacted by intersectional oppression), strategies are being formed to further reach, mentor, and advocate for carcerally impacted scholars.[5]

Just as people involve with crime interpret crime from their cultural perspective, subcultures of system-affected academics view the issue of how to address criminal legal system problems from their own cultural lens. The SAA population's perceptions of their relationship to the criminal legal system are viewed through the filter of their own experiences. While I am not stating that all members of the diverse SAA movement view the criminal legal system and criminality through the same lens (they do not), all are at least influenced by their contact with the justice system. The life experiences and SAA media and scholarship presented in this book will bear that out.

FOUNDATIONAL THEORY AND SCHOLARSHIP OF SAA: CAPTURING THE DIVERSE UNDERPINNINGS OF SAA THOUGHT

The establishment of scholarship that fits under the umbrella of the SAA paradigm is multifaceted. In addition to the far-reaching impact of intersectionality (Collins, 2000; Crenshaw, 2017; Desmond & Emirbayer, 2009; Emirbayer & Desmond, 2015) on the SAA population, there is a massive body of scholarship of movements to improve, transform, or reform the CLS within the U.S. and internationally that can be traced back to the nineteenth century (Bentley, 1998; Vázquez, 2018). Yet because a complete history of the scholarship of criminal justice reform is outside the scope of this book, I focus on the era (and thought) that has served as the theoretical underpinning of the SAA movement, primarily the second half of the twentieth century through the present. The ideas that in varying capacities support the development of SAA actions are drawn from multiple areas of thought, including the (a) new criminology, (b) cultural criminology, (c) prison abolition literature, (d) peacemaking criminology, (e) insider perspective on overuse of mass incarceration, and (f) feminist standpoint theory. Then, after the presentation of theories of support, the subsequent two sections explain the relationship that much of the SAA movement has to the prosocial capabilities of both activist scholarship and critical scholarship.

The New Criminology

From the tumultuous protest era of the 1960s came a criminological perspective from the U.K., *new criminology* (Taylor et al., 1973), which sought to emphasize that crime is motivated by people's relationship to and places within the social structure, and situated in systems of power and authority. This was an attempt to explain crime using the sociology of C. Wright Mills (1978), reframing crime from the sphere of a private problem to that of a public issue. New criminology was a criminological discipline whose intentions were humanistic and focused on prosocial change, not just research for the sake of additional lines in a vitae and professional accolades.

Cultural Criminology

The *cultural criminology* of Ferrell (1999) and Ferrell et al. (2015), which is founded in the work of new criminology (Taylor et al., 1973), attempts to "integrate the fields of criminology and cultural studies or, put differently, to import the insights of cultural studies into contemporary criminology" (Ferrell, 1999, p. 396). It strives to place the motives for deviance and crime within culture and cultural processes and qualitatively analyzes how individuals construct meaning in regard to the inclination to cross moral, ethical, and legal boundaries within systems of power (e.g., passing laws to define an action as a crime or not a crime, moral entrepreneurship). Through the SAA movement, the culture of criminal justice lived experience is interacting with social institutions including higher education, public justice policy, and the CLS, with the potential to assist in transformative progressive change. Through their unique insights into the subcultures of crime, deviance, and the CLS, SAA people may be able to more effectively illuminate problems within these systems and propose more effective solutions.

Thomas Mathiesen's Perspectives on Prison Abolition and Positive and Negative Reforms

Regarding the solutions proposed by SAA people working within and outside of society's major institutions of power, there are differing views on what it means to "reform" the justice system. Mathiesen (1974, 2008) spoke to continual and gradual abolition-informed action and policy change, framing this process through the concepts of positive and negative reforms. Positive reforms are implemented to change policies and practices within existing social institutions (e.g., the CLS), to help that system function better and/or more efficiently, thus further perpetuating that system. Alternatively, the goal of negative reform is to consistently and gradually diminish and shut down components of an oppressive system of power, introducing abolition-informed changes to the justice system that are subtle enough to avoid being rejected outright as being perceived as too radical. Thus, the long-term goal is eliminating the institution (prisons) that creates the social inequality, while at the same time continually constructing better alternatives to the current system through measures of decriminalizing society (eliminating the need for prisons through addressing the social factors that create them).

As far as how to address the many problems within the CLS, the goals and intentions of the SAA population are varied in type and intensity, with support for both positive and negative types of reform, including (among other things) complete and immediate prison abolition, adding more educational programs to existing prisons, and helping people postincarceration. For example, during anecdotal discussions with many SAA colleagues over the last few years, some have described witnessing the negative impacts of internalization of institutional cultural norms of prisons among fellow SAA members. Comparisons have been made to the oppressed (SAA people) having been deluded into supporting the abusive behavior of the oppressor (correctional institutions). In stark contrast, SAA members from countries (outside the U.S.) that have strong social welfare networks have explained (in casual conversation and during the course of qualitative research) that their prisons actually facilitated their rehabilitation and educational efforts while they were incarcerated.

Peacemaking Criminology

The broad and diverse SAA movement also encompasses many of the concepts of *peacemaking criminology* (Pepinsky, 2013; Pepinsky & Quinney, 1991), which is a movement to address crime through the use of peaceful means of restoring society, instead of the harsh punishments utilized in punishment-centered carceral institutions. In regard to listening to others as equals instead of speaking down to them, Pepinsky (2013) stated, "By definition, peacemaking as praxis defines control as moving from people speaking to or for others, to letting people speak for themselves, giving priority to stories less heard in discourse about a social problem" (p. 336). This dynamic forms the very backbone of much of the actions and impact of the SAA population, whether through openly disclosing their criminal justice backgrounds and experiences or through the influence of their lived experience–informed efforts and research on social institutions. Through the methods of healing, honest communication, listening to others, and reconciliation, peacemaking criminology seeks to overcome the structural inequalities and systematic oppression perpetuated by the current punitive CLS. Yet as I have already stated, the SAA movement is diverse and broad; and consequently, the fine points of action within this population are not always perfectly synchronized. Nonetheless, it would not be an overstatement to point out that peacemaking ideals are in alignment with much of the work of the SAA movement.

John Irwin on Extreme Overuse of Incarceration in the U.S.

In the prolific work of the late criminologist and founder of Project Rebound, John Irwin (Irwin, 2005, 1987, 1980; Irwin & Austin, 1994), the reader gets both an insider's (in his youth, Irwin served five years in Soledad Prison in California for armed robbery) and a critical criminologist's perspective at the same time. His work does not shy away from directly taking the U.S. CLS's policy of mass incarceration to task for its detrimental impact on both society and the individuals who are confined within. Irwin (Ross & Richards, 2003, pp. xvii–xxii) also brought attention to the swinging pendulum of public and subsequently political sentiments about how to approach system-affected people and the harm that this constantly fluctuating and inconsistent process wreaks on society.

While expressing a need for all forms of criminological research and avoiding a purely essentialist stance on the insider perspective, Irwin has emphasized that conventional research on FI populations is often at least partially inaccurate and thus very susceptible to purposeful political manipulation and media sensationalism (e.g., the Willie Horton myth).[6] This is an important area in which the input of system-affected people in criminology can provide invaluable perspectives and insights to expand the reach of correctional scholarship. Such scholarship might otherwise be open to misinterpretation by those who have not experienced incarceration directly. Irwin's own impact as a lived-experience scholar lends powerful street cred to the utility and value of use of carceral insider perspectives that establish often overlooked commonalities among the system contacted, while at the same time highlighting fascinating subjective phenomena that can lead to new avenues of knowledge discovery.

Feminist Standpoint Theory

Another theoretical perspective that informs the SAA movement is feminist standpoint theory (Harding, 2004; Hartsock, 1983; Smith, 1987).

Standpoint theory, initially developed and used quite effectively by feminist scholars (Harding, 2004; Hartsock, 1983; Smith, 1987), argued that feminist studies was best conducted by women, because women had actually "lived" and experienced the concepts being studied. They were best suited to understand and interpret their own realities. This premise has been compared to the actions and scholarship of certain SAA groups that present criminology through the vantage point of the FI, primarily CC (Earle, 2018; Larsen & Piché, 2012). In other words, when applying the standpoint perspective to the broad SAA movement in a general sense, the system-affected social location of many in the SAA population could be framed as presenting a criminal justice lived-experience position.

I have presented a diverse body of scholarship, research, and academic literature that lends theoretical support to the SAA movement and is important to the integrity and durability of any long-lasting, progressive social movement. Building on this diverse platform of academic concepts, SAAs have found a means to put the scholarship to work (helping carcerally impacted people) through activist scholarship.

SUCCESSFULLY HARNESSING THE POTENTIAL OF ACTIVIST SCHOLARSHIP IN THE SAA MOVEMENT

Activist and critical scholars such as the voices in this book are directly involved with the issue we are exploring. Nicole, an FI college instructor and active SAA group member, gives a spirited shout-out to activist work: "I became an activist, I just wanted to follow something that made me passionate, something that made me feel alive and that my life was not being wasted." For example, we may actively take institutional and political stances in support of progressive social change within our own academic institutions and/or work toward enacting justice for the research populations that we are part of. In the primary argument of this book, I state that a powerful means to eliminate the dysfunctional punitive CLS is through the growing activist scholarship movement of system-affected academics. This is not to discount nonactivist scholarship within or outside the SAA movement that collaboratively focuses on building a humanistic system of grappling with justice issues alongside activist scholarship. The work of the nonactivist academic who aims for purely objective and nonpolitical scholarship (Lennox & Yildiz, 2020), although that is a difficult target to hit, can alter the social and systemic landscapes of social justice in powerful and meaningful ways. Such work has helpful effects in constructing pathways to social equity in the midst of the current broken CLS (in the total sphere of social justice–focused scholarship) (Bowling, 2006; Lynch, 2000; Naegler, 2022).

In order to build a successful activist movement, certain components need to be present. While vigorous and emotional appeals for rights and justice are powerful tools to draw attention to issues in the social and political spheres, such action does not seem to be as successful in building powerful, sustained social movements. Luhtakallio's (2019) research on Finnish bicycle activism indicated that in order to endure, group activism needs more than passionate appeals. To succeed, long-lasting movements must be founded on an underpinning of rigorous evidence-based research supported by the discourse of experts in the topic/issue of the movement over a prolonged period of time, *in addition* to including emotional and spirited pleas for justice and/or change.

The formation of some of the early SAA actions involved discussions of FI scholars (who identified themselves as victims of oppression, bias, and injustice), who generally hailed from criminology, criminal justice, and adjacent fields in the social sciences (Richards & Ross, 2001). There were many spirited conversations in which some group members, having been victims of systemic oppression, made emotionally charged appeals for reform and change within the justice system (Newbold & Ross, 2013). Thus, such SAA groups combined the qualities Luhtakallio (2019) emphasized as qualities of activist movements that are prosperous, comprising both experts in the field (who produce rigorous research) and those making fervent appeals for justice. In many examples, people from the SAA population encapsulate these components of successful activist movements in their scholarship (Davis, 2003; Dietsche & Kilmer, 2024; Herzing & Piché, 2024; LeBel, 2009; Ortiz et al., 2022; Richards & Ross, 2001; Ross & Richards, 2003; Smith & Kinzel, 2021; Soto, 2020; Sudbury, 2015; Tietjen et al. 2018; Trivedi & Ray, 2024; Woodall, 2020), being formally educated experts in their field who also ardently speak truth to power in search of justice.

Scholarship Meets Activism

In the definition of *activist scholarship* employed in this book, Hale (2001, 2008) described the concept in three parts: first, it provides an improved comprehension of the foundational causes of oppressive social forces; second, such research is done in collaboration with groups of people who are the subjects of such oppressive social forces; and third, the results of such research are used in cooperation with impacted populations to bring about prosocial, progressive, and/or transformative change. Sue, a system-involved scholar and SAA group member, defines activist scholarship this way: "I think also with being in a, in the academic route, I think you'd agree, it's like, there's a lot of flexibility there, too, right? Like, you can teach and do all that. Which I love to do, like, don't get me wrong. But then for my heart is really at which is like community organizing activism and like, lets me do both."

Activist scholarship has been used to further multiple causes, including social justice, human rights, anti-racism, and anti-imperialism (Hale, 2008). Such work aligns itself with Marx's (1845/1978) famous statement, "The philosophers have only interpreted the world, in various ways; the point, however, is to change it" (p. 145). The activist-scholars presented in this book have generally focused on issues surrounding criminal justice reform and transformation and incarcerated and FI people. Many of the SAA people interviewed have interacted with an oppressive system and through that interaction have become motivated to change the system. During the process of forming organized activist and critical-scholar groups or in engaging in activism individually, SAA members have aligned themselves with "organized groups in struggle" (Hale, 2008, p. 26), thus slowly building up the SAA movement. In a powerful statement that further delineates the uplifting process that develops as system-affected people seek out each other for support, LeBel (2009) asserted, "Therefore, it is thought that the more FI persons identify with similarly stigmatized others, the more they will endorse advocacy/activism as a coping orientation" (p. 169). Whether part of a formal SAA group or an independent SAA individual, members of the movement are likely to be working with others with similar worldviews.

Activist scholarship is a mechanism through which the SAA population utilizes and/or accesses "the radical potentialities of the university as a site occupied by communities of resistance" (Sudbury & Okazawa-Rey, 2009, p. 2). For many centuries, activist scholarship has been engaged in seeking material changes for various facets of society, premised on a multitude of complex political issues.

In America and Europe, many academics who engage in activist scholarship are from marginalized and/or oppressed populations and work in academic fields such as critical and/or social-inequality areas of criminology, sociology, and anthropology. They also reside in criminal justice, ethnic studies, and women's or gender studies programs, which commonly study such populations. Hale (2008) pointed out that when making the argument for activist scholarship (which is often qualitative), one must contend with criticisms that such research lacks the rigor, objectivity, and positivistic qualities of conventional research methods (quite similar to the critiques of scholars who use their insider perspective in their research). But activist-scholars make strong arguments for why their work challenges such notions, questioning the imbuing of quantitative data (without critically examining its value and accuracy) with value it may not have, the use of objectivity as a means of subterfuge for agreement with authority, and the use of positivism (when it doesn't examine the origins and causes of positive facts). Responding to claims that qualitative activist researchers' work lacks objectivity, Davis et al. (2019) pointed out that activist scholarship moves beyond rigidly maintaining objectivity, challenging dominant and/or commonly perceived forms of knowledge production and leading toward prosocial impact. Activist scholarship, much the same as work informed by insider perspective, does not abandon the furtherance of knowledge, empiricism, or researcher objectivity, but instead calls into question how such concepts are defined in status quo academia, reconceptualizes the outcomes of status quo knowledge production, and attempts to weaken systems of social inequality and oppression.

"Positioned Objectivity" within Activist Scholarship

One of the primary critiques used to marginalize and denigrate the lived-experience perspectives within SAA activist scholarship (including written work and classroom instruction) is that it lacks objectivity. Such narrow attitudes within academic disciplines such as criminology and criminal justice have attempted to disregard the SAA member's unique knowledge of specific situations, in favor of purely quantitative analysis of crime and deviance phenomena. These unique insider viewpoints potentially contain compelling insights into why many criminal legal policies are failing, insights that are missing from the supposedly "objective" works of mainstream carcerally focused scholarship in multiple disciplines.

There is a significant body of literature, which I subsequently explore, that reframes the research of lived-experience ethnographic, autoethnographic, and qualitative scholars as more aptly suited to reach many oppressed populations. The outcomes of such researchers' efforts are more likely to help marginalized populations, and many scholars informed by carceral lived experiences argue that their lived-experience-informed research is valuable because it is objective within the specific situations that their experiences and observations are focused on. Hale (2008) explained that activist-scholars do not seek to eliminate objectivity from the stance-driven research process and replace it with ubiquitous subjectivity, but instead present the concept of *positioned objectivity*. With this stance toward objectivity, the activist researcher considers their political positions and unique insights in their focal topic. Also, this practice emphasizes the value of the researcher's situated knowledge (Haraway, 1988) when interacting with those they are both studying and collaborating with in order to further the central prosocial or social justice cause(s).

Davis et al. (2019) addressed investigator *answerability* to the populations studied in activist research, noting that researchers are not only working with the people/groups/movements they are studying, but also answering to them. Thus, the interactions and communications of the research process take place between the researcher and the researched, not from the perspective of the academic expert lecturing down from the ivory tower to all others involved. In the research presented in this book, answerability takes place from the perspective of my being involved both in an SAA group and in SAA activist scholarship, as well as the participants being part of the SAA movement and producing activist scholarship. Thus, I am positioned as an SAA activist-scholar studying other SAA activist-scholars. I have spent my career collaborating with other activist-scholars, and I attempt to remain answerable to the movements that I am concurrently working with and researching. Such answerability to the SAA movement entails vigilantly centering my scholarship around the actual matters that affect people impacted by the carceral system, based on the direct lived-experience voices of our population. It also involves openly dialoging with our members, having honest conversations about our struggles, and helping to guide the movement toward inclusive and supportive values.

In addition to highlighting activist scholarship's components, outlining how it stands up to systems of power, and explaining why people engage in this work, Davis et al. (2019) pointed out that scholarship that uses "activist" and "radical" language may not actually be activist, but more the work of "armchair revolutionaries." Such reputed activist-scholars use diluted language and vague concepts to address serious issues of oppression indirectly, without actually taking a stand on the issues through their scholarship, thus hiding safely behind their research.

Often activist academic scholars must create their own spaces for work in environments in which such scholarship is not the norm. In many cases, the dedicated practicing activist-scholar is placed in a potentially compromising situation, in which they must both produce scholarship that promotes their universities in order to gain tenure and at the same time point out systems of oppression and/or critique structural inequalities that exist within their institutions (Davis et al., 2019). Mainstream academia is traditionally and historically white, cis-heteronormative, and patriarchal. If an activist-scholar is from an intersectional background or identifies with a marginalized or historically oppressed group (e.g., race, record of criminal conviction, ethnicity, non-CIS sexual orientation) and chooses to study such identities/issues, their scholarship is often denigrated or devalued by their institutions and the academy as a whole. The type of research methodology they employ also matters (Christensen & Jensen, 2012).

The Importance of Building Supportive Spaces for SAA Scholarship

In many cases, the methods of study needed to capture the organic human experience of oppressed groups is qualitative in nature (e.g., ethnographies, semistructured interviews, participatory action research). Nonquantitative forms of research are frequently viewed as less rigorous, not empirical, and/or less credible; consequently, activist researchers' scholarship is more likely to be excluded from more prestigious academic journals. This hierarchical value system of research (Tewksbury, 2009; Kleck et al., 2006; Gelsthorpe & Sharpe, 2005) is actively and aggressively promoted as the gold standard by which research grants are funded, professional accomplishments are recognized, awards are granted, institutional support is distributed, and faculty promotions are earned. Subsequently, activist scholarship is often less likely to receive such positive attention and the privileges and awards that accompany it.

Aspiring student scholars and junior faculty within SAA groups who practice activist scholarship need the support of senior faculty. Sue, a system-affected junior faculty member, activist, and dedicated SAA member, explains how a lived-experience faculty member (and leading scholar) reached out to her as a graduate student and brought her in on a major funded research project at a large university: "'Do you want to be the lead research assistant on my gang project for [large western city]?'" She quickly made the decision, stating, "So I started getting involved in that research project." This changed the trajectory of her academic career, plugging her into a powerful network of resourced support.

Senior faculty can, of course, offer their wisdom, but more importantly, they can provide institutional social capital to support and legitimate the activist work of new scholars and researchers struggling to gain an academic foothold in institutions and academic disciplines that may not be entirely open or welcoming to the politically or socially controversial topics they are researching. Sudbury and Okazawa-Rey (2009) stated that the need for radical spaces in academy was urgent and needed to be protected. Given the increase in the anti-intellectual, anti-science segment of conservative political climate in the U.S. (Peters, 2019; Motta, 2018), this need has increased exponentially in importance. In order to establish such radical activist spaces, an institutionally supported and reliable pathway between activism and academia must be forged across academic disciplines.

There are several criminology and criminal justice academic programs aligned with conservative political and theoretical definitions of criminal justice that function as a means to further proliferate the socially destabilizing and oppressive components of tough-on-crime, mass-incarceration, and CLS policy. Often well-resourced with large grants from institutions of power, the programs can function as mechanisms of oppression, cranking out mountains of publications from "studies" designed to legitimate the mission of the U.S. CLS, which is known to perpetuate institutionalized inequality. Such departments form relationships with state and federal criminal justice institutions to access their data and research grant resources (Wincup, 2017; Hillyard et al., 2004). Forging such relationships creates conflicts of interest that strongly discourage critique of such carceral institutions, much less taking active political and/or idealistic stances against them, as doing so could endanger the academically fruitful relationships and revenue streams generated from such arrangements. Such profitable arrangements that benefit universities during this era of ever-tightening state university budgets (Richards & Ross, 2001) may seem attractive to criminology and criminal justice academic departments, but they often function to continue or even expand socially destructive impacts of the prison state.

It must be noted that social activism versus the structural realities of institutional policies are where critical movements, students, and the university institution run into real structural conflicts. In an era of shrinking college funding from states, students and faculty reasonably expect to use their academic credentials to find viable employment, while universities, in addition to offering their degree programs, are scrambling to find money to operate academic programs in general. To further frame this, there are socioeconomic, cultural, and political forces affecting both university financial issues and the academic social justice efforts that take place within these institutions. This creates an academic and social environment of tension that can impact the SAA movement. For example, degree programs that are perceived as not contributing to revenue generation (i.e., in the social sciences, arts, and humanities) within the university structure are commonly undersupported and gradually defunded (Ikpe, 2015; Patel, 2015), while more resources are given to academic areas that can lead to high-income careers (i.e., in professional fields, business, and finance). A large portion of SAA members whose voices have created this book work in these underresourced social science and adjacent fields, where much of the important work of social and carceral transformation is done. Thus, some of the work of the SAA movement should focus on demonstrating to universities and society how our work and our empowered population strengthen society (Hall, 2015). When system-affected people are provided with educational resources that include the critical thinking abilities of social sciences education coupled with professional skills for careers, as well as support to facilitate full reintegration back into society after their legal system contact, their contributions add social and economic value to their surrounding communities (McCorkel & DeFina, 2019). Stronger and healthier communities and economies can lead to similar positive effects in society's institutions of higher education (Alonso, 2023).

Sudbury (2009) emphasized that activist-scholars within these academic departments have taken action to discontinue and/or challenge the problematic/dysfunctional relationship between universities and formal institutions of the criminal justice system. Antiprison scholars who work on a firsthand basis with incarcerated activists and people in antiprison activist groups are organizing academic events through university channels and services that directly engage the academic institution with progressive causes (Sudbury, 2009).

To delve further into the working relationship that many activist-scholars cultivate with the groups with which they collaborate, it is important to point out that activist-scholars often include those they are researching in their research process, giving them a part in constructing and writing the scholarship itself. In some cases the activist-scholar is actually part of the focal marginalized or oppressed group being studied, as is the case in this book. In many traditional qualitative studies, even among the work of well-meaning social justice–focused scholars, the research process can function to directly or indirectly exploit the stories of the research populations (Sudbury, 2009). For example, a researcher may solicit qualitative interviews from their research population, collect the data, and then disappear back to their university to personally interpret and record their observations and digitally recorded data. Then, without seeking feedback or advice from their study participants, the scholar may write up the journal article, book chapter, or book and subsequently collect the professional accolades, privileges, and benefits associated with producing such research. The researched population may be left out of the benefits of the study, or their benefits may be delayed and perceived as secondary in importance.

Another benefit of the collaborative and interactive relationship established between the researcher and researched group in the activist research process is overcoming what Haraway (1988) referred to as the "God trick": when the scholar's voice becomes the omnipotent and objective message of reason, explaining the nature of reality to both the reader and the populations studied, based on their own distanced interpretations, without feedback from the researched participants. In contrast, the SAA researchers (of which I am one) and the SAA people we are studying possess shared experiences. We interact with each other as peers collaboratively working toward similar goals.[7]

Activist movements have found support within the often open-minded and progressive ideas and culture that can commonly be found in university environments. Although the relationships between universities, activism, and scholarship are often complex and fraught with conflicts of interest, including differential distribution of power between the faculty and the institution, institutions of higher education have been fertile sites for social and political movements dating back to the thirteenth century (Carlton, 2022; Jason, 2018; Muir, 1981).[8] Jason (2018) pointed out that as youth protest has increased in recent years, students in the U.S. have been asking what the perfect strategy is for effecting change. For example, a 2016 UCLA survey indicated that one in ten students expected to be in a protest at some point in their college career (Jason, 2018). Further, Marshall Ganz, a lecturer at the Harvard Kennedy School who provided perspective in the Jason article, indicated that youth come to college with the best tools to effect social change: youthful vibrancy, energy, and open-mindedness unpolluted by the rigors, harsh realities, and struggles of adult life.

In addition to youthful vibrance, many also note the mind-opening impacts of university degree programs (Taylor, 2017; Hare, 1979), which often include courses in humanities, liberal arts, and social sciences—fields that include addressing issues surrounding oppression and social injustice, support progressive and prosocial concepts, and are more likely to generate equality-motivated movements (Beattie, 2018; Broido & Reason, 2005; Cancian, 1992). Additionally, a strong body of literature points to the evidence-based potential that higher education has to lift the oppressed out of disadvantage and provide the marginalized with the tools to fight against injustice and systems of inequality (Berila, 2015; Furlong & Cartmel, 2009; Harkavy, 2006).

Successfully Harnessing the Potential of Critical Scholarship in the SAA Movement

Critical scholarship exists alongside and within the activist scholarship footprint of the SAA movement. Such critiques often harness the spirit of lived experience to produce research that frames how critical scholarship practices produce destructive and counterproductive individual and societal outcomes. Critical scholarship has a wider history in the criminological field, especially in SAA-affiliated literature. The critical perspective of criminology this book presents took root in 1970 with the work of Richard Quinney and states emphatically that the public's preconceived images of crime and those who commit crime have tangible impacts on the entirety of the CLS. More specifically, critical criminological scholarship explains that the CLS serves to oppress those under its supervision, functioning to criminalize, control, and incarcerate the powerless while protecting the power elite (Mills, 1956). The critical scholars in this book speak to the past quashing and/or marginalizing of formally incarcerated viewpoints within conventional criminological scholarship. Their academic training, coupled with possession of carceral insider perspective, creates the potential to develop unique capabilities to recognize, deconstruct, and formally critique systematic suppression of FI communities.

Much of SAA group research and scholarship is critical activist work that does the heavy lifting in regard to delivering the message that mass incarceration is a broken system. It would be appropriate to present the work of this movement as an amalgamation of activist and critical scholarships. SAAs commonly use critical scholarship and critical academia, presented as an academic perspective to question and critique conventional criminology's alignment with and support of the mainstream systems of power (Foucault, 1977b). Much of the research produced by SAA individuals questions the impact of status quo criminal justice scholarship (Tietjen, 2019; Ortiz & Jackey, 2019; Richards &

Ross, 2001), whose topics of study and findings are often aligned with and sympathetic to the large state and federal criminal justice institutions from which they are receiving large research grants. Josh, a busy SAA member and directly impacted academic, speaks to the SAA movement's critical mission: "I see us as the critical challenge to the division of, to mainstream correction views of corrections within academia." Many SAA group members would argue that the findings of criminological scholarship would be more comprehensive in scope of research findings and more effective in impact on policy if they were informed by the carcerally impacted perspective. As Jones et al. (2009, p. 153) explained, "The convict perspective is also based on perceptions, experiences, and analytical ideas that originate with defendants and prisoners, which are then developed by critical scholars (Richards & Ross, 2003a, 2003b)."

In their literature production, many SAA scholars (Abeyta et al., 2021; Anderson et al., 2024; Fox et al., 2023; Kilty & Fayter, 2022; Quach et al., 2022; Smith & Kinzel, 2021), while writing the foundational work of the movement, have openly identified with the critical theoretical perspective. The critical scholarship produced by these SAA members attempts to illuminate the exclusion of system-affected perspectives within status quo and managerial criminological scholarship and policy development, especially when such research influences correctional policies and practices that interact directly with incarcerated people and FI people. Stephen Richards (2013), one of the cofounders of CC, emphasized that for FI criminologists, a critical stance toward the justice system was already established during their carceral exposure: "For those of us that have suffered the prison, there is no intellectual debate about the relative merits of mainstream versus critical criminology. We know what side we are on. The journey to prison and back informs our ontological understanding of the horror of imprisonment" (p. 384). Even though many SAA group members who actively engage in scholarship through research and in the classroom take a critical stance, much of the legitimacy, academic acceptance, and accomplishments of SAA academics would not have been possible without the actions and scholarship of supportive academic allies outside of SAA groups. Richards (2013) also explained that standing up for carcerally impacted academics sometimes placed the non-SAA academics' careers at risk, yet many such scholars persisted in taking a stand against systemic bias by defending their SAA colleagues' critical stances.

Earle (2016) posited that the stresses and strains of the prison environment may actually create more effective critical thinkers. Incarceration forces an individual to withdraw into the self as a defensive-coping measure, thus giving them the opportunity to introspectively examine their feelings and thoughts continually over the course of their prison sentence, which in some cases may span many years. Criminologists and other academics who have had direct system contact are potentially more practiced in engaging in reflexive and critical analysis of some criminal justice–related issues, thus producing more insightful findings and analyses to inform effective policy development. Jones et al. (2009) explained, "CC also challenges commonly held beliefs; thus, it is coterminous with many of the epistemological approaches found in critical criminology, which tries to deconstruct myths and look for deeper meanings" (p. 156). This article then explained that critical criminology was part of the intellectual legacy of this particular SAA group. This critical position, much of which is based on Richard Quinney's (1970) *The Social Reality of Crime*, views the formation of criminality and deviance of individuals as attached to broader social structural forces such as punitive criminal justice policies, economics, politics, and systems of oppression, in place of attacking the character, immediate family, or moral failings of the system-affected person.

Another, deeper point to emphasize is that critical scholarship and activist scholarship often function together to tear down oppressive hierarchies of power, overcome injustice, and create more altruistic and humanitarian environments. The work of activist scholarship (including activism, academic literature, and instruction) and critical scholarship (including scholarship and instruction) operates in partnership to generate transformative justice (Arrigo & Bersot, 2016). Through a Nietzschean concept called "transpraxis" (Nietzsche, 1961, 1966), Arrigo and Bersot (2016) explained, "We argued that the revolutionary academic activism sufficient to advance the struggle of mutual, collective and interdependent human existence depends on a critical pedagogy for a people yet to be, and we reconceived the educational terrain of criminological activism as the pedagogy of becoming" (p. 561). Thus, SAA critical and activist scholarship and actions can work together to generate nondiscriminatory, supportive, and egalitarian environments for system-affected people, who are struggling to become a legitimate and accepted part of society. It must be noted that the process of "becoming" for those involved in the emergent SAA movement is greater than just gaining higher education, although this transformative process can use such academic institutions as the foundation from which to build revolutionary concepts, groups, and coalitions focused on creating equality and legitimacy for CLS-affected people in general.

The hard work of activist-scholars in the activist movements on which they are focused can function heuristically through the cumulation of their scholarly findings to build a means of understanding how to overcome and/or navigate oppression. This process of overcoming can be activated through critical scholarship and thought, the outcomes of which can function to provide guidance (education) for oppressed/underrepresented people to arrive at transformative and liberatory solutions. Arrigo and Bersot (2016) explained that the process of building a legitimate identity through scholarly activism established on hard-earned equality is not a straightforward linear process but is built within the movement through a multitude of fluctuating and varied creative actions by the group. From a transpraxis perspective, SAA groups forge their social justice–focused realities by overcoming the power structures and bureaucratic entanglements that function to suppress and suffocate progressive/prosocial change and collectively construct their own means of justice and equality for people oppressed by the CLS.

WALKING THROUGH THE DOOR

The idea of system-affected people discovering higher education as a door of opportunity has the potential to lead to humanistic and transformative changes in higher education and the legal system. George, an FI professor and SAA group leader, explains what SAA-motivated system changes he is advocating: "I'm a prison abolitionist, I believe, we should slowly reconstruct the system, you know, to utilize transformative justice." He believes in dismantling the current carceral archipelago and replacing it with something markedly different, using alternatives to punitive justice.

When I discovered an SAA group that advocated and mentored FI people like myself, I broke through a societal barrier that had been imposed on me by the CLS. This interaction informed me that legitimate opportunities existed, and that perhaps I could escape the stigmatizing constraints of a criminal conviction. Yet to realize the full potential of the SAA movement, I still had to engage through such actions as acquiring educational credentials, advocating for system-affected people, producing scholarship, and doing social justice work. I had to be shown how to *walk through the door.*

As this chapter presents, for individuals with direct carceral contact, the process of walking through the door of potential that the SAA movement provides can be a positive and life-changing experience, but the journey is not easy and is often littered with obstacles such as structural inequalities, intersectional discrimination for BIPOC populations, and systemic bias. Enduring several decades of mass incarceration has traumatized millions of people, and they have returned (and continue to return) to society as a disenfranchised population, left to fend for themselves. Subsequently, many have turned to education as a means of overcoming the stigma and collateral consequences of criminal convictions, only to discover that such consequences also extend to institutions of education. Although through their own hard work, their academic ability, and good mentorship several system-affected scholars have found their way through higher education to careers in academia and the professional sphere, the other part of the story is that because they found very little support from society, they had to forge their way through structural obstacles largely on their own (with the support of a few dedicated allies). Then, when some educational successes were attained by early SAA members, many turned around and helped others overcome academia's structural obstacles, constructing their own networks of support through the SAA movement. Further, using activist scholarship that harnesses their unique lived-experience perspectives, I framed how SAA members can humanistically transform both the academic and legal systems. As discussed, they are discovering the power of activist and critical scholarship to effect prosocial change and are mobilizing the immense resources of institutions of higher education to secure support for future SAA members.

While this chapter has set up the background, catalysts, and framework of the SAA movement, including the value of the insider perspective, group formation, and foundational theory, and the importance of activist scholarship, in the next chapter I begin to think about the relationship that system-affected people have with the social institution of higher education. While education can be a saving grace for this population, these bonds/connections can often be tenuous, complex, and quite vulnerable to external social forces such as stigma and bias. I emphasize that segments of the SAA population vulnerable to intersectional oppression (e.g., people socialized as Black, Hispanic, LatinX, or Chicano; the economically disadvantaged; women) often experience greater structural obstacles within higher education More specifically, in chapter 2 I dig into the first half of the important reciprocal SAA/university transformative dynamic (which underlies and reinforces the movement's growing humanistic impact on higher education) presented by this book, *the effect of the university on the SAA individual.* The journey through the powerful impacts of college credentials and engagement, though laden with social structural obstacles, can both signify to the carcerally impacted that *the door is open* to opportunities and/or lead to the discovery of this *open door.*

CHAPTER 2

The Journey of Higher Education

I was a few months into my two-year prison sentence, and it was a day for an epiphany. Sitting in a crowded and loud cellblock in a holding facility for federal and state incarcerated people, the stress level was high. Negativity easily takes hold of the mind, as your cellblock peers tell stories about the difficult issues they are enduring. People in prison are rarely living their best lives, and for most, their lives have taken a drastic turn for the worse. I was stone bored and full of despair. This was my first time experiencing incarceration, and I was not dealing with it well. I was facing a serious drug charge in federal court and had just simultaneously lost my freedom and all of my worldly possessions. While desperately trying to find some hope and a reason to move forward with my life, it had occurred to me, after listening to some surrounding conversation among my sixty bunkmates, that maybe I should try going back to college. Through the prison grapevine, I had learned that educational programs in prison were few and far between. Later, when I arrived at a federal prison, I learned that there were long waiting lists if you were lucky enough to be at prison that had a college program. Also, you often had to pay for the college credits yourself, because at that time (early 2000s) federal education grants and loans were inaccessible to incarcerated people. To further compound this issue, I was seriously short on financial resources. The one thing I did have plenty of was time, yet it was quickly becoming apparent that prison as an institution was not going to help me do anything productive or positive with my time. Consequently, in an attempt to generate some hope in the midst of a dark time, I became focused on figuring out a way to access some sort of education, of any sort. I had no grand strategy, or long-term goals, as of yet. My mind was still too overwhelmed with the hopelessness of incarceration to allow for that. The only plan I had formed was that I was going to try to take some college courses that might nudge me closer to a college degree at some point in a distant and unknown future.

Fast forward to about nine months, approximately a year into my sentence. I had been placed in Yankton Federal Prison Camp. It was mail call, and I was anxiously anticipating a package. In federal prison, the vibe of the environment was similar to the holding facility I had been in nine months earlier: there was a vast surplus anxiety, while hope was usually in extremely short supply. As a rare exception, mail call could be a hopeful time for all of us. It was a connection to the outside world. If mail was received, it was a brief moment when we perceived a link to others outside of the stifling and isolated prison ecosystem. We waited as the guard called out fellow incarcerated men's names. I heard my name called; I walked to the front of the group to receive my mail and was handed a large package I had been anticipating for several weeks now. It was much larger than the envelopes I usually received from family, and I knew what it was from the university label stamped on the package.

The process to access these courses from within a federal prison had been arduous. There was a lot of red tape to cut through. After spending several weeks researching colleges to find affordable distance learning tuition and signing the institutional clearance paperwork to gain permission from the prison, my correspondence course materials had finally arrived. Educational Pell Grant availability for incarcerated people had been abolished several years before my prison term due to early 1990s tough-on-crime legislation, yet I was able (barely) to scrape together enough financial resources to pay for these classes. Otherwise, such opportunities would have been unavailable to me.[1]

This was the beginning of my journey back to education. Being a precocious youth, I had excelled academically in my grade school and high school days. Then, after I graduated from high school, I fell into a period of personal troubles. For many years I was separated from education by my intensifying struggles with substance misuse disorders and the subsequent slew of legal problems that eventually landed me in prison. Yet I turned a corner when I began to reengage with the pursuit of academic learning. I became energized and accessed a sense of happiness, enthusiasm, and purpose that I had not felt since childhood. Further, this gave me a means with which to see through the disheartening fog of incarceration. I now had a purpose for moving forward toward an accomplishment that I perceived as a positive goal, something that could help me improve my life.

I would spend the next ten years engaged with higher education on the pathway to my doctorate. It would be an extreme fabrication to state that my journey through my undergraduate and graduate degrees was seamless, easy, and entirely smooth. As an eager but naive undergraduate student, I struggled to find academic direction and lacked confidence in myself. Finding an area of scholarship that would lead to a career open to FI people was paramount, but I felt like a ship without a rudder. Yet as I slowly improved my academic grade point average with continued good academic performance in my sociology courses, I began to regain some confidence in my ability to succeed at something once again. But . . . I lacked a mentor. One day, after an inspiring lecture in one of my favorite sociology courses, Sociological Theory, I self-disclosed my background to the professor. I had already discovered that this professor advocated for incarcerated people, and I felt confident in placing trust in her acceptance of me. From that point, this professor worked closely with me as a mentor throughout my time as an undergraduate student. In addition, I accessed the general academic counseling available to all students, and the university's academic counselors helped me find opportunities. I began to put together a strong résumé of scholarly accomplishments. Through interacting with my university, I built a support structure of accomplished scholars, acquiring both life-course and academic guidance, and found confidence in myself. College helped me overcome several of the structural hurdles of reentry that my criminal conviction had placed in my path.

CROSSING THE TERRAIN OF HIGHER EDUCATION

The dynamic of higher education's impact on SAA people can be a complicated reality, with much variance often based on the forces of intersectional oppression. The transformative pathway through collegiate attainment functions as a two-pronged experience, introducing carcerally impacted students to levers of empowerment while at the same time presenting them with systemic biases. Thus, while system-impacted scholars still encounter many biases and collateral consequences, higher education can function as a means to potentially overcome and more successfully navigate many of the difficult structural hurdles in their path. SAAs also encountered both pronounced and subtle prejudices and discrimination, well documented within the U.S. university system, against many historically oppressed groups such as disenfranchised minority people, women, and low-income people. Yet through academia they also have the opportunity to access a wider array of new resources, which when coupled with additional systems of support can help expand their potential to experience general life-course and reintegration success, while also being given more tools to stand up to the structure of inequality that surrounds criminal convictions. In this book I present a dual transformation, as system-affected academics and the university institutions they are affiliated with change, influence, and interact with each other.

This chapter presents the first half of the reciprocal transformative effect between SAA individuals and institutions of higher education, the impact of academic institutions (i.e., universities, colleges, and professional schools) on the system-affected academic. Initially, SAA participants define how and why they made the choice to interact with higher education as a life choice and speak to the importance of mentorship from academic faculty members in leading them to educational success. Then, drastically varying impacts of system-contact stigma for those with direct and indirect contact within higher education are set forth, from the SAA members' interpretations of marginalization, intersectionality, and privilege. A person with *direct system contact* has been convicted of a legal offense, with or without incarceration. Someone with *indirect system contact* is without a formal legal conviction but has a family member or loved one who has been convicted of a legal offense.

Next, I discuss the way that many SAA members are prone to personal struggles that often stem from their legal system contact. This process affects how the university system influences students. Thereafter, group members provide views about how the often intersectional (Crenshaw, 1991, 2017) factors of social inequality (focusing on class, gender, race, sexual orientation, and age) interact with previous system contact when they encounter higher education. Study participants also parse out the influences of varying combinations of bias and/or acceptance they may have encountered within their institutions of higher education because of their CLS contact and/or involvement with the SAA movement. The higher education–associated influences they experienced shaped both the transformative processes and the types of scholars or professionals they would become (or aspire to become). In regard to impacts on SAA members, higher education provided the opportunity to flourish from a general life-course and scholarly standpoint, while simultaneously perpetuating and dispersing prejudicial/marginalizing forces. Consequently, many participants were still significantly hindered by larger obstacles associated with societal bias and stigmatization attached to criminal convictions (which also existed within higher education), but they also gained awareness of further opportunities available to them and accessed a network of like-minded others who could provide support and advocacy for them.

NAVIGATING THE HALLS OF ACADEMIA: A MULTIFACETED, TRANSFORMATIVE JOURNEY

In this section, SAA participants define how and why they made the choice to interact with higher education as a life choice, speak to the importance of mentorship by academic faculty members in leading them to educational success, and describe where they want their education to take them. At some point in the life of SAA group members, they chose to engage in higher education. Yet the reasons for the initial contact, the academic path, and the experiences encountered on this journey are varied and nonlinear.

Encouraged by a Friend, Family Member, or Educator

A powerful part of many SAA group members' academic journeys was encouragement and advice from family members, mentors, and acquaintances to engage with education. Family played an important role in this process for many. Families without previous formal contact with higher education often functioned in a vital general support capacity (i.e., emotional, financial, shelter, childcare), while family members with academic credentials provided advice on how to successfully maneuver through academic processes.

Many participants spoke about guidance and encouragement from mentors who had experience and expertise in a specialized scholarly or professional area that required higher education as a means to engage with this field. SAA members who encountered such guidance described a wide array of mentors and mentorship styles. Some mentors were more directly involved with providing opportunities and giving directives (well-meaning) that were to be followed. Bernard speaks of a mentorship process as a system-affected academic. Describing his initial mentor, he states, "He remembers me, and he kind of just walks me through everything, introduces me to everybody. The guy who would become the dean, who would become my supervisor, introduces me to the vice president, who will become like my mentor as well." Bernard built up a mentorship network that he credits with introducing him to further mentors and that gave him focused and in-depth educational guidance.

Another type of mentor that was referenced was those who had shared life experiences of system contact with the SAA mentees. For example, some people spoke of receiving educational mentorship from others they were incarcerated with, breaking with the stereotypes of shiftless "convicts" who think of nothing but criminal exploits and mayhem all their waking hours. For example, George, along with a small group of the people he was incarcerated with, took some correspondence courses while serving a prison sentence. When asked what his fellow students thought about him taking college courses in prison, he replies, "They were, they were down with it, man; it was some of them that encouraged it and gave me the information on how to do it. They actually provided me with like, social capital, you know, they hooked me up with the information." Thus, respondents indicated that education within the prison subcultures of incarcerated people was viewed as a means to improve their lives, or to "go straight" (Irwin, 1987) and "make good" (Maruna, 2001) in carceral jargon. Others pointed to the guidance of experienced SAA mentors. Such guidance from lived-experience mentors was often described by SAA members as a beneficial dynamic that forged a uniquely empathetic and supportive connection not present in more conventional mentorship relationships. Joanne, an independent SAA individual from the U.K., describes the advice a fellow woman independent SAA mentor (who later became a friend) gave her:

> So, one of my colleagues and one of my fellow students. I said to her, get on [social media site], start following people around, start telling people to follow you and they'll help you. . . . I said, I'll help anyone, anyone who's got an interest in criminal justice and . . . wants to make a difference.

Not only is this an example of SAA women helping each other, it also demonstrates how mentorship networks start. Joanne and her mentor went on to become good friends outside of social media, and both actively work to help (such SAA helping dynamics are discussed in the subsequent pages of this chapter) other SAA women in the U.K.

Practical Reasons Such as a Means of Support or to Earn Credentials Needed to Find Employment

While mentorship served as a powerful means of encouraging engagement with education, several SAA members pointed to the more practical motivation of acquiring a means to support themselves. Arriving at this scholarly inspiration was motivated by both personal and external origins. From the personal/individual perspective, many explained that they arrived at the desire to engage in education of their own volition, without the encouragement of others. Included in this reasoning was the belief, after being blocked from many other conventional avenues of self-improvement, that formal education was the only option available. When asked why she began to pursue higher education, Madeline very succinctly points out that she went back to college "because I couldn't get a damn job." Due to a felony conviction, many employment opportunities had been blocked, so she chose college as a means to overcome these impediments. Other pragmatic reasons for attaining academic credentials were also encouraged by mentors, system-contacted peers, and supportive friends and family members. Sue explains that her parents strongly encouraged her to pursue education. She wanted to pay her parents back for all the support they had given her:

> But my parents were always like, school, school, school, school, right, like, keep going.
>
> It's very rare to meet someone that's first gen [BIPOC] parents that doesn't take advantage of school or the opportunity . . . parents make happen by them leaving their country and like, you know, pushing school on you or whatever, like, so school itself and undergrad was a fucking breeze.

She points to the struggles and sacrifices her parents, first-generation immigrants, made for her, urging her to go to school. This gave her the strength of conviction to apply herself so effectively that she performed very well in school.

To Overcome and Manage Stigma Attached to Criminal Convictions

The desire to overcome the stigma of a criminal conviction was expressed in association with many of the other explanations for academic engagement. Also, through the attainment of educational credentials (i.e., college degrees), SAA people attempted to manage the stigma of incarceration. Carl, a direct system–contacted SAA group member and graduate student, explains why he is pursuing a PhD after incarceration:

> And I hope to bring that voice to the conversation as that expert who has that PhD that is recognized in academia as well that can say this guy isn't just some crackpot former incarcerated defendant. He's got a degree, he's got experience, and maybe that'll be the difference between being taken seriously and just being another guy with an axe to grind.

College degrees signify a positive life achievement while also providing the degree recipient with a recognized document of expertise in their subject, further legitimating their voices within academic and public spheres.

To Help Others, to Give Back

For some SAA group members, attaining education was a means of accessing the tools needed to help others. Some people were involved in helping others in an educational capacity before their formal education started. For example, Clara, when speaking about education while incarcerated, explains that while she was still serving her short prison sentence, she was working with other incarcerated women as a tutor, "[This] is why I think I ended up doing more sort of peer role type stuff, like helping other people."

Also, through educational credentials, SAA group members perceived that they could further help others in need within their own communities, or who might have experienced forms of oppression similar to what they had. Diego, a graduate student and active SAA group member, emphasizes that he works in higher education to help his community. Stressing that criminologists need to do more, he makes his views clear:

> We're not changing anything by continuing to research the community, because we're just researching the community. We're researching gang injunctions; we're researching these shootings. But how are we changing it? There's people in the neighborhood, activists and activists, I call them activist-scholars, organic intellectuals, that are actually fighting against the system of mass incarceration, where they're fighting against the system of policing. . . .
>
> And for me, a lot of . . . at least academia, especially when you get into PhD level. . . . [A] lot of these researchers don't even, again, don't even set foot in academia, didn't even set foot in the barrio, they don't even . . . , and how they don't even know the prison conditions.

While many study participants knew of the suffering and problems in their own lives and neighborhoods, their experiences within the CLS often expanded their awareness of the pervasiveness of inequalities that existed in society. Consequently, several SAA members developed the desire to help improve their world in some capacity.

WHY PARTICIPANTS CHOSE THEIR FIELDS OF STUDY

Encouragement or Advice to Go into a Field

For study participants, an important part of successfully navigating the process of higher education was receiving social support in the form of academic mentorship. Faculty in academia provided specific/detailed academic guidance and opened doors for scholarly and career opportunities. Many SAA members mentioned varying degrees of mentorship at the institutions of higher education that they were affiliated with. In some cases, they identified the support and encouragement provided by such mentors as the key factor in their academic and career progress. For example, Tera is moved to tears as she describes the importance of her faculty mentor going to bat for her:

> Fortunately, for me, and I think if this hadn't have happened, I may be in a very different place.
>
> I think she took me under her wing, because she really, really wanted to help me, and she really wanted to give me a chance to be the best that I could be. But she was also really mindful, which I really liked about her, to see me as a student, and not as someone that had been to prison.

This level of support that Tera found at her university gave her confidence in herself. Her professor looked out for her and assisted her in gaining a position in a graduate program.

In regard to why SAA members chose their fields of study, in many discussions it was pointed out that academic mentors advised them to go into their fields (often humanistic and social science fields, such as sociology, social work, humanities, and criminology). Holly explains that one of her professors advised her to go into sociology because they believed that she would not be able to use her criminal justice degree: "So it's one professor, who basically told me, 'Why are you doing this? You have a felony?'" She goes on to explain what she learned from sociology:

> Sociology, I really started learning the criminal justice system, which, my rights and all that, the sociology part plays into the surrounding, my areas of my people, the, you know, the community, that's why sociology fits in.

> And I took sociology and behaviors. There was some criminal criminology in there. So it's [*sic*] kind of work together.

Holly discovered that sociology gave her a broader perspective on many issues including people in her community. Advisers explained that the mentee's potential might best be realized within certain areas, and that such fields might be more likely to result in employment opportunities.

Many chose fields that aligned with their value systems, such as wanting to lift up others, creating social equity, and promoting egalitarianism. For example, Bernard, a multiple SAA group member, points out why he chose his area of study:

> I went with sociology, and I didn't know what I was gonna do with that sociology. Yeah. But it was perfect. It was perfect for me. I noticed that a lot of my classes that I did really well, there were social science classes in sociology, and, and I took to it, you know, and I was there around people who were actually doing sociological work around reentry . . . and changing the narrative around formerly incarcerated people and advocacy, and just all the things that we're doing. So I just kind of fell into that. And then through that network, I got the job I'm working at now.

As they had explained about why they chose to engage with education, many system-affected academics chose their fields to help others. This desire often tied in with their value systems. Through education, they were made aware of academic and professional fields through which they could most effectively provide help to oppressed others in society and in their own communities. Also, others without legal convictions (acquaintance contacted), who already worked in a humanistic field and were knowledgeable about the oppression and struggles of system-contacted people, wanted to put that knowledge to use helping others through activist scholarship. Other SAA members already had previous college exposure before their experiences with the CLS, and they subsequently returned to their fields after their carceral contact.

Taking College Classes in Prison

Engaging with college while incarcerated was contingent on certain factors. In prisons in the U.S. prison system, educational program coverage is quite inconsistent. Subsequently, access to higher education while incarcerated is far from certain. Participants' reasons for not having access to prison programs varied. For example, their sentences were too short to engage with prison education programs in overcrowded and underresourced prisons with long waiting lists to get into college programs. Other reasons were that they were not qualified to take the college classes due to lacking educational support and resources before incarceration, lacked monetary resources to pay for college classes in prisons where college was only provided at cost, were not interested in higher education yet, or had already obtained advanced educational credentials before prison. In a few cases, incarcerated SAA members were able to access mail-order or online correspondence courses, if they had the financial resources with which to do so (which many did not).

In correctional systems such as that of the U.K., SAA members could access well-established college education programs such as the Open University, which provides educational coverage in prisons. Bob, an SAA group member from the U.K., talks about taking college classes in prison: "So in the, in the U.K., we have the Open University. Yeah. They've been around to celebrate the fiftieth anniversary, actually. So I was like, seven when it started, but it's always been a big part of the prison education system, because obviously people can study from the cell." The U.K. prison system requires a sentence of over four years to be eligible for this program.

WHY PARTICIPANTS CHOSE TO WORK IN ACADEMIA

To Help System-Affected People and Others through Higher Education

While I have previously discussed why people chose to become engaged in higher education, the choice to work in education as a career embodies another sphere of commitment to helping. Many participants discovered that the wisdom and knowledge they discovered through academia were enlightening and empowering, and they felt a strong urge to impart helping/empowering wisdom to others, including those with life experiences similar to theirs (system-affected people), who had been oppressed and suffered as they had. Anna, a system-affected professor, explains how she had a change of heart about teaching during graduate school:

> And I was forced to teach that as part of the PhD stipend, okay. And I fell in love with being in the classroom, okay. I told my husband [I] was like, I'm gonna hate this, shitty kids, they're not going to give a fuck, its [*sic*] going to be miserable. He still brings up to this day that I said that. And then once I got in the classroom, I fell in love with teaching students.

> I could be in the classroom and change the mentality of the people going into the system. And I just enjoyed being in the classroom. So I really say that I became a professor kind of [by] accident. Like it wasn't my intent to actually do that, but it became my passion.

This experience drastically and unexpectedly changed her life, and she has subsequently gone on to become a charismatic advocate for system-affected people. Through exposure to higher education, SAA group members such as Anna realized that academia was something they had an aptitude for and really enjoyed doing. Sometimes this realization of academic capabilities, an educational epiphany in other words, is also associated with the transformative potential of higher education and the aspiration to help others.

To Progressively Transform the Legal System through Higher Education

Transformation ties in with the key ideas of this discussion. SAA group members often chose to work in academia because they believed in the transformative potential of their chosen field of study to change the CLS in a progressive manner. Anna, a faculty member with direct system contact, points out the transformative potential she possesses in the classroom:

> So [correctional] officers had like, they could just use the free [college courses]. So, I had a lot of them [in the classes she taught] and seeing like a light bulb go off in their head when they learned about things. I was like, "Well, I can, I can change it in the classroom," like I could be in the classroom and change the mentality of the people going into the system.

As she explains, Anna discovered that she could use the knowledge she had acquired from both carceral experiences and formal academic training to illuminate differing viewpoints of prison reality. In this instance, she exposed a new perception of prison to those who had already experienced prison as employees and staff, which she viewed as opening their minds to other ways of understanding people who are incarcerated.

WHY PARTICIPANTS CHOSE TO WORK IN PROFESSIONAL CAREERS

Among the one out of every five SAA members within the scope of this book who used their educational credentials to access various professions outside of academia (often academic adjacent), the motivations for working in their fields often overlapped with the reasons given for working in higher education. They were especially focused on the helping factor, transformation potential, and discovery that they enjoyed doing the work. Such nonacademic helping careers included law, social work, and psychology. Also, there was a realization that they had an aptitude for doing the work. Tomás, a degree-holding professional and SAA member who at the time of the study was applying to graduate schools, describes how he arrived at his current position:

> I created my own job position. Job developer became the vocation education manager at the time. Okay. And I just, I would just tell people like, hey, go to school, I will take them to trips at [local university] colleges, right? We'll see [visit local university] like, I develop a lot of networking with professors.

In addition, individuals engaged in nonfaculty jobs within academia for practical reasons, such as a means to support themselves and/or to gain experience on their way to other life goals, such as a better career position. Tomás has aspirations of attaining graduate-level degree credentials in order to access greater opportunities.

STIGMA AND SUPPORT ON THE SAME BOAT

As SAA people travel through their lives after direct and/or indirect system contact, many grapple with the drastically varying impacts of this stigma. From the vantage point of higher education, this denigrating social mark interacts with the dynamics of achievement, marginalization, intersectionality, and privilege. The strategies that are used to overcome and/or manage the stigma of system contact can influence the educational trajectories of SAA people, functioning to both empower and disempower.

When they chose to be open about their legal backgrounds, many SAAs received greater support from the academic faculty, while others received passive forms of resistance and pushback from faculty and fellow classmates. Yet others preferred to not disclose their criminal justice involvement and thus did not grapple with open bias except when they were forced to reveal their records during institutional administrative processes. Most study participants reported trauma due to their carceral contact, yet also noted that it was generally their past criminal records, more than sentence length and type of crime they were convicted of, that were likely to hinder their educational progress upon reentry. While recognizing the powerful transformative impact that university education can have on system-affected academics, the stigmatization of a past legal conviction is still a considerable stumbling block for students.

DIFFERENCES IN HOW HIGHER EDUCATION INSTITUTIONS RECEIVED THE FORMERLY INCARCERATED

Participants Received Different Levels of Support; Some Experienced Bias

Among the thirty-eight out of forty-six participants I spoke with who were FI, most reported receiving support yet also indicated that the biased reactions they received in higher education related to their carceral contact was tied to factors of inequality such as racism, classism, sexism, and type of crime they were convicted of. The majority of FI and system-involved SAA members I spoke with indicated that they were not treated in a different capacity as far as oppressive experiences such as discrimination and bias. Interestingly, many described receiving more support in academia than they did in society in general (in the outside world). Faith, an SAA college student with graduate school aspirations, recounts the support she received from faculty who taught her in college: "So, and their [her university faculty] intentions were pure and good and beautiful. And I love them. Right for, for the care and the support that they've given me, [large university] was really like, the only place I've ever felt connected to society." Even with the genuine support and good intentions of her undergraduate faculty, due to systemwide discrimination within her academic field, she has been unable to gain access to a graduate program or advance in her academic field. This has effectively stopped her progress, but she continues to fight for inclusion of carcerally impacted people within her area of study.

Coinciding with Faith's experiences of both support and exclusion, it must not be understated that bias was present within academia. SAA members pointed out that their carceral contact led to differential treatment within the academic institution. This was often exacerbated by the intersectional impacts of issues based on class and race and drastic disparities in worldviews because of their traumatic CLS and class/race lived experiences. For example, Mark, a system-affected African

American university faculty member, describes an undergraduate experience he had in which a prominent faculty member changed her mind about writing a graduate school letter of recommendation for him, "Because she had this warped mentality. I don't know, I just believe that she didn't think I was good enough, or because I was a Black male with a criminal record that I was never going to make it. And here I am sitting, sitting in the academy." He explains that after a verbal exchange in which he perceived that she was speaking to him in a condescending manner, she would not have treated him this way if he was white and did not have a legal conviction. In certain cases, participants described openly prejudicial treatment during consideration for prestigious scholarships.

Some Participants Did Not Disclose Their Backgrounds, to Avoid Negative Reactions from Colleagues and Peers

A certain segment of SAA members did not disclose their backgrounds to the public for fear of bias and discrimination, thus hoping to avoid the topic and some potential problems that could come along with it. Neil, an SAA group member, describes that he did not want his fellow college classmates to know about his record: "The fear of people finding out was there too." He further explains, "At the time, I liked it [not revealing his criminal justice record]. And then after I was done, I realized I may have been, I may have been hurting myself from not embracing it a little." When he looks back on his graduate school courses, he ponders whether he should have revealed his background, as he believes that his system-affected student peers received additional support because of their disclosure.

Yet many SAAs still ran into complications when they were forced to reveal their backgrounds (i.e., when checking the legal conviction box on applications) in the enrollment, admittance, and employment documentation of certain universities and colleges (not all institutions of higher education require this). Isabel, an SAA group member in graduate school, explains, "Because I always kind of had to account for my felony. So it's like, the opportunities they're talking about is [*sic*] not necessarily translate to like an opportunity for me. So that's why I always had felt just like a little bit on the outs." Continually being placed in situations in which she had to explain her criminal justice background exposed her to public judgment. Thus, completely avoiding the stigma of carceral-impact has been difficult for many.

STRUGGLES IN HIGHER EDUCATION: ARE THEY ABOUT TIME OR THE CONVICTION?

The Criminal Conviction Itself, not the Length of the Sentence, Primarily Impacted Participants' Experience after Incarceration

The majority of SAA members explained that it was primarily the subsequent myriad consequences (formal and collateral) of their felony conviction that hindered their educational progress. They did not describe the direct experience of incarceration as affecting their ability to interact with education. Heather, an SAA group member and doctoral degree–holding professional, had correctional contact but did not serve a prison sentence. Yet her legal past continually interfered with her educational progress:

> So, I felt like just having a felony, regardless of my incarceration, and not having that felony [her wish to not have the felony], impacted everything, also. Because you have to check the box, whether you went to prison or not. If you can't get past the box, it doesn't, you can't even . . . explain to somebody that you were incarcerated, because you click the box. And I looked at some schools, and as soon as I saw the box, I didn't want to check it, I just, I was like, I don't feel like explaining, I don't want to jump through the hoops, I don't want to have to, you know, I just don't want to do that. I want to be able to go to a school that can accept me for who I am.

Having to indicate on educational documents that she had a criminal record by "checking the box" was the source of much more strain than her correctional contact.

Participants Experienced Time and Trauma Subjectively

Many FI people described experiencing traumatization from the carceral experience, yet the amount of time that was deemed to be a long sentence was quite subjective. Within this sample, it would appear that any sentence length could be a traumatizing experience. During interviews I conducted in previous research focused on how FI people used higher education to overcome stigma (Tietjen, 2013), participants expressed that three years of incarceration is the estimated point at which damage from carceral institutionalization becomes irreparable. Alisa, an SAA group member, when discussing her long prison sentence, says, "I think the length of time stunted me. I had a parole agent tell me six years and over, and you're not going to be able to assimilate back normally. That was his, he said personally, this is my opinion." She goes on to say that she did not think that many of the women (whom she viewed like family) that she was incarcerated with were ever assimilated into society even before prison, due to systemic racial and class inequality. She was very aware of the intersectional struggles (including racism) of People of Color within the legal system and was skeptical that any of them would be given the opportunity to fully assimilate back into society. Within this research, participants expressed that they had been traumatized by far shorter lengths of incarceration than the three-year mark. For example, George, an SAA group member and professor who served a short prison sentence decades ago, recounts that he still experiences recurring, vivid dreams in which he is standing in a courtroom as a judge is sentencing him to decades in prison.

Society, Not the Prison Time, Does the Damage

Several people in this sample did not perceive that they were badly traumatized from the experience of serving their prison sentence, citing very short sentence lengths (sometimes only a few months or days in a county jail for a felony offense). This is not to discount the importance of their experiences. Even short stints of incarceration impact people in many powerful ways. Not all people convicted of felony offenses serve long stretches of incarceration, even though the courts reserve the right to make them do so. While generally not viewing the correctional system (whether prison or community corrections) as beneficial, several people spoke as if they had attempted to make the best of the situation while under correctional supervision, perhaps as a coping mechanism or form of resistance against the system. Thus, they perceived that it was the reentry into society after their legal sanctions had expired that exposed them to harm; society was inflicting penalties, bias, and exclusion upon them due to their criminal conviction.

The Time after Prison Time: How Parole and Supervised Release Impact Access to Higher Education

Results regarding parole and probation were mixed. In one group, their educational journey was detrimentally affected by the parole/probation process. They spoke of being constrained by the confusing mass of restrictions set out by the supervised process of postincarceration parole often required of people who have served a prison sentence and/or people who were sentenced to the noncustodial sentence of probation.

These restrictions often functioned to limit their ability to interact with the academic process. In addition, some SAA members explained that their individual parole/probation officers (POs) were not interested in their reentry success and even actively worked to see them fail, going as far as to discourage them from engaging with higher education. After incarceration, Alisa (a graduate student) was discouraged from engaging in education by her PO, who referred to her college efforts as "a nice little hobby." On the other side of the equation, a noteworthy group received support from the parole/probation process. These individuals had POs who actively attempted to help them successfully reintegrate back into society. A couple people mentioned having mixed experiences from parole and probation, experiencing multiple POs, some of whom were helpful and some of whom were not. Heather had both supportive and unsupportive parole officers, as she explains:

> So my first probation officer was really supportive. He, you know, like he if, like, anything I wanted to do to like, classes or workshops, you know, he was pretty flexible. Then I, then I switched [he switched parole officers, from a male PO to a female] and I got an, I went, somehow I got on, like, most supervision [he was placed under a higher level of supervision], but it became more restricted than regular probation, and so she just made it very difficult.

A common issue was interrupted educational progress created by the discontinuity of dealing with multiple POs during the legal process.

Type of Criminal Conviction

The most common response was that the type of crime participants were convicted of did not significantly hinder their educational progress. The lack of significant obstruction in the educational journey from type of criminal conviction may be due to the fact that the most common types of criminal convictions (e.g., drugs, property, white collar) are often less socially stigmatized (Rickard, 2016; Uggen, Manza, & Behrens, 2013); more stigmatized types of crime are also the less common types of criminal convictions (e.g., sex crimes, severely violent crimes). While some of the participants whose crimes did not hinder their progress experienced minor hurdles or inconveniences during their passage through education, these issues were not powerful enough to derail their progress.

Similar to what SAA members discussed in regard to the far-reaching stigma and effects of a criminal conviction being more impactful than their sentence lengths, many people convicted of less-stigmatized types of crime (the majority of participants in this study) pointed out that their legal records produced more negative types of consequences than the type of crime they were convicted of. Moving to a discussion of crimes socially defined as more severe, it must be noted that most convictions are for crimes labeled as less severe (Gramlich, 2020), which reflects general crime trends.

For a certain smaller group of SAA members for whom the type of crime was heavily stigmatized for various reasons, their educational progress was severely limited. People who were convicted of sex crimes, crimes involving high-profile cases, or certain types violence (defined as more severe within the legal code), stigma management was used to protect them from the harms of negative stigmatization, or they risked facing further bias, possible physical harm, and discrimination due to social perceptions of their convictions. For example, Warren, convicted of a crime that involved violence, describes being denied access to a volunteer program that was part of the requirements for his graduate school program. He was open with them, explaining,

> "Hey, I'm a felon, will that interfere with my volunteering?" And they said, you know, "as long as [it's] not like sexual assault or anything? I don't think so." . . . [B]ut then they called me and said, they couldn't let me volunteer. And I said, "Well, I told you guys, I was a felon." They said, "Yeah, but we didn't understand it was for a violent crime, we can't risk."

Even though he was always open and honest with his university, he continued to run into roadblocks in his academic progress due to his legal record, which resulted in the eventual discontinuance of his education.

Another small group within the SAA movement is struggling to overcome structural and institutional hurdles because of specific restrictions against felony convictions in their fields (e.g., the medical field, the practice of law; rules at specific universities) that do not exist in other fields. While the majority of people in this research have generally had successful experiences in education, many still face stigmatization on multiple fronts. I do not want to mislead the reader into believing that our pathways through higher education are expected to be a perfectly smooth process. SAA members have overcome many obstacles even in the face of difficult social structural hurdles due to societal and institutional biases against system-affected people, yet they commonly encounter blockages to progress along their journeys. As those involved in the SAA movement grappled with stigmatization from system contact, they also discovered that the rigors of system contact were intertwined with their own individual struggles, a common issue in system-impacted populations. This presented an additional level of challenge to navigate within higher education.

OVERCOMING INDIVIDUAL STRUGGLES

The ramifications of the past and present personal struggles of and obstacles facing SAA members are often tied to system contact and issues associated with it. This process affects how higher education influences the people involved in our movement.

In any capacity, contact with the CLS produces its own set of personal struggles and obstacles for system-affected people. Regarding attempting to engage with higher education, this group, while highlighting many types of issues, emphasized certain struggles that focused on economic resources, mental health, incarceration-induced trauma and PTSD, substance misuse disorders, and what they described as self-imposed barriers. It must be noted that many of these personal struggles are interrelated, as personal problems that affect carcerally impacted populations often occur as closely grouped constellations of issues (Pinard, 2006; Wakefield, 2016).

A commonly mentioned struggle that system-affected academics face is lack of economic resources, as people with criminal convictions are more likely to come from economically deprived backgrounds. This is coupled with the widely known fact that higher education is extremely expensive. SAA members pointed out difficulties in struggling to find housing, paying for basic living expenses, and paying for college expenses (i.e., tuition, books, housing, fees). Coupled with the lack of economic resources initially faced by many SAA members within the educational process was lack of access to educational resources. People described being deficient in sound academic advising, family members and acquaintances with knowledge about and connections to higher education (social capital), and not understanding how to navigate academic processes (e.g., enrollment, applying for scholarships, how to write in a scholarly manner, networking with other academics).

Mental health and prison-induced traumas may be associated with one another (DeVeaux, 2013; Haney, 2003). This was continually referenced as a major issue confronted by SAA people. Mental health was often discussed as a lifelong issue that was worsened by the rigors of prison confinement (Haney, 2008). The strains of serving time in the often anxiety-producing commotion of the correctional institution often weighed heavily on the well-being of many individuals, who commonly described continued suffering from these problems years after their release from the CLS (Purvis & Devine, 2023). Postcarceral struggles such as anxiety around groups of people, experiencing trauma triggers when near places that remind them of correctional facilities, and vivid dreams/nightmares about incarceration were described (Murphy, 2004, 2012). Many people also pointed out that they had preexisting mental health issues that were aggravated by their contact with the justice system, as they often did not have adequate mental health treatment while incarcerated. They pointed out that addressing mental health issues in the justice system was not considered a priority, so many people who were suffering were undiagnosed and/or untreated. Thus, the individual mental health problems, coupled with the traumas of incarceration, may have functioned to create a synergistic negative impact on those who endured these experiences. Substance use disorders were commonly mentioned as personal difficulties by SAA members. For those with criminal convictions, addiction commonly had started before their carceral contact, and many had sought out assistance in managing this struggle, through resources such as twelve-step programs for alcoholism and addiction (e.g., Alcoholics Anonymous and Narcotics Anonymous).

Major obstacles SAA members commonly pointed to were self-imposed barriers. Many talked about situations in which they attempted to manage anticipated stigma and suffered from the symptoms of impostor syndrome. Isabel, an SAA group member and graduate student, describes how she limited herself: "So really thinking back over, I think, probably myself, and like, the limits that I put on myself, in my own mind, is probably like, the defining thing that held me back." Then she describes how her educational experiences were part of the process of overcoming her personal fears that were holding her back:

> Like, I'm not, I used to be scared of my future, like, "Oh, what is it gonna look like?" I'm not like that now. So like I was working on, when I graduated, I started working there as program coordinator for [SAA group] at [major university], then I got accepted to [another major university] in their [professional graduate] program.

In the educational process of working through the issues that were limiting her, she was able to access her potential. Additionally, many SAA members received unsolicited advice from correctional and probationary staff, discouraging them from seeking out higher education. They were informed, in what some considered to be a condescending manner, that college was not going to be a realistic option for them. Instead, they were told to join the manual workforce and not waste their time on education that correctional staff perceived they would not be able to use. Intertwined with individual struggles, many in the SAA population concurrently grapple with multiple forms of social inequality.

GRAPPLING WITH INEQUALITY

In the U.S., it is common for groups heavily affected by social inequality and intersectionality to be overrepresented in system-involved populations due to long-standing systems of direct and institutionalized oppression (Western & Petit, 2010). When discussing how social inequality influenced their educational journeys, SAA people mentioned issues of privilege, race, economic class, gender, and sexual orientation. The impacts of intersectional oppression were also discussed by many SAA people from historically oppressed groups. Under the umbrella of this concept, issues of racism, classism, gender, and privilege (in varying combinations) impacted a large proportion of people in this study. Anna points out how the concepts of race and social class affected her in graduate school:

> I was definitely: race and social class. So social class in the sense of I was in a classroom, especially the PhD level with predominantly middle- and upper-class individuals. And it felt as though whenever I tried to bring in the perspective of people from a lower class, it was almost like, well, well, you're just biased. It's like, well, we're talking about my people. How the fuck am I biased?
>
> There was a running joke. At that every year, there was one token person of color, like every cohort had one. Okay. And so, when you were the one, everybody looked at you like, you must get a scholarship; kid was the one who like didn't earn their way.

This educational experience had a very powerful impact on Anna, forming her perceptions of the academy as an institution: "Loaded with structural violence, it's loaded with oppression."

Struggling with economic issues was common, but perhaps from a more personal perspective. Those that did report economic bias said that because they came from working-class backgrounds, they often lacked the middle-class and elite academic cultural capital that is expected in conventional academia. Women in this research mentioned bias against them within higher education because of their gender. They expressed that they were aware of the social inequalities that exist for women in society in a structural sense. Some women reported that they found support and inclusiveness within higher education in some spaces but not in others. Heather, a doctoral degree–holding SAA group member (African American/woman), gives a nuanced explanation about social inequality in regard to gender:

> I just felt like, inside women don't have oftentimes the same number of resources and support as men. I think come home, though. Like the programs or the programs, I don't think that they like said, you know, like, this scholarship is just for men, and this is just for women, you know, think it was open.

Postincarceration, Heather described her academic experiences as nonbiased, yet she expressed that there was a dearth of educational programs for women within the correctional system.

At least two women SAA members pointed to some discrepancies in how women were treated specifically within their SAA group. They indicated that women were stuck with the unappreciated and unacknowledged task work while men were given more appreciated and high-profile public roles and took credit for a lot of the organizational accomplishments made possible by the work of the women members.

Socially defined definitions of race had a powerful impact on academic experiences among the SAA participants. Fran (African American/woman), an SAA group member and university faculty member, describes grappling with lack of acceptance at her institution:

> I'm not going to convince anybody that I'm supposed to be in a space, because if I wasn't supposed to be in this space, I wouldn't be in this space for real. So, my thing is, you're just gonna have to get used to a young Black woman being in [this] space.

Fran was able to take a stand against this dynamic, yet this also added a further level of struggle and expenditure of energy to the already challenging responsibilities of being a new faculty member. Within the scope of this study, racial bias was commonly encountered by minority group members in higher education, while white participants did not encounter racial bias.

Some people identified themselves as personally troubled about their age. Because of the obstacles and limitations experienced by FI and system-involved SAA members based on their carceral contact, many engaged with the advanced levels of education somewhat later in life than traditional students. Some SAA members pointed out that they were interacting with younger academic peers (students, faculty). They expressed concern about their starting later in their academic or professional careers limiting the length of their careers and anticipated rejection or stigma from their younger educational peers, yet generally encountered acceptance from their academic peers regardless of their age.

BIAS IN THE ACADEMY

Interacting with bias in their educational pathways was common among the participants and was often heavily intertwined with the other obstacles and struggles experienced by this group, including stigmatization, structural inequalities, and individual struggles. The SAAs' journey to education includes system contact, and members with system contact were doubly susceptible to marginalization both within the correctional system and within the university. Entering advanced levels of higher education while grappling with the biases discussed in this chapter made the educational journey more difficult and added more pressure to an already challenging academic process.

Although the purpose of this book is not to rank the experiences of SAA people in a hierarchy of severity, it must be noted that many who are faced with the multiple intersections of oppression coupled with direct system contact (e.g., long-term incarceration, multiple incarceration, multiple legal convictions) discussed being heavily impacted by bias. Perhaps because of their encounters with inequality, they were more acutely aware of the effects of discrimination and marginalization.

There was a lot of variation in how SAA people perceived and encountered bias within higher education generally, attached to issues of structural inequality. A large group of participants stated that they did not experience bias, oppression, or discrimination within higher education because of their system contact, and they tended to align with experiencing a lot of support within higher education. Among the participants who did not disclose their past system contact, bias and discrimination was avoided. Yet there was a strong contingent of people who chose to disclose their legal convictions (or were involuntarily exposed) who encountered differential treatment within higher education because of their system contact.

For many SAA members, in place of the bias and discrimination frequently encountered in society, they discovered an environment of support within higher education. While experiencing varying degrees of societal stigmatization outside of academia because of their criminal records, many individuals who were open about their backgrounds reported that they felt safe in school and could be themselves without fear of reproach. Yet it must be noted that some people chose not to disclose their system-contact backgrounds in the context of their educational engagement due to fear of rejection and stigmatization. The individual complications of deciding whether or not to disclose a criminal record within the formal academic setting need to be considered here, as a fragile status (Tietjen & Kavish, 2021) may negatively impact the academic journeys and careers of SAA members with direct system contact.

Several SAA group members reported experiencing bias and exclusion from academic programs, such as doctoral programs, research labs, and internships. One FI individual, convicted of a less-stigmatized type of crime, was told that their presence would tarnish the reputation of a research lab. It was later revealed that this incident was not the policy of the research lab but due to the personal opinions of the lab director. Other SAA members (TRAC members) were excluded from clinical doctoral programs, even with top academic performance (and no subsequent contact with the justice system after their prior convictions), due to their felony convictions. Other SAA group members experienced marginalization and denigration of their lived-experience opinions and perspectives within the classroom. Some people pointed out they were told that their classroom discussions and opinions put other students on edge and were asked to change their tone or were not taken seriously by faculty.

Most SAA members reported experiencing strong support for SAA groups. The current social perceptions of rehabilitative and progressive criminal justice policies and practices may be more of a supportive environment that welcomes SAA groups, in both the sphere of higher education (Mukamal et al., 2015; Quach et al., 2022) and society in general (Maruna, 2017). Yet a group of people affiliated with a specific SAA group, CC, reported a certain amount of bias. Members spoke of being told by other academics that they disliked the word *convict*. CC attempted to assert ownership of the word *convict* as an act of language reclamation during the tough-on-crime era of the 1990s. This was a direct action taken as a form of activism to stand up to the oppression and inequalities faced by the founding members of CC, in an era when system-affected people were openly discriminated against.

THE UNIVERSITY AND THE CARCERALLY IMPACTED SCHOLAR: A COMPLEX RELATIONSHIP

Higher education's impact on SAA people is a dynamic yet complex reality subject to the forces of privilege and intersectional oppression. The transformative pathway through collegiate attainment functioned for the study participants as a two-pronged experience, introducing carcerally impacted students to levers of empowerment while at the same time presenting them with systemic inequalities and social-structural hurdles.

Overall, SAAs spoke of institutions of higher education as generally acting to assist in transforming their lives through the provision of means to overcome many of the structural barriers and obstacles faced by system-affected people. Yet it must be strongly noted that intersectional bias against system-affected people present outside of education was also present in colleges and universities. Examples of how the lives of people in this study were improved within higher education included support in overcoming the stigma and limitations of incarceration, increasing social capital, establishing academic and professional careers, finding the resources and skills to help others, and broadening their worldviews. Major barriers faced in higher education were lack of knowledge about available opportunities, systemic blockages, limited access to social and human capital, mental health and carceral trauma issues, and economic disparities. Participants also described overcoming self-imposed barriers of anticipated stigma and/or impostor syndrome, and many emphasized that this was an ongoing battle that they were still struggling with.

In summary, while the relationship that SAA members had with higher education was beneficial in many aspects, it must be noted that the emotional tone purveyed from various circumstances encountered within academia could be interpreted as ambivalent. SAA group members still grappled with many other obstacles in their lives. For example, several SAA members spoke of encountering experiences that could be defined as structural violence (Galtung, 1969) in the academic environment. In the narratives of some SAA members, universities were perceived as extensions of the carceral system, continuing to carry out the mechanism of punishment through collateral consequences such as excluding certain students when using such measures as checking the box and discriminatory campus policies and rules. Thus, while higher education functioned to open up doors and provide many types of resources to system-contacted scholars, it could also simultaneously perpetuate the traumatizing impacts of incarceration and criminal legal contact, through collateral consequences that can be imbedded in misguided institutional policies and practices. Overall, those who made it through the difficulties of the academic maze to become system-affected faculty and professionals experienced a sense of empowerment and social and self-improvement. Attainment of educational credentials was perceived as a means of overcoming at least some of the stigma of system contact. Many were on track to establishing careers in both academic and professional settings, had created strong social networks, and had developed meaningful relationships with supportive mentors. Also, after realizing the advantages and privilege they had obtained from their educational experiences, several SAA people gave back to their own communities, possessed with a strong desire to pull their people up.

This chapter examined how higher education impacted and transformed members of the SAA movement, including increasing their social and human capital, expanding worldviews, and giving them the tools to give assistance to others. The next chapter looks at the other side of the same coin: how the building and establishment of SAA groups could influence institutions of higher education. This cyclical journey starts with building peer support groups, progresses to mentorship of like others within higher education, encompasses the passing of humanistic lived-experience informed knowledge within the classroom, and finally expands SAA work outside the classroom to communities.

CHAPTER 3

Building a Prison-to-School Pipeline

We're Connected

College before and after Prison: Different Types of Struggles

As a college student in my late twenties, recently released from prison, I was on fire with enthusiasm. After spending several years of my life struggling with debilitating substance abuse issues culminating in a felony drug conviction with a two-year federal prison sentence attached to it, I was finally back to hitting the books for real. I had more dedication to my education now. I was able to summon a level of seriousness that I did not possess during my first failed college attempts after high school. I eagerly jumped into every academic activity and volunteer internship opportunity that presented itself. In my college courses, I arrived early to class, responded to the professor's questions, and would often stay after class to discuss interesting points from lectures. I was trying to make up for the time I had wasted in my prior attempts at college.

When I attempted college right out of high school, addiction issues (alcohol, methamphetamines, cocaine, pills, hallucinogens) dominated my life. Basically, the eight years from the end of high school until I found my way into federal prison were a chaotic struggle. I would go on binges of drinking and drugs, intermittently dispersed with periods (from one to eighteen months) when I would try to clean up or get sober. During a binge, I would often stop going to work, quickly drop out of college, and lose any job I had, while subsequently rapidly depleting my meager savings. I burned through my small college savings in a matter of a couple of years. When the money ran out, I would desperately scrounge around to find another source of money to keep the party going. If I couldn't find work (which was often), I would end up in an inpatient or outpatient drug rehab program to keep myself from ending up homeless, then try to stay clean for a few months while reenrolling in college and working for a while, until I could save up enough money to go out and party again. I quickly tired of this cycle and attempted to "remedy" the impossible problem of finding a more reliable means to fund my cyclical binges. Consequently, I entered the world of drug dealing. By this point I had tried college three or four times and had given up on ever earning a college degree. I could not hold my life together long enough to accomplish any major life goals. After a couple of years of selling drugs, I found myself at the wrong end of a federal indictment for methamphetamine distribution, which quickly resulted in my conviction and subsequent two-year prison sentence.

While still in prison, I made my mind up to pursue college. Initially, I focused on simply obtaining a single college degree. I needed a success, an accomplishment, after so many years of failure after failure. Consequently, I became singularly focused on education. Because of my felony conviction, I perceived that I had few other options outside of education, and I told myself this every time I started getting tired and considered giving up. I was terrified of what would happen to me if I were to fail at education. While I knew there were manual labor jobs out there that I could access with a criminal record, and I respect those who work in such jobs (having done this type of work myself), I was not inspired by this type of work. I was fearful that if I found myself unemployed or back working on a poorly paid factory line, I might give up, make poor life choices, and end up back in prison. As a result, I developed the mentality that I could not afford to fail, a sentiment conveyed to me by many of my system-affected colleagues in past casual conversations. Thus, I shifted the focus of the meaning of *conviction* from the process of being formally found guilty of a crime, to a strong belief in the value of educational credentials. My conviction was that education would be a pathway for me to achieve life-course success.

In the midst of my bachelor's degree studies, my academic mentors encouraged me to go on to graduate school. So my educational journey continued on to a sociology PhD program, where I found a whole new world of support as a system-affected academic. My literal job was to study, learn, write scholarship, and teach others; and I enthusiastically jumped right into this process. But to be honest with the reader and create a realistic picture for future carcerally impacted scholars, I admit that I still struggled with personal issues, including addiction (alcoholism) and mental health. Those issues do not just disappear after we are released from prison. They remain with us for the rest of our lives, and many system-affected people continue to grapple with these invisible struggles.

Higher Education Gets Real

Many years into the academic process, I would learn that I was at least partially idealistic in my educational convictions. While I maintained a strong sense of dedication to my studies and believed that I better appreciated the value of my education compared to before my incarceration, I found that my reality would not be rendered perfect by striving for college degrees and faculty positions. As a system-affected academic (both as a student and a faculty member), I was exposed to the actualities of the university world in two capacities—structural inequalities within higher education and experiences similar to microaggressions—while concurrently seeing my intersectionally impacted colleagues endure more severe inequalities. This was an educational cycle of continually crashing up against my own ignorance and naiveté, then attempting to learn from it.

After working within academia for many years, I began to view the university system in many ways as broken, from the perspective that it functioned more like a business designed to attract as many students as possible. Instead of focusing on a mind-expanding liberal arts education, the institution concentrated on creating degree programs designed to service free market capitalism, pursue monetary gain, and provide employees for the technocratic elite. All this, while devaluing the humanities, the arts, and social sciences. Essentially, I had stumbled onto the neoliberal university model (Slaughter & Rhoades, 2000). For example, as a junior faculty member, when I asked fellow colleagues why certain market-focused academic programs were receiving more resources from the university than the arts and social sciences, I was given a hopeless shrug and sigh. They explained that the institution wanted to give more focus to programs that they believed would be more likely to "generate revenue" for the university, even though the institution had been founded on the liberal arts, which include arts and sciences. Within this historically strong focus on the liberal arts was a rich history of social justice action by dedicated faculty. Yet over time the university had lost its focus on social equity and moved toward a capitalistic market emphasis, while only mentioning social equity when convenient for the business-centered programs. Unprofitable liberal arts, humanities, and social science programs were shoved over into older buildings, their resources were cut, and faculty members' salaries dwindled in comparison to more "favored" programs. I began to observe that the tradition of universities as bastions of protected free thought and social justice (which had drawn me to higher education) was veering off course toward profiteering and consumerism (Ball, 2012). In addition, I have been working in a political era when universities have fallen under attack from anti-intellectual and anti-science, conservative politics (Newfield, 2011). This form of academic attacks, politically speaking, is swinging dangerously close to fascism (Stanley, 2020).

Spoken and unspoken experiences, known as microaggressions (Sue, 2010), are defined as intentional or unintentional subtle rebuffs, actions, gestures, or insults expressing belittling or antagonistic viewpoints directed toward members of marginalized and/or oppressed groups. Examples are an offhand comment demeaning ex-convicts or prisoners, uncomfortable silences after self-disclosure, and being encouraged to keep my system-affected identity "low-key" for my own protection. I have been subjected to all of these events during my employment in higher education. Being trained as an academic, the sense of something being "off" yet not being able to clearly define it is frustrating. Because of their quiet subtlety, such slights are often ignored or disregarded by members of privileged groups, yet they function to sustain and perpetuate systemic inequalities for groups who have been denied social and cultural advantages.

When interpreting the situations in which I felt subtly insulted or stigmatized as a carcerally impacted person, I asked myself if I was blowing things out of proportion, and immediately begin second-guessing myself. I wondered if my background is the reason I was not awarded certain scholarships or awards. I knew that being encouraged to keep my background low-key or quiet by a peer was often intended to be well-meaning, yet I also heard that internal voice whispering to me, "That's not fair, those experiences are yours and they're meaningful to you, you should be able to be open about them if you choose." I tried to capture this uncertain feeling through my scholarship, writing about a theoretical concept called *status fragility* (Tietjen & Kavish, 2021), in which a criminal conviction weakens the usually prestigious status afforded tenure-track academics, placing them in a state of constant precarity, vulnerable to social-structural impediments that marginalize their careers and weaken their academic potential. Of course I could speculate indefinitely about how my profession as an academic may have been limited or diminished by the felony conviction in my past, yet at the end of the day, I am mostly left with lingering doubts and suspicions that are difficult to confirm. So I have attempted to channel my energies and anxieties toward issues that I can directly change, and that is how I began to engage with transformative actions.

What I Add to Higher Education

Thinking about how my lived experiences and work within academia perpetuate transformative dynamics within higher education is not an easy task. Of course, any academic trained in the positivistic school of research will seriously question the reliability of assessing oneself from one's own subjective perspective. So the first action I take in framing my discussion is to acknowledge and embrace my subjective stance. Through introspection within the context of my own insider perspectives and experiences, I attempt to identify, reflect upon, and understand my subjective biases and worldviews with a focus on interpreting how they influence my perceptions of self.

The first and most powerful experience through which I view my reality is from the perspective of being FI. This event was a seismic shift in how I viewed myself and the outside world. Whether directly aware of it or not, the social events I encounter and personal thoughts I interpret are now filtered through the experiential lens of incarceration.

The Transformative Dynamics of the SAA Movement

In examining how my work within academia and higher education may have added to processes of progressive change, I first reflect on how I learned that such change was possible and subsequently developed these capabilities. I discovered social justice motivations through progressive social sciences academic training, compassionate mentorship, and contact with the SAA movement. I gained an education in sociology, a social sciences discipline that I perceived to be populated by many compassionate researchers and professors. Many academics with whom I aligned myself placed value on making the world a better place for others, and their research topics and actions reflected this. One of my mentors during my undergraduate studies was a Marxist scholar and activist focused on equal rights and justice for Indigenous people. She showed me how my social sciences education could be applied to standing up for the rights of others. I was told that I could better understand the issues and problems that FI people face through the sociological (and criminological) study of inequality. This mentor not only produced scholarship in support of Indigenous peoples, but also actively used such scholarship to support her activist efforts, continually traveling long distances to tribal reservations to lend support. Also, she invited me to assist in her scholarship. Through her work, I attained my first academic citation as an undergraduate student.

I had to be shown how to effect change for others through effective mentorship. I was fortunate to find, in addition to my undergraduate mentor, several additional mentors during graduate school and as an early-career faculty member. Some mentors were from the SAA population, while others were caring faculty from my university. Each provided expertise and advice from different perspectives and in different contexts, from general to specific. For example, the faculty mentors I encountered in graduate school demonstrated how to instruct college courses, advise students, write proper research projects, and navigate the academic job market.

Yet there was another level of transformative knowledge I would encounter in my academic career: finding the SAA movement. Working with members of the SAA population imparted vital wisdom to me, in regard to how to maneuver through the academic world with a felony conviction. This built the foundation of knowledge from which I was able to harness the human-centered potential of my lived experience and subsequently teach this dynamic in my university. The SAA group I was part of invited members to join in collaborative research projects. I was encouraged to join in special topic issues of journals and given opportunities to speak to major news sources about SAA-related issues. Eventually the network of carcerally impacted scholars I was a part of expanded in membership and developed into more SAA groups and independent SAA members. Now we are connected across the U.S. and across the globe. This has created a large bank of social capital from which SAAs can draw. For example, I can ask various SAA members for assistance on such wide-ranging topics as how to develop effective academic programs, advise system-affected students, or engage in a successful job interview. In regard to overall scholarship and advocacy, being part of an interconnected group of supportive academics increases the ability to share ideas and interactively help others. From interacting with mentors and supportive SAA peers, I learned how to advocate for others too. Just as carcerally impacted peers spent hours advising me in past years, I now give time to working with mentees.

How I Attempt to Create Change as a Blueprint for the SAA Movement's Potential to Transform Higher Education

I have attempted to facilitate bringing active social justice back into my university through advocating for social justice within an academic criminal justice field (where many SAA members work). This work occurs through my actions as a "scholarvist" (see Green, 2018), classroom instruction, student advising, and involvement in institutional initiatives and committee work. There is much work to be done here, as many criminal justice programs in modern colleges heavily promote teaching practitioner-based managerial style programs that do not emphasize social equality, the oppression/harm of the CLS, or social-structural explanations for crime-related issues.

Green (2018) used the term *scholarvist* to refer to faculty and formal researchers involved in activism who use rigorous research to inform their social justice actions. A significant portion of my research (and others' research that I engage with) is used to inform my advocacy undertakings. For example, I work with SAA mentees and often use the findings and research from an article I wrote about mentorship with two SAA colleagues (Tietjen et al., 2021). Our research is about our experiences in mentoring, as both mentors and as mentees. When mentoring, I use concepts gleaned from this research to inform discussions with mentees, such as how to manage the bias often attached to students and faculty with legal convictions, a concept we identify in our article as *professional fragility*. Such activism is focused on enabling SAA members to overcome some of the obstacles of their legal convictions, while encouraging supportive academic environments to flourish within academic departments.

Because I am a faculty member at a teaching-focused university, classroom instruction and advising is how I interact with my students. Based on a research- and insider-perspective-informed belief that the current legal system does not operate to serve actual justice, I teach my students that the purpose of the CLS should be to eliminate the need for it, not to further perpetuate this unjust institution. Wherever possible, I go beyond only making students aware of social inequalities to actually teaching the means of enacting social change. For example, I serve on boards and directly work with local social justice advocacy groups and nongovernmental organizations on issues such as successful reentry for FI people and the rights of youth in the juvenile justice system. Consequently, as a criminology professor who was formerly in an academic criminal justice program (I am now in a criminology and justice studies program), I taught students about how criminological theory (a course I teach) informs policy, then taught them about how legal system policies are enacted at the community level. Some of my former students have gone on to engage with these organizations in professional or activist capacities.

Also, in lectures, class projects, and advising, I encourage criminal justice students to stand up for system-affected people's human rights and focus on ways to improve the lives of people in the legal system. I want them to see their roles as CLS practitioners as a means of helping all people, both the people in jails and prisons and the people in society. Yet we simultaneously discuss advocating within the CLS for policies that support alternatives to incarceration, promote rehabilitation, and encourage social support for system-affected people.

Through involvement in institutional initiatives at my university, I have also found means of attempting to communicate advocacy for system-affected academics. During discussions and workshops on how to increase diversity equity inclusion (DEI) and cultural awareness, I emphasize issues and questions that focus on students who have been carcerally impacted. Of course, I realize that the process of implementing institutional-level measures in an academic institution to help system-affected students requires a lot more action than asking some questions or making a suggestion at a faculty workshop. It requires strategizing, being proactive, advocating for and building support, and bringing proposed initiatives before various institutionally sanctioned committees. I also lend support to my colleagues attempting such actions at other universities when possible.

BRINGING CARCERAL KNOWLEDGE TO COLLEGE

Similar to my gradual odyssey from prison to higher education, then to involvement with the SAA movement, most of those involved have followed roughly similar pathways. Additionally, the growing institutional support, legitimacy, and protected space that we have built in universities has created a stable grounding for members of the SAA population to prosper. Because of the establishment of such secure places, many SAA faculty members and professionals have been able to start the work of dispersing and expanding social justice transformation through humanizing carcerally impacted people and expanding awareness of legal system injustices at their respective institutions.

In this chapter I address the other side of the reciprocal transformative effect that exists between system-affected academics and institutions of higher learning: the SAA population's humanistic transformative influence on the university. I argue, in four parts, that the SAA movement can assist in revitalizing social justice within the modern neoliberal university system, an institution that overemphasizes satisfying the needs of capitalism while forsaking its humanity. This process occurs through active engagement that starts at the organic level and moves upward toward institutional work, then further outward to communities and society. First, SAA people organize groups for peer support, both within and outside of universities. Second, system-contacted people mentor others in education. Third, students interact in the classroom with SAA instructors passing knowledge about general humanistic and equal justice perspectives informed by lived experiences. Finally, involvement (and engagement of students from classrooms) of SAA members in institutional and community initiatives are a possible means of enacting advocacy and justice for system-affected academics.

There are multiple pathways to SAA involvement. Groups not affiliated with academic institutions have formed in many contexts from the collective actions of people who align with the general concepts I am defining as the SAA movement (i.e., academics, professionals, activists). University-affiliated SAA groups were generally formed by system-contacted people to provide support networks, to establish a safe space to associate with those with similar experiences, and as a form of social capital, yet several also went on to engage in justice-centered activism work. Also, independent SAA individuals are firmly part of the movement, yet they take an alternate approach, forging their own pathways through higher education while carving out powerful impacts within their spheres of interaction outside of the group setting.

The transformative impact that SAA has on higher education is not a flawless or smooth process. Sometimes the SAA movement may change higher education through growing pains experienced during its establishment and subsequent evolution. Often, SAA groups and people have to engage (much of this is an ongoing process) in periods of reflexivity and introspection, in attempts to recognize and address their own struggles with the forces of privilege, oppression, elitism, and many other additional forms of social inequality. Yet through this imperfect but constant struggle to effect change in higher education, the SAA movement's transformative potential is given the opportunity to expand.

BUILDING THE SAA MOVEMENT: WE CAN HELP TRANSFORM HIGHER EDUCATION

Among carcerally impacted faculty and students, the initial strong sense of aloneness on the university campus and in their social spheres was palpable, especially among the already marginalized groups that are disproportionately represented in system-affected populations. While they were happy to be engaged in higher education, the very insulated and privileged institutional environment of academia placed many SAA members in a symbolic rowboat in the middle of an ocean, wanting to make contact with a protected refuge of acceptance. Part of the motivation to join the SAA movement was to find a means to overcome the feeling of being detached from the wider academic community and a means of support from those with similar backgrounds. Isabel, a scholar and student with direct system impact, describes how her SAA group builds support for new SAA students on her campus: "So it's just like helping show them, these kind of things before they're even like really a student at our campus, it's already kind of making them feel like welcome connected and like to have friends on campus."

Accordingly, SAA group organizing that begins in diverse environments influences higher education in varying capacities.[1] The university-affiliated organizations (i.e., Underground Scholars, Rising Scholars, TRAC, FIST, CC at Westminster, Project Rebound) have the most direct connection to specific educational institutions. These groups were generally founded by students, faculty, and staff on individual university campuses, and some of them (i.e., Underground Scholars, Project Rebound) have branched out to other campuses too. Yet students and faculty in non-university-affiliated groups (i.e., CC, FICGN, From Prison Cells to Ph.D.) also directly interact with higher education through members who are university faculty and initiatives that they may facilitate to support system-affected people in academia. Jared, a system-contacted faculty member, explains why he helped to found a non-university-affiliated SAA group:

> I started that because I kind of found in my life to better understand the possibilities that, that formerly incarcerated people imagine for themselves and how that limits our opportunities and how to expand that. And then also, on [*sic*] the end, also help people sort of realize, expand their possibilities and realize their possibilities through, like a support program.

Jared believes that the SAA group can could help lived-experience people improve their lives through their higher education and beyond.

Increased Awareness of SAA Issues

With the increased presence of actively justice-engaged SAA people on college campuses both here in the U.S. and internationally, potential for increased awareness of the existence, issues, and problems impacting this group may increase. Often, just as is the case among the general public, the marginalization and oppression faced by carcerally impacted populations is unknown to much of the university community. This phenomenon may be similar to the lack of public awareness about the massive problems that plague our current prison system. By illuminating these problems, the SAA movement can create an environment of consciousness about the unique struggles that many disenfranchised carceral citizens (Loyd, 2015; Miller & Alexander, 2016) face in higher education. As Nicole, a PhD-holding faculty member who is system impacted, states about problems with awareness (even among the SAA population) about SAA-related issues:

> There's a lot of misunderstanding among, among us all, as convicted people, as people who were, I like to say, who were carceral citizens. I like that, that I'm going to be using that phrase a lot. I think that that's probably something we can begin to use. That status is, very little is known about.

Building Prosocial Change Ourselves

With increased consciousness of issues and struggles facing SAA students, the opportunity to build and expand networks of support can take root. Establishing activist-scholar work comprising lived-experience people (Aresti & Darke, 2016) increases the presence of social-equity and humanistic scholarship within the university space. This can have impacts that affect the general university structure and specific academic spheres, such as the often very prosystem and positivistic worlds of criminal justice and criminology departments located on college campuses. As described by members of the SAA population and through my own experiences as a carcerally impacted faculty member in a criminal justice department, we can bring lived-experience-informed perspectives of social change into our workspaces as educators, scholars, and professionals. Tomás, a directly impacted SAA member and student, explains how lived experience impacts scholarship, higher education, and the public:

> We see things in a completely different lens, and so we can also put our lived experience part intertwined with some of the theories. So, I think we're both, we're educating the public, we're educating you in ourselves, but we're also scholars in the sense that we are able to be at the same level as any other person who's in academia or . . . even in [an] organizational field.

Tomás is attempting to describe the strength in this process as an interconnected system. He speaks to the versatility of the SAA movement's potential to generate egalitarian change, through education of students and the public, while at the same time living as members of the groups we are advocating for.

Lived the Nightmare, Living the Dream: We Have Seen Oppression; We See a Need for Change

As lived-experience academics, SAA members present the potential of a high-impact combination of scholarly knowledge and insider perception. Generally, people who have lived through oppression and disadvantage are more aware of structural inequalities and privilege (Hernandez, 2019; McIntosh, 1989). Anna, a directly impacted faculty member, explains how directly relating to the real struggles of other system-contacted people gives her insights into their struggles:

> So honestly, I have, I have a love-hate relationship with academia, were it not for what I call my fellow deviants. I would not be here, I would not be in academia, I would not be doing this, for not, for knowing if there were other people like me, in academia, going through the same things.

Within the SAA movement, motivated students and credentialed faculty members have trained in various forms of critical thought and research, yet the attainment of degrees and skills is not enough to motivate them to continue. Having the peace of mind that others are struggling and succeeding along with them can be a powerful motivator to continue on in their academic pursuits. They, as carcerally impacted individuals, are closest to the social problem they are studying. This expanding network feeds insider-informed discourse production from a population that has often experienced forms of social inequality and oppression firsthand.

More and Different: SAA Engagement over Time

The roles and missions of the people within the SAA movement (whether in groups or as independent individuals) evolve and change over time, for a multitude of reasons. Yet for many, the trend is to become more involved the longer they engage with SAAs. Further, this involvement can function as a springboard to other endeavors and more diverse forms of participation. This can be a means of framing how our movement influences higher education. Many people, myself included, became more engaged with SAA work, including scholarship, SAA mentoring, and advocacy, over time as our stores of social and human capital expanded, increasing our prosocial capacities as activist-scholars and agents of change.

This is a good place to point out that SAA groups and the people in SAA groups are not without flaws or growing pains as scholars, activists, and scholarvists. They are susceptible to the forces of systemic inequalities and oppression just like any other movement, and there were times when such issues crept into what was often originally crafted as well-intended efforts. Sue, a system-impacted member of an SAA group, points to dysfunction within her organization:

> Like, clearly y'all still don't understand how oppression works, because you're doing that shit to each other amongst men, and they are doing that shit to women in the space, and to people who are queer identified, right? There's a reason why there's a lot of people who are queer, that aren't part of the space, right? And those that have been critiques that have been voiced and expressed by people, but because of their lack of like, credibility or prison, bucking status or whatever, like they get, like, we get pushed out.

If actions were taken to correct these inequalities, opportunities for growth and improvement were created. Through this journey of healing, SAAs attempt to learn from and avoid (when possible) the very destructive forces that brought about the social problems that motivated the creation of the movement. A process of continual egalitarian and humanistic correction and regeneration in system-affected organizations is necessary to build ever-increasing territories of equality- and justice-focused academia.

Through involvement in the work of the SAA movement, whether group initiatives or individual actions, members of this population discover that they may be skilled in certain areas such as organizing events, research and scholarship, networking with other activist-scholars, or various forms of leadership. Anna, a very active SAA group member and university faculty, is involved in multiple roles: "So first as a mentor, but second, like, as a leader." She is aware that her system-contacted status and academic training gives her a wide array of skills and knowledge that is valuable to SAA people.

Further, as an SAA group member, I became involved with an SAA group as a basic member of a loosely formed network of academics; over time, I and the SAA group evolved. The group became more formal and structured, and I became more focused and organized as an academic. I chose to focus more heavily on activist scholarship. Also, there was evolution beyond just the organized network I was affiliated with, to conducting broader scholarvist (Green, 2018) work and engaging with advocacy for the directly contacted outside the formal SAA group format. This emphasizes the role complexities of involvement in the SAA movement, as I was acting as both as an independent SAA individual and an SAA group member. Taking on multiple roles is common among SAA members, potentially for a couple of reasons. First, their unique insights are often helpful in many capacities that organized transformative actions need. Second, as discussed throughout the book, the helping traits that many carcerally impacted scholars develop on their journeys to higher education may motivate involvement in many facets of SAA-related service.

Many people involved in the SAA movement also described expanding their engagement in various areas including mentorship, teaching lived-experience concepts, activist research, and participation in progressive initiatives in their communities and universities. Also, while it must be noted that the increased reach of their actions/work was not always focused (even though they often were) directly/entirely on transforming higher education, the impacts of such actions can still affect the university environment in meaningful ways. The next step after establishing an SAA presence in higher education is to engage it with helping others through working with other lived-experience people through mentorship.

SAAs AND MENTORSHIP

While *mentorship* may be a term that gets thrown around so much in academic conversations that it loses some of its meaning or is viewed as "common knowledge," the impact that this process has on lived-experience students is of vital importance to successful trajectories within education. Norma explains: "It's also like, a way for people to give back, right, like, so I mean, people who have gone through academia can provide support for folks who are embarking on that process who have criminal records. So like, there's kind of like this mutual support."

To support my emphasis, SAA mentorship can have what could be described as an exponential effect on higher education, as the cycle of lived-experience academic mentees transitioning into mentors who mentor new cohorts of scholars is repeated (Tietjen et al., 2020). As Anna, a university faculty and an engaged SAA member who works with system-contacted graduate students, says, "I see my role as mentor. Mentor is trying to mentor people that are in the process of getting a PhD, and or trying to get an academic position." She gives her lived experience to others.

When considering why system-impacted students and scholars are so eager and willing to work together to support one another, perhaps look to their experiences in incarceration. Some of the lived-experience scholars in this study reported that they were part of similar educational peer support networks while they were in prison (Richards et al., 2010). For example, Alisa, an FI graduate student, states about when she was incarcerated:

> So then I started tutoring women. You know, in the unit, they're like, "Hey, you know [prison nickname], you think we could meet and you know, you can help me with social studies and all that kind of stuff in the unit, because I feel like I'm not getting enough from the programming here."
>
> I held little study groups on the side.

She worked with other incarcerated women, who studied together and supported each other.

Dante describes another example of peer support while incarcerated:

> I was getting near and getting ready to my GED, I told the same individual again, "let's do college courses, man, because I'm down but I just don't have the money." He said "don't trip; I'll have my mom pay for everything. All we need is one book. We can share it."
>
> We just need one books order, you know, order the books will show up. We don't have to buy double books.

Dante also points out that his carceral peer support taught him good study values: "I'm adequately prepared. Because don't trip. I'm gonna help you. I took all the classes already. You know, one thing he never did? He never cheated."

Fellow incarcerated people supported each other and gave of themselves, without asking for compensation or recognition. These were often small groups organized and composed entirely of fellow incarcerated people who were interested in gaining education. These groups often emphasized rigorous and disciplined study habits and encouraged one another.

Opportunity Innovation and Carceral Capital from Inside to Outside

Prison is designed to be a harsh and restrictive total institution that creates environments of deprivation. To punish incarcerated people, many amenities and possibilities for success are denied. Yet as I discovered in prison, we attempted to overcome these limitations through innovation and creative means and became quite adept at creating our own storehouses of what I refer to as *carceral capital*. Unlike when Kropotkin (1913), an early system-affected academic, first referred to prisons as "universities of crime," speaking of some of the damaging qualities of prison, the action of carceral capital was composed of SAA people taking advantage of any opportunities they could find in the carceral and correctional spaces they were in, where opportunities were very often sparse or unavailable. If they could not find any opportunities within their prison, they constructed their own, through opportunity innovation.

This process of finding opportunities, which I refer to as *opportunity innovation*, is often honed in the prison environment and is then transferred to the higher education environment as carceral capital by way of the SAA population. This undertaking can also include building peer support networks where external support may be minimal or lacking. For example, Toby, a multiple-degree-holding justice advocate, explains his experiences collaboratively (along with other incarcerated peers) building an informal literacy group while incarcerated:

> I sort of thought, you know what, let's, let's try and actually do some informal education stuff, because the school in there wouldn't let us actually do anything formal. So, myself and another guy with a decent level of education, both did a similar course and thought, you know, what we might be able to help guys actually, not only write functional things, but write things that could help themselves out when they come out.

Additionally, some segments of the SAA movement are becoming more successful at constructing transformative organizations and attracting societal and institutional engagement. Not to imply that prisons are somehow beneficial to those they hold, I want to emphasize that the development of this carceral capital is the product of the concentrated efforts of confined people attempting to overcome adversities and oppressive conditions in prisons.

Coupled with the potential of opportunity innovation and carceral capital are the efforts of outside people, who volunteer their own time and energy and physically enter prisons to provide educational resources. Such support can come in the form of teaching college courses inside the prisons, tutoring in various academic disciplines, helping incarcerated people access educational resources, and teaching basic skills such as literacy and mathematics. Their efforts working with incarcerated people can further augment and strengthen the academic capacity of SAA members.

Another example of the reciprocal effect between the SAA movement and higher education is the educational advocacy work of many SAA members. Many of the lived-experience people within this book come from environments in which educational opportunities did not exist. Their epiphanies in regard to realizing the power of education can be life changing, and many have become powerful advocates for the benefits of education for the carcerally impacted, consequently drawing more SAA people, scholarship, and influence into the academic world.

Mentorship takes place in SAA groups and among the SAA movement's independent actors and can take many forms. Some independent SAA people focus on identifying and developing leaders and leadership qualities among carcerally impacted scholars and activists. The work of identifying and cultivating the gifts and skills of lived experience is often hidden, yet this might be some of the most vital work in the mentorship process. For example, Ramona, an independent SAA individual in the U.K., uses her skills and graduate-level education to develop new leaders amid system-affected people, as she explains:

> I also have to spend 50 percent or more of my time on galvanizing lived-experience leadership, and therefore what I've done now is talk to more about lived-experience leadership I've invested in. . . .
>
> I mentor and really invest time in lived-experience leaders in the U.K. to connect them up with each other.

Alongside mentorship, another level of SAA direct impact in universities takes place in written research and the actual classroom, as lived-experience scholars and instructors transmit transformative concepts to wider educational audiences.

SCHOLARSHIP THAT TRANSFORMS

For many carcerally impacted scholars, whether in organized SAA groups or independent individuals, there was a great deal of enthusiasm and ambition focused on being involved in scholarship projects. It is common for members of the SAA movement to engage with multiple academic endeavors within their educational institutions. Many expressed a strong desire to maximize the benefits of education, gaining as much experience and knowledge as possible in college. SAA scholarship efforts can include theoretical work, various types of research, thought pieces, collaborations, and research workshops.

It is common for SAA members and groups to collaborate on scholarship, bringing together multiple lived-experience interpretations. While collaboration occurs across academia, certain members of the SAA population identified a unique dynamic of scholarly camaraderie among themselves. Pete, an established faculty member with experience in the SAA movement, explains the dynamics of working with people who are incarcerated and system contacted: "I don't talk about prisons and say that I can talk for people that are in prison now, right? So what we do is, we do the collaborative research, right? So what we try and do is, is actual research, where you're sort of doing it together, you know." Many networks of SAA support often encountered a greater sense of cooperative action on scholarship projects and a desire to work together. They perceived that these dynamics were not as readily apparent among many other scholarship groups.

Such working relationships can also function as part of the mentorship process in which more experienced researchers and scholars work on projects with newer academics and students (Tietjen et al., 2020). This process was fundamental to my learning how to construct scholarly work; more importantly, how to encounter and engage with different interpretations of system contact; and how to then effectively and meaningfully incorporate lived-experience concepts into research.

While the reciprocal dynamic of transformation between institutions of higher education and the SAA movement provides carcerally impacted academics with the tools and skills to produce influential scholarship (as discussed in chapter 4), the subsequent impact of the scholarship that SAA produces can reshape the knowledge terrain of social equality within higher education. Through changing the cultural norms regarding who can produce knowledge and who should be "allowed" to produce knowledge, SAA scholarship can illuminate the often-unseen perspectives of those disenfranchised and marginalized by society. Kim, a heavily engaged university faculty member, discusses how the justice system contact in her past was given new meaning through involvement in her SAA group: "By being part of this group, it gave me the ability to turn over into research, my experiences into real research, legitimate research." She perceives that she was able to unlock more of the potential of her lived experiences in higher education.

Further, the stances of lived-experience intellectuals often do not align with conventional prosystem scholarship. Adding the observations of people with legal system lived experiences constructs a human-centered base of knowledge, which can change the course of dialog and policy about legal and justice issues.

TEACHING THAT TRANSFORMS

Many faculty and instructors are affiliated with the SAA movement. Teaching and instruction may be one of the most powerful means to directly transform higher education in a more humanistic capacity through the direct classroom interactions of the student and professor. Lessons informed by lived experience can add context to how the CLS is conveyed to students, potentially painting more critical and comprehensive pictures of how institutions such as courts, prisons, jails, and the reentry industry operate. This may illuminate facets of dysfunction or carceral realities that a textbook would miss. Academic instruction that is sensitive to an inside viewpoint creates awareness (among students) of perspectives of incarcerated and lived-experience people to compare to the more commonly taught concepts, which are often curated for criminal justice administration by prosystem scholars. This introduces a more diverse (often critical) knowledge base into discussions of the legal system and can problematize viewpoints that are often accepted as "settled" issues by conventional criminology and legal system practitioners.

Some instructors use in-class activities to help students break through biases about people convicted of legal offenses. For example, Alex, a professor who is open about being FI, says, "I share my story. I developed a stereotyping exercise about convicted felons that I use. And we had a few students who approached me afterwards and told me they were FI; they wanted [to know] were there any resources."

Pete, a directly contacted SAA group founder and faculty member, explains how he experienced the dynamic of classroom instruction from a reciprocal perspective: "I mean, you know, when I started teaching,

I did actually enjoy, you know, having that knowledge and sharing that knowledge and engaging with, with students and sharing knowledge and listening to what they have to say and learning from them as well." Other SAA faculty members bring the insights of lived-experience people directly into their classrooms by bringing in guest lecturers. For instance, Deb, a system-impacted faculty member, routinely invites a directly impacted family member to speak to her classes about their experiences with the correctional system as part of her lesson plan. "I actually started like, having my dad come in as a guest speaker." She points out that students enthusiastically engage with this experience: "I don't tell them that it's my dad until like, halfway through, and then they're like, 'Oh, my God, it's your [Dad].—Wow, that's cool.'"

George, another scholar who is FI, invites carcerally impacted academics to talk to his criminal justice courses. Through this process, students have the opportunity to interact with people who have existed under the system's control, instead of just with the more commonly taught viewpoints of those who have controlled others. This can introduce the often-ignored reality (within criminology and criminal justice fields) of those who are marginalized, unseen, and unheard into classroom discussions. He emphasizes, "We're going to talk about it, we're going to bring up those issues, and we're going to deal with them, in everything, institutionalized racism or whether it's overt or whatever, you know." Introducing such conversations into the classroom can serve to redirect academic fields like "criminal justice" toward thinking about actual equity measures that consider wider social-structural forces that impact people in the system, away from the prosystem, tough-on-crime mentality that incorrectly focuses on "free will" and the supposed flaws of the individual. A more humanistic shift toward criminal legal issues in the social sciences and humanities points to building a legal system that emphasizes justice measures as a means to improve the common good, not to serve a capitalist state that uses correctional systems to control and warehouse people that the market no longer has use for (Davis, 2003; Irwin, 2005; Sheldon, 2008). Further, refocusing our priorities on the critical thinking and embrace of collective good often found within a more liberal focus on higher education would create a stronger and happier society, in which more people would be given the support and resources to prosper.

It must be noted that instructional strategies often change as academics' viewpoints evolve over time. As I engaged more extensively with SAA-focused "scholarvism," the SAA movement, and critical (but solution-focused) scholars, my approaches to teaching also shifted.

I introduced more critical and conflict-focused scholarship into my course readings. Part of this process was moving beyond simply learning about social problems by teaching students that they actually have the capability to improve society. Thus, I created activities that engage students with finding solutions to systemic justice problems. Early in my faculty career (ten years ago), I taught from the perspective that the brokenness of the CLS could be solved through reform measures, and I even accepted to some extent the "that's just the way it is" justifications for the existence of prisons. Yet after years of interacting with newer generations of SAA scholarvists, reading more lived-experience scholarship, and watching the institutions of law resist any meaningful efforts to change them, my criminological worldview has drastically changed. The cycle of reform for the sake of reform is not working. Consequently, the message I purvey to students has also significantly shifted to complete transformation, reimagining entirely different processes that center on the common good of people and society as the only means to bring about real change to the legal system. In this vision, the system of mass incarceration cannot exist (Davis & Rodriguez, 2000; Gilmore, 2009; Kaba, 2020), and we are moving beyond endless cycles of often minimally effective practical reform toward alternatives to prisons (Kalica, 2018), as well as to the construction of a society in which we fix the social problems that have led to inequality and oppression.

DISCLOSURE AS A LEARNING TOOL?

For SAAs who are college instructors, disclosing in the open classroom their legal system lived experiences, if they are comfortable with doing so, can be a powerful means of transformative potential. Yet I want to be careful to point out that divulging such information is a very personal decision, strongly tied to many sensitive social-structural dynamics such as the presence/absence of structures of privilege; the intersectional impacts of race, class, and gender; and the presence/absence of social support networks. Thus, this action should not be expected as a requirement of scholars with system contact, and they should not be pressured to do so. This process is only for scholars who have willingly made the choice after critical deliberation.

Some explain that revelation of system contact should be presented as contextually tied to the subject matter currently being taught in the course, so that it becomes a teachable moment. In these circumstances, the knowledge provided to students may be more impactful and provide unseen insights otherwise not encountered in standardized textbook readings. George explains how his graduate students react to his disclosing that he was FI: "They're cool, you know, they're open, they ask questions about it, they, you know, they engage with it, I think some of them appreciate it, some of them who even came forward to talk to me about their own experiences, you know." The experiences that can be passed on to students from SAA instructors who are in a position to *come out* about previous parts of their lives may have the capacity to uniquely illuminate the system's human dynamics. George imparts to his students that the CLS and all of its vast institutions are composed of actual people, and that it is important to keep this idea central to how to approach solving societal problems that involve justice. To be more direct, this human component is often missing from many of the "by-the-book" criminal justice departments that tend to resemble job training programs, rather than full academic programs that critically grapple with the humanistic problems that plague the U.S. legal system (Delgado & Stefancic, 2007). George indicates that framing his criminal justice courses around humanity and compassion teaches students how to approach conceptualizing criminal justice as an effective and legitimate alternative to the tough-on-crime model.

The SAA movement can also transform higher education beyond the classroom and literature, through engagement with measures in the wider frameworks of institutions and the community.

SAA MEMBER INVOLVEMENT IN INITIATIVES IN COMMUNITIES AND EDUCATIONAL INSTITUTIONS

SAAs' influence on higher education manifests at the institutional level too. As the SAA movement further engages with higher education, faculty, and scholars (some of whom are now involved in administrative roles); the avenues toward humanistic transformation also increase. This can include committee service (often required of tenure-track academic faculty), and organizational involvement in various types of wide-ranging institutional initiatives involving people in any position in academia, from students to staff. One SAA leader and faculty member, Jared, uses his committee planning skills and vision to enact organizational plans,

> like academic societies, and how there are sort of like committees and social like members that sort of like often like lead things, oftentimes through committees, but I imagine their being like strategic action committees, that

> strategy sort of like developed collectively from the membership and then sort of committees to enact that strategy.

Most faculty members at universities are required to serve their institutions on committees of many types, including educational policy formation, promotion of other faculty, hiring, and academic integrity (and many more). This gives SAA faculty opportunities for connection with many often unseen moving parts of the institutional bureaucracy that impact everyone connected with this process. Deb, a very active newer SAA member proactively reaches out to others: "I've told other members who are in leadership that I would love to, like, volunteer for committees and become involved." Pointing to examples of organizational initiatives, she explains that she works in multiple areas: "Like the committee and social justice work I get involved with is kind of involved with legal issues a lot of times." Her breadth of work allows for a dispersive level of SAA interaction.

Herein lie many possibilities to advocate for system-affected academics in higher education. For example, serving on a faculty hiring committee for a professor position in an academic department allows for direct advocacy to consider and hire people who have system contact. In another scenario, SAA faculty on educational policy committees may be able to construct institutional policies that provide greater opportunities for system-contacted students or eliminate oppressive guidelines. In a variation of committee-based transformative potential, many activist-scholars also choose to become involved in justice-focused organizations in their surrounding communities.

Shaun, a directly contacted SAA member and university staff member with aspirations to work in academic administration, describes committee work in wide-ranging environments: "I participated in the formation of committees, served on committees locally, my area wide and region wide. So I did a lot of work. I've done a lot. I kept consistently [*sic*], always worked on myself." He feels that such engagement is how he can help reach the community, especially marginalized students, while building his abilities as an effective future administrator. The SAA movement can benefit from wider social exposure, as carcerally impacted academics represent their institutions and advocate for system-contacted people in nearby neighborhoods and regions.

Engaging students in organizations on campus and in the community that engender awareness and acceptance of system-contacted people can also function as a powerful conduit for humanistic transformation in the legal system and society. Many SAA instructors pointed to coordinating opportunities and experiences that involved their students in initiatives focused on helping system-affected people. Tomás, a system-impacted academic working in university administration, explains an institutional initiative he is working on with faculty:

> I develop a lot of networking with professors. And they will give, they will sit in class, and I said, "Look, I don't want my guys or girls to sit in a class and be tokens." I want them to sit in a class and treat them like a student so they can get the full scope of what it is to be in college life, right?

He is integrating wider circles of university faculty into transformative work that can improve educational conditions for directly contacted students.

In another example of this type of work, Edward, an SAA leader and university staff member, asks:

> How do we build this infrastructure before the students get here and also serve the needs of the students who are already here, right? How do we have that sort of support available to students when they come right, so that they can advocate for themselves, they can advocate in the community?

He works toward higher education advocacy for SAA people within his institution and in the political sphere.

Isabel, referring to SAA members' desire to engage with wider social actions, explains:

> I think so many of our students and so many of us, like we understand like the, the trials we went through and all the hardships and all the like wandering around. What can I do? That I think so many of us enter the program with this want to give back to those of us and to make it easier for others coming behind us definitely.

She points out what motivates SAA members to engage with transformative action, which ties in with the movement's goal of helping to pull others up.

For example, some instructors referred their students to internships in organizations that support SAA-related issues. In a similar situation, George was open with his graduate students about his system background and his actions to help system-impacted people. He was approached by a student who was interested in helping youth in the legal system and then introduced the student to a local social justice community action group. The student subsequently became actively engaged in this group. While motivating a single student's engagement may seem inconsequential, an expanding population of carcerally impacted instructors in academia may cumulatively influence humanistic change.

CONCLUSION

In a statement about the potential of activist scholarship to radically change market-driven higher education, James and Gordon (2008) captured much of the intent of this chapter: "We are arguing for activist scholarship not as therapeutic but rather as a radical, potentially revolutionary, alternative to the corporate university" (p. 367). Changing the massive and complex institution of higher education at the level of full humanistic transformation (from the current market- and profit-beholden university system) while finding viable employment opportunities for system-contacted people is no small task. Yet the movement has to address this task strategically, working to implement change in targeted areas where we can have the most effect, such as in classrooms and through our community activist—centered research that amplifies and centers the lives and experiences of system-contacted people. We, as a movement, are not naive enough to state that we could carry out this task entirely on our own, this chapter has provided many poignant examples of how the SAA movement's potential for multiple avenues to transformation is there. We can push the dial.

The processes of SAA movement building, mentorship, teaching practices, and influences on institutional and community initiative work have been tapped in this chapter as potential means of creating meaningful humanistic changes within higher education. Considering the forces that motivate such changes (which will require further research to determine), the cluster of SAA transformative undertakings presented in this research could be the product of the powerful peer support networks formed by people who are incarcerated in correctional institutions. The SAA members in this book are bringing the peer-support dynamics they forged through legal system contact with them into their communities and educational institutions. Their academic presence and activist scholarship work can motivate institutions of higher education, which often pride themselves on inclusivity and diversity, to engage in an introspective look at themselves. This can force universities to grapple with pivotal questions, such as how they meaningfully practice acceptance of groups that have been historically marginalized and stigmatized by society. An example of this is the Huskies Post Prison Pathways (n.d.) (HP3) program at the University of Washington–Tacoma (UWT).

This organization, run by a strong representation of FI faculty, alumni, and university staff, has strongly and vocally advocated for the rights of system-impacted students on campus and in society. Their work has been recognized and supported by UWT administration. HP3 has now begun to advance the cause of system-impacted students in the sphere of higher education, through the development of resources, mentorship, and guidance for system-impacted students, alumni, staff, and faculty. If the existence of dynamics of social inequality are exposed, then SAA groups can work with colleges to find solutions.

This chapter concludes by reemphasizing that through the powerful outcomes of members' interactions and work within their universities, this movement can function to bring the importance of standing up for social justice back into capitalism-mesmerized institutions of higher education, also referred to as the neoliberal university (Grimaldi, 2012). This sets the stage to examine in the next chapter how SAA uses the powerful instruments of critical and activist scholarship (Aresti et al., 2012) to build support for decarceration and progressive justice measures that advocate for the system affected.

CHAPTER 4

Reaching Hearts and Minds and Eliminating the Social Need for Incarceration

The Man Who Was Never Going Home

I remember talking to a man while in prison who was never going home. He had a sentence so lengthy that he would have to do more time than even the longest of lifespans. Being a relative short-timer (prison nomenclature for having a shorter sentence), I had to learn how to talk to him. He would not discuss events in the outside world or the prospects of being released and returning home, because these concepts no longer had any meaning to him.

His convictions were from when he was a very young man, and he was conversing with me after decades in prison. He knew about institutionalization and how serving time changed us, speaking of it with a thousand-yard stare.

He had given up on a society that had forgotten about him. Few know of, value, or care about the many millions of incarcerated people serving pointlessly long sentences as "residents" in thousands of U.S. carceral institutions. Further, coupled with the everyday hardships of prison are the additional hurdles of overrepresented marginalized groups that our society chooses to send to prison. Years later, as a student, I learned that many critical criminologists explain that the purpose of prisons is to serve as warehouses for "storage" of unwanted segments of society that the status quo does not value or instead of addressing serious social problems (Irwin, 2005; Sheldon, 2008). Yet the insider perspectives of SAA members can bring these social problems and forgotten lives and experiences to the outside world. This can give the public an insider-informed view of the social trauma that incarceration wreaks upon the confined (and the waste of human potential).

Because of my past carceral experiences, my current life is heavily influenced by conversations and experiences with people I will likely never see again. The world wants to forget about such people. Yet even after twenty years, I cannot stop thinking about these discussions. Incarceration is not just a qualitative interview that I, as an academic, mine for gold nugget quotes to use in some career-advancing article. No, these are actual occurrences from my past that became life-defining moments for me. I directly experienced the humanity of my fellow incarcerated peers. We discussed our fears and lived through being ground down by the endless numbing boredom and senseless frustrations of everyday life in the correctional environment. We are all real people, whether within or outside of the legal system, struggling with common problems, worries, and hardships.

Having been asked to share my life experiences with students, mentees, and concerned community social justice groups, I know that the lives of the people I was incarcerated with have value. As an SAA, I interpret my carceral contact as more than basic lived experience I can draw on casually from time to time to frame a point. Its potential for greater aggregate impact is much more than that. My lived experience (carceral contact) was forged by multiple factors: the carceral impacts of trauma and social/psychological deterioration and learning a new set of cultural values and how to live in a new social environment, coupled with a later rebuilding/reintegration process. My carceral contact is an alloy of experiences that had a synergistic effect on me.

I was given an opportunity to illuminate often unseen human and social realities contained within my experiences of incarceration through a reflexive lens. In plain terms, in my training as a qualitatively inclined academic, I learned to acknowledge the influences that my personal stances and biases would have on the research process. Using this knowledge, I harness the subjectivity of my own views not as a limitation but as a strength. Additionally, I carry within me a library of discussions and interactions with people I encountered in prison; I now bring the stories of their lives (which might otherwise be unknown and unheard) to the world outside of walls and barbed wire. Thus I can serve as a human window into an otherwise closed-off microcosm, building a narrative of the deep personal harms that prison inflicts on the incarcerated. Bringing these perspectives and knowledge to wider spheres, including communities, academic scholarship, students in the classroom, and even state institutions may function to increase humanistic understanding of the carceral system. The damage of incarceration can then be presented at a more empathetic and human level that broad audiences (including the general public) can relate to.

Unlike academics without lived experience, as a system affected academic I perceive myself as having something in common with my still-incarcerated and reintegrating peers. I saw the grit and grime of prison and experienced some of the harm it inflicts on the human condition. This provides me with a means to empathize with portions of their complex carceral experiences, suffering, and trauma of prison. From this, I have worked to build a compassionate activist scholarship informed by personal interactions that have endured the destructive dynamics of confinement.

HARNESSING THE POTENTIAL TO TRANSFORM BOTH CARCERAL AND EDUCATIONAL SYSTEMS

The SAA movement was generated from the seismic forces of two major social institutions, the CLS and higher education. Thus, it does not come as a surprise that SAA both influences these systems and is influenced by them. This chapter focuses on the potential the movement has to tranformatively influence both of these systems.

The SAA's activist-scholar–informed presence in universities comprises people who have endured carceral-centered traumas and social inequalities, who have survived marginalization and oppression and are now attempting to use their lived experiences to improve the life chances of others. The collective presence of their energies and impact on college campuses can show contemporary market-driven business models of higher education the way back to channeling their vast resources toward social justice and the common good. Many SAA members, by attempting to build larger structures of opportunity and inclusion in schools and prisons, are advocating for the rights of all system-contacted people within and outside of education. Further, members of the SAA population can function as an effective vehicle for advancing *high*-impact critical and activist scholarship (in research, teaching, and community engagement) that shines a bright light on the intersectional oppression of and problems perpetuated by the CLS. Such discourse can assist in pushing the dial toward overcoming deficit perceptions of system-impacted students (Abeyta, 2022), deconstruction of mass incarceration, and creation of prosocial alternatives.

BY PEOPLE WHO ARE SYSTEM CONTACTED, FOR PEOPLE WHO ARE SYSTEM CONTACTED

Those who have experienced confinement in the correctional system speak of being socially isolated and marginalized during and after incarceration or system contact (Schliehe et al., 2022). These negative impacts carried over into the college campus, where many who subsequently found SAA support spoke of feeling alienated and lost before contact with the movement. Study participants indicated that issues such as frustration at lack of representation in academia; the need for educational support, resources, and mentorship; marginalization of their research and scholarship in the academy; and being ignored by policymakers were often mentioned as issues that motivated engaging with the movement.

To summarize views on why SAA groups were formed is not a simple task. SAA members present many varying opinions. Mark, an SAA group member and member of a historically oppressed population, captures one of the more commonly shared viewpoints: "So I believe [SAA group] was created to give us space, a space for us, we run it." This process has been framed as effective, as Trivedi and Ray (2024) pointed out that FI people are successfully developing spaces through organizing to fight against social injustices and defend their human rights. Further, being part of a dedicated space gives SAA members a sense of agency and empowerment, a marked positive change in contrast to the world outside of this space that often excludes and stigmatizes them.

Vickie, an FI graduate student and active SAA group member, shares this sentiment, but also expands on this discussion:

> I'll say the payoffs of like, being a part of the group. And I can imagine some of their motivations was [*sic*] like, to have, you know, a support system within the, within higher ed, but also to have a resource, like good information, because it's so hard to find good information about, like, you know, what's possible for us what, you know, laws really allow or curtail or whatever. So, that's another huge benefit, I think, and, like, impetus to join a group like that.

She points out that those who join the SAA group gain not only access to camaraderie and general support, but also the collective knowledge and wisdom of others who have already navigated the mazes of higher education and society. This is similar to the funds of knowledge concept theorized by Vélez-Ibáñez and Greenberg (1992) and González et al. (2006), which builds on the concept that regardless of the presence or lack of material wealth, groups of people have skills and bodies of knowledge that they have accumulated and acquired over time through the aggregate of their lived experiences and the historical memories embedded in their culture. Moll et al. (1992) also applied funds of knowledge to education as a useful tool for teaching. While this study focuses on the family dynamic, this concept could certainly be applied to educational cohorts of system-contacted students and scholars. Faith, an involved SAA group member and current student, continues this discussion of the impacts of building spaces for SAA members by adding an educational element: "I think that's my ultimate goal is to raise awareness from all aspects of it." Such SAA work can help inform public knowledge about the issues that people in the movement face. The point of such awareness is not to present this population and their struggles through the lens of a deficit model, but rather to demonstrate that with sustained support, system-impacted students and scholars are capable of achieving at a high level.

Tomás, an SAA group member and aspiring graduate student, points to group formation as being motivated by a need to create a means of expression for our population: "I think one of the things, there was no voice for the people that were system, that were formerly incarcerated." He continues an important vein of the SAA movement, vocal activist work and advocacy. This projects our viewpoints outward, from spaces of support. Carl, a graduate student and SAA group member, continues this discussion: "Because of all of this stigma, and all the hurdles, and all the barriers that exist in life, for formerly incarcerated people, we saw an opportunity to kind of maybe take down some of those barriers and show that higher education could be all inclusive." He points to an SAA purpose of taking apart systems that oppress SAA people and building more inclusive educational environments. This frames the multifaceted functions of the SAA movement, working on multiple fronts toward greater opportunity and equality for people with system contact.

Bernard, a graduate student with direct system experience and a very involved member of multiple SAA groups, explains that each of his SAA groups has very different visions. His well-established university-affiliated SAA group was founded to create a space of support for students with system contact. He states, "There was no space for us, there was no support for us." Before the formation of the SAA group, students on this college campus had felt isolated and somewhat marginalized. Through their own efforts, this SAA group built a campus-based program for themselves, informed by their own lived experiences (Antojado, 2023).

If no space exists, SAA groups create their own space. Yet when speaking about another non-university-affiliated SAA group he was part of, Bernard points to a broader explanation for its founding: "It was more . . . just want[ing] to see a national network." This group had a firmly national focus, wanting to create a nationwide network of support for college students who were FI. Thus, being able to reach out to a broad audience could enable them to create a larger system of support and resources for college students and graduates who were FI that did not have the limitation of being attached to only one college campus.

The perspectives of independent SAA individuals about why they decided to engage in SAA-aligned work brought many illuminating insights into this discussion. Within this research, many of the independent actors were from the U.K. and Australia, regions of the world with a growing SAA movement presence due to many factors, such as their unique and often oppressive carceral histories. This small but dedicated group explained that SAA-type organizations have not had enough time (yet) to develop as fully as in the U.S., but the believed that there was often an urgent need for the influences, work, and expertise of scholars and activists with lived-experience perspectives in their countries. As in the U.S., if international SAA groups cultivate opportunities to partner their lived experiences with the resources and support of willing university systems, this can increase opportunities and social capital for marginalized groups (Smith, 2013) in higher education in their own countries, too.

SAA APPROACHES TO EDUCATION AND THE CLS

One of the defining lynchpins of the SAA movement is interaction with higher education. SAA people position themselves as educators, producers of activist and/or critical scholarship, reformers, and representatives of other perspectives. When incorporating such views as critical and cultural criminology (Ferrell, 1999; Ferrell et al., 2015), social inequality, and feminist standpoint theory (Harding, 2004; Hartsock, 1983; Smith, 1987) into their work, SAA groups have engaged in higher education stances such as being producers of rigorous critical/activist scholarship, rigorous researchers, and educators bringing the lived experiences of system-affected people to the public and to classrooms in both universities and prisons.

Higher Education

To establish the initial connection (or linkage) between education and the SAA movement, Faith, a graduate student and system-contacted SAA group member, elucidates using rhetorical questions:

> And what the difference might mean for them, right? If they send somebody to prison for five years, or if they, you know, give them a grant for college? What's the difference? Right? If they're going into law, if they're going to, going into policy, what the difference is between having an education versus not having an education?

She has experienced both the benefits of higher education and the damage of incarceration, and subsequently asks society to consider a world in which incarceration for a legal sanction could be replaced with programs that would give people options to learn how to improve themselves and change society.

Viewpoints among and within different SAA groups and independent SAA individuals varied. Those who viewed themselves and/or their groups as activist-scholars pointed to many reasons for this. Within the population interviewed for this book, oppressed and marginalized groups explained that they were aligned with more critical and radical educational stances than demographics that had experienced more privilege. Diego, an SAA group–involved faculty member with direct system contact, comes from a background of oppression. He points out his SAA group's stance toward higher education:

> We try to push revolutionary theory and radical and critical education, but at the same time, we're not going to force it on the party, because that's the, that's the important part of being the society, right? We're all different, we all have different aspirations we push for, is [*sic*] revolutionary and systemic change. But if you want to be part of the status quo, okay, but just know that we're gonna critique that.
>
> Also try to push revolutionary theory, we also try to push political education.

He also goes as far as explaining that his group respects differences of opinion among individual members, yet the spirit of the group itself will remain focused on more critical and radical forms of politically focused education. This dynamic speaks to robust variation of worldviews among individual chapters of some SAA groups, yet Diego points to a sense of moving forward together with a common purpose.

Furthering this discussion, differing intergroup opinions on how to move SAA people forward were quite prevalent. Campus-affiliated organizations had different focuses, and the groups were large enough to have multiple chapters on numerous college campuses that also experienced fluctuation in their educational perspectives. For instance, some SAA organizations with more funding and resources can demonstrate that their students are academically high performing. Dean, a member of such an SAA group, makes this clear:

> So we tend to be more [a] mature classroom, because we already screwed up. You know, we don't have time to screw up again, we mean business. We read everything that that is prescribed to us. Because we, you know, we're eager to succeed, and we have a lot to prove to [the] community.

A strong emphasis is placed on the SAA members' desire to demonstrate ambition and accomplishment. He also points out that within his group, members achieve higher than average GPA scores when compared to the general student body.

Among independent SAA members, viewpoints ranged widely on subjects such as how to approach academia and activism, including varying stances on community advocacy and activism, peer mentorship, administrating social justice nonprofits, and direct focus on in-depth research (just to name a few). For example, in regard to the varying ideological stances on SAAs' purpose within the university and mentorship relationships within the SAA movement, it is worth noting that the mentor and mentee experience can be influenced by this process. To illustrate, some mentors, when advising new tenure-track SAA faculty, might emphasize adhering to a more conventional scholarly role and avoiding any controversial stances, especially before receiving tenure. Conversely, other faculty with a more public-facing and advocacy stance on SAAs' place in academia may advise mentees to speak out to systems of power and take positions on issues. Variations in mentor ideological worldviews on how carcerally impacted scholars should interact with higher education may also influence how mentees are advised to approach disclosure of their legal backgrounds within professional academic contexts, including in the classroom and among colleagues. These dynamics may warrant further research. An article by Tietjen and Kavish (2021) addressed the potential of additional fragility of some SAA members' position in academia due to the ever-present legal convictions in their backgrounds, a factor that could influence how informed mentors would approach counseling mentees on this issue.

The important point is the power of the wide scope of SAA focus. We as a movement are addressing issues across a spectrum of social justice–focused work. Of course it must also be noted that there is significant overlap in educational focus between independent SAA members and those in more organized groups.

The CLS

Overwhelmingly, SAAs view the CLS as broken, but there is a range of perspectives on what to do next. I found a couple of prevalent perceptions of how to approach this system. The first is drastic reforms. The second is various stances on prison abolition, supported by works of current scholars and outspoken proponents, such as Angela Y. Davis (2003), Dorothy Roberts (2019), and Ruth Wilson Gilmore (2022). In addition, many people within the scope of this research were often focused on decarceration, or stated in other terms, wanting to use incarceration far less. Thus, a spectrum of viewpoints was expressed, from supporting a gradual decrease of people confined in corrections, a form of the attrition model of prison abolition (Knopp et al., 1976), all the way to completely and immediately abandoning incarceration (Knopp et al., 1976; Zinn, 2014). Additionally, there were mixed perspectives among participants on whether to work on reform and transformation from within or from the outside of the CLS.

In regard to working within the system to bring about change, Isabel provides some advice an academic mentor gave her:

> If you're that person throwing rocks at the box, you're never gonna get inside the box. You want to work within the box and push those limits out.
>
> So now you're inside the box. That means like, he's basically like, work within the system and push as hard as you can, within it, to your capacity to try to keep pushing to get it where you want it to be. Versus like openly confronting it, going against it. Like, you're, they're never gonna let you in really to be able to make some of these changes.

Isabel voices that she was supporting her peers who advocated total abolition measures, yet she struggles with fully embracing the concept and has been encouraged by her abolitionist peers to read more about the topic. She alludes to abolitionist scholars having to spend much of their time envisioning a world without prisons while reformists are actually going into the prisons, describing a more boots-on-the-ground sort of engagement to create change.

Many SAAs younger system-contacted scholars/students, who expressed that they perceive their own approaches to how to deal with the legal system as more abolitionist and revolutionary than were previous generations of system-contacted scholars. Pete, an SAA group member and professor, states:

> You know, there's a whole generation of [SAA group] members now coming after me now, you know, and they're, they're doing great work. They work hard and they're really bright, you know, brilliant people. But yeah, some of them are a little more, they're more radical or they're more not, I don't say radical in like a negative way. I just mean. . . . Yeah, I mean, it is a term of respect but yeah they have they have some different ideas you know and I'm cool, I'm like let's work let's all work together we can work.

Another interviewee, Sue, an SAA group member and graduate student who supports total abolition of the prison system, quotes Audre Lorde:

> Like, it's like what Audrey [*sic*] Lord says, right? Or if it's her, Bell Hooks [*sic*] like. . . . There's that saying that . . . you know, use the master's tools to dismantle the master's house or something, but I'm like, I don't, I don't believe that you can ever really use the master's tools to dismantle the master's house. But I mean, it's good to know like what tools the master has.

In another addition to the abolition discussion, Bernard, a member of multiple SAA groups, speaks about an SAA group he is part of, affiliated with a large state university: "[SAA group,] is about abolishing. They don't want to work with it in any form of [*sic*] fashion." This group is firmly against the correctional system and will not work with any facet of the CLS (or sit down with those who do), including law enforcement.

Among independent SAA members, viewpoints ranged widely, from reform-centered accommodationists to more critical viewpoints of decarceration that look to deconstruct the system. In certain instances, SAA groups espoused multiple viewpoints simultaneously. Madeline, a doctorate-holding scholar and SAA group member, provides an example of this: "So publicly, we're, we're more like progressive, let's change the system. Privately, we're a little bit more like, okay, the system has got to go." She also offers an explanation of how incremental reform over time can act as a precursor to major abolition efforts:

> It's what makes it palatable for the people in power. And you know, Audrey Lorde [*sic*] said, you can't use the master's tool to dismantle the house or whatever. And it's like, we have to, like, we're not going to change anything, unless we're doing it incrementally right now. Because it is so powerful. It's such, it's such a firm, deeply seated, structural issue. But these little incremental changes are not only changing the system, but also empowering more people so that we have more people power when we're ready to finally take it all down.

She explains that this paves the way for larger, more transformative changes. It gradually introduces the process of change without creating excessive resistance from the power structure, which could completely derail their efforts.

VISIONS OF THE FUTURE: PLANTING THE SEED

There was a lot of hope for, and some constructive criticism of, what lies ahead for the SAA movement. In the broadest terms, many discussed hope for expansion of their organizations and desire to see the movement help more people, and they listed initiatives that their networks or themselves were planning to begin (or should implement). Yet in discussions of the future directions and visions of SAA groups and individuals, there were also worries. As is common in new movements, concerns were expressed over maintaining and recruiting members and how to find enough resources to operate and carry out initiatives. There were also more group-specific issues expressed, such as dealing with internal struggles and difficulties. This process of SAA progress, full of stops and starts, intermittent successes and failures, is reminiscent of the concept of *wild seed justice* emphasized in the book *Abolish Criminology* (Saleh-Hanna et al., 2022). The authors' concept is based on the books of Octavia Butler and emphasizes a form of justice that exists outside of the oppressive systems of white colonialism and the carceral dreadnaught that was built to protect the wealthy castles of privilege and power. It is a form of justice that cannot be controlled or corrupted by the existing state and criminal legal systems, because it operates outside of them. Yet the process of implementing this form of justice is also susceptible to the immense corrupting forces of the long-standing and powerful state and carceral establishments that surround it; thus, the SAA members' progress is often full of peaks and valleys and often not neatly linear and smooth.

Hopefulness among those interviewed often centered around the movement maintaining, expanding, and continuing the ability to help current and future generations of system-contacted scholars engage with education, thus improving their lives. Bernard speaks about his desire for the newer SAA organization he is part of "becoming like a support for formerly incarcerated people . . . . That's my hope and desires for it." He imagines his group having the capacity to become more capable of assisting FI people. Tomás optimistically points out where he envisions his group going: "So I think it's just gonna keep on moving forward and growing, as long as people are planted the seed that they can achieve a degree and see by examples of other people, there's going to be more people applying and being part of it." Much of this sentiment of hope is fueled by the perception that the SAA movement has the potential to continue to help others who have not arrived yet.

Kim, a system-contacted faculty member who is heavily involved in the movement, would like to see her non-university-affiliated SAA group branch out to other organizations and form connections outside of the academic disciplines of criminology and criminal justice (e.g., psychology and sociology). She points out:

> There's also wings of sociology and psychology that do work, that are about criminal justice; it would be nice if he even knew [of] our existence. And like, yeah, we had a little so I could see like pieces of that possibly happening, of being able to reach out and have new connections in those kinds of ways.

Yet intermixed with hopeful and supportive sentiments, SAA members have also voiced concerns about their organizations' futures. Sue talks about issues her group needs to address regarding internal disputes within their ranks: "There's already fucking people who are rallying to make sure that organizations like this don't exist. Right, right, right. You don't need to fuck ourselves over and the people that are yet to come to benefit from this organization, if we don't address the fucking mud in the water." She offers her concerns as constructive criticism, emphasizing that she is concerned about their vulnerability among already established social biases. She wants to see her network flourish as a supportive space and continue to help future members.

For people involved in the SAA movement, whether in groups or independently, looking into the future was an exercise in envisioning the means to harness and direct the energy and potential found among themselves and system-contacted colleagues. Often they were working within nascent groups and networks that were just beginning to discover their strengths and capabilities; thus the experience was simultaneously exciting and unnerving for them. This can be perceived as stage 1 of a larger two-part transformative process of collective lived experiences that translate into the energies the SAA movement generates to potentially impact higher education and correctional systems.

First Stage of Transformation: The Alchemy of Turning Toxic Waste into Valuable Activist Scholarship

The gaze of the FI and system impacted looking back into the carceral past is filtered through the events of years. The mind-set we had while in prison becomes unrecognizable to some of us over time. In those barren locked rooms, a motivation or mentality often forms that comprises the will to survive. It is an environment of strain, pressure, and fear, coupled with correctional staff continually telling us we are worthless. For many of us, our worldview became battered and distorted.

That is the insidious nature of prison: it slowly grinds its captives down over time. Many walk out feeling like jaded, beaten-down people, scared individuals dragging their traumas along with them. Yet for several people whose lives are presented in this book, the encounters with the SAA movement, coupled with postprison education, gradually converted their carceral experiences from what they saw as worthless toxic waste (Brown, 1991; Ebaugh, 1988), something to be shamefully concealed, into a valuable currency of lived experience. This currency could subsequently be used as the building materials needed to develop growing networks of action-focused scholarship to advocate for transformative justice and increased social justice focus in higher education. Engaging with a supportive network of system-contacted scholars can serve as a functional form of alchemy (unlike the failed attempts of medieval times), transforming something initially perceived as worthless into something of great value. This experience was shared by several of my SAA colleagues and peers (Richards & Ross, 2003b).

The first level of transformation takes place as a synergistic process within and between the people directly involved in the movement. Whether in groups or independently, looking into the future was an exercise in envisioning the means to harness and direct the energy and potential of themselves and their system-contacted colleagues. Often SAA people were working in nascent groups and networks just beginning to discover their strengths and capabilities. Thus, the experience was often empowering, supportive, life changing, and cathartic for them. Many of those interviewed described processes of personal and communal change through various types of engagement with the SAA movement.

This process can involve such things as peacemaking processes (Morris, 2000; Pepinsky, 2013; Pepinsky & Quinney, 1991), camaraderie, and direct confrontations of systems of oppression through processes of scholarship, organizing, and activism.

Vicky, an SAA member who has overcome many struggles including addiction and incarceration, frames how SAA networks influence their members: "It's like, it's such an investment in each other, too, which is just really empowering. You know?" She emphasizes that fellow system-contacted people are sharing their energies with each other in a process of building each other up. Nicole, an SAA member with carceral lived experience, also stresses this line of thought: "So . . . we need each other. Because I know I learned that I wasn't alone." As an activist-scholar and faculty member with many years' involvement in the movement, she found many forms of social support (House, 1981) in her SAA group. Marie, a system-impacted faculty member, further reiterates the powerful impacts of collaborating with peers: "I think that the more that of us that there are, it's motivating to kind of be organized and stick together to try to make some change." For the people engaged in SAA organizations, such support can provide the stability needed to access and utilize transformative resources.

SAA group members describe this synergy of encountering social support and actively using resources to create change through helping fellow peers solve problems. For example, Carl, an SAA group organizer and graduate student, narrates this process:

> Here's an advocacy group that will meet on your behalf with whomever. Yeah, whatever the case may be doesn't matter. You have an issue with finances? Well, we've got somebody who's a financial counselor, who's an advocate of ours, yeah. In touch with them, they'll get in touch with you; we can synergy together to make this a simple solution.

Through a network of system-contacted people, those with legal convictions are helping other people with legal convictions work through the unique problems they grapple with.

Their insider knowledge informs others how to navigate the bewildering minefields of collateral consequences that the FI step into after prison. Yet in addition to creating unique networks of support that enable individual transformation, the SAA movement can engender change through other avenues, such as emotion. Pete, an established faculty member with direct system contact, sheds light on this point: "So what we've got is the ability to empathize, we've got the academic ability and the academic skills." He emphasizes that in addition to classical academic training as scholars, his SAA peers identify with each other and care about each other's plights.

This change occurred at the personal and the communal level (peers and colleagues). Examples would include discovering such strengths as organizational skills, research abilities, teaching the system-contacted, and mentorship of FI students.

Second Stage of Transformation: Using the Cumulative Value of the SAA Dynamic to Create Change That Lasts

In the second stage of SAA movement transformative impact, the collective energies of members of the SAA network can be focused on potentially impacting higher education and correctional systems. This process occurs through the organized initiatives of SAA groups and independent members and actions that they take to directly engage with transforming the institutions of higher education and the CLS (often focused on corrections).

Incarcerated people quickly become aware that prison is damaging them and those around them. Within this grinding process of trauma and suffering, many found the motivation to strive for more effective systemic change, subsequently consolidating their energies within the SAA movement. Through the value of lived experience–informed actions in the form of legislative advocacy efforts, research informed by system contact, and educating students and practitioners, the SAA participants in this book are working toward constructing a compassionate and prosocial justice system.

Hard-fought and promising policy changes, after they are achieved, are often simply discontinued when a political regime shift takes place. In order to avoid this pitfall, the work of the SAA movement needs to go beyond engaging in political machinations that grind down and dilute our missions, then subsequently attempt to co-opt us into the very systems that oppress us. To strategically avoid simply attempting policy changes that are so often temporary and unsupported by society, we need to move toward a more revolutionary focus and the hard (but worthy) work of changing societal beliefs and perceptions. Therefore, SAA groups are building structures (e.g., mentorship programs, funded community initiatives, scholarships) to reinforce the revolutionary activism and transformative changes of the future, so we can work toward overcoming oppressive processes holding us captive and limiting our potential.

Transforming Higher Education

Similar to Arrigo and Bersot's (2016) transpraxis concept, in which critical scholars of the present build a revolutionary activism for those yet to come, SAA members are working in various ways to lay the groundwork to enable continued progress, acceptance, and opportunities in higher education. Alisa, a graduate student SAA group member who is FI, demonstrates the movement's forward-thinking mentality and work when asked about her SAA group's stance on higher education, "I feel like it's a huge purpose and a responsibility that we have, as a criminologist and as academics, to foster an environment of inclusion and to promote the next person that comes behind us that's been justice impacted."

This is the point at which SAA groups move beyond self-transformation toward using activist-scholarship to motivate targeted institutional- and societal-level transformation. Such strategically focused transformative efforts can manifest in many forms, such as building knowledge and scholarship that can lead to helping system-contacted people. Alisa further discusses how she perceives her SAA group's potential when coupled with learning, "So to me, [SAA group] and education, to me goes with that feeling I have that, you know, it can save lives if we can build a theory, you know, to better understand people." She possesses a strong belief in the promise of her group and its relationship to higher education, believing it can rescue lives.

Many of the SAAs in the scope of this book describe the linkages between the SAA group and affecting institutional change, potentially mapping out an effective pathway for future activist-scholars to follow. Anna, an engaged SAA group leader and faculty member with Chicana heritage, points to bringing about large-scale changes in higher education: "I realized that academia is loaded with structural violence, it's loaded with oppression. Yeah. Which is why I, like I'm so focused on that idea of like eradicating the structural violence within academia." She speaks to oppressive processes within educational institutions that marginalize and discriminate against system-contacted and FI students and faculty as a form of systemic violence that produces social harm. Anna, as an activist-scholar, also works to reduce or eliminate oppressive long-term consequences perpetuated by the CLS:

> Our role is really as like scolarvists [*sic*], scholar-activist[s]. And so obviously, our job is scholarship, right, that, that's what we get paid to do for real, but making our scholarship make a difference. Yeah, actually do something,

> okay to get into that activist role. So, like, for example, I am advocating for reinstating voting rights in the state of [state name].

She refers to a key point in regard to moving beyond research and scholarship to actually activating scholarship to create change on a broader societal scale in both universities and the collateral consequences of the carceral system.

Tomás, an active SAA group member and system-contacted student, illuminates the multifaceted relationship his group has with education: "So I think we're both educating the public, we're educating even ourselves." He describes a transformative educational process that operates at both the macro and micro levels.

Transforming the CLS

Coupled with the SAA movement's efforts to shift higher education toward a stronger social justice focus are diverse sentiments and efforts to drastically change, rebuild, or replace the CLS. Marie, a system-contacted scholar and SAA group officer, describes how she views fixing the correctional system. She explains a long-term process viewed as more likely to succeed:

> So while I would love to tear down these systems, I think I'm somebody who maybe, ideally, maybe I'm like, tearing them down in tiny steps by working within them. If I can work with people, and maybe like, influence them in ways to kind of think about other things to do. That's something I'm down for.

She speaks to multiple viewpoints on how to grapple with the legal and correctional systems within her SAA group, with some members leaning more toward an immediate dismantling of these institutions and replacing them with alternatives.

Sue, a dedicated SAA member and Chicana graduate student, takes a passionate stance against the CLS:

> Fuck the system. I mean, fuck the police, fuck prison, fuck the whole system, you know, like, the U.S. Empire. But the U.S., you know what I mean? Like, if it was me, we've burned this motherfucker down. Right? And we . . . cause a revolution, is like you're trying to either work within the suit, like take the resources of the state and like, redistribute them away. But like, if you really want some, I think some change, then you're talking about abolition.

She fully embraces the concept of abolition yet later admits that she does not think that abolition of corrections can take place all at once:

"Although I do understand that this is not going to happen overnight, right. I do get that like some of us are going to have to work within the system." Anna's thoughts capture the substantial complexity of the decarceration process. She understands that deconstruction of an institution as well-established and socially ingrained as mass incarceration may require multiple strategies over an extended amount of time.

Ramona, an independent SAA and advocate who has organized her own networks of activists and academics who are FI, describes the transformative process of empowerment needed to engage oppressive institutions of justice:

> And so then when you come out and you want to help, you, what you want to do is help other people not to get in that situation, right? But you're not questioning the system. You might go, prison doesn't work, but you don't have that, have a real sophisticated understanding beyond that. You can't build a political strategy because you don't have the contextual knowledge.
>
> And this is why our job, for me my job through my network is to identify prisoner leaders, do community organizing in prison, build them, build up contextual knowledge, send out, send papers into them, create ally-ship [*sic*] with scholars, build a different, like coauthor papers. So, when people read about, when people in prison read about themselves, they're not participant A and participant B, they see themselves in print, and then that creates the confidence to lead, that creates the contextual knowledge that you need to battle with the system.

She describes helping her FI peers overcome the institutional indoctrination she endured in prison, by engaging them with knowledge and scholarship focused on systemic oppression and structural inequalities. In other terms, she describes this process as a means of liberatory empowerment. Instead of fighting the power structure using the master's tools, she works to give activist-scholars the skills needed to deconstruct oppressive systems and construct humanistic egalitarian processes. This can be more than mere resistance, taking a college course, or writing a scholarly paper; this can function as revolutionary changemaking for system-contacted people.

WE VIEW OURSELVES AS OF THEM AND FROM THEM

The people of the SAA movement are shaping uniquely impactful means to transform the societal institutions (e.g., prisons, universities, professional organizations) that have at different times functioned to oppress or exclude system-contacted people. Here are some thoughts on why the movement is uniquely impactful.

We share many identities with our system-impacted peers, and while all our viewpoints are not identical, we can generally state that we view ourselves as of them and from them. Due in part to our shared experiences, we possess an unconventional means for understanding our peers' complex personal experiences, including both the suffering and trauma of prison and the stigmatization of society that openly discriminates against us. Informed by an aggregation of knowledge that has survived destructive pressures, SAA members have provided examples of taking actions to not only construct an empathetic activist scholarship, but also engage directly with proactive change. Yet this ongoing movement of transformation has not occurred all at once as a single seismic leap; rather, it has involved a multitude of strategic individual and group actions. These small yet cumulatively powerful actions often come from system-contacted students and scholars, most of whom do not hale from the academically elite classes but from underresourced communities and marginalized groups.

The impacts of their many individual actions can both encourage and build larger systems of opportunity and social change. As I talked with and listened to many SAA members, I was told that when they worked together with similar individuals in networks, groups, and supportive collaborations, they perceived greater strengths and capabilities to accomplish their own projects and effect social good. Similar to Ruha Benjamin's (2022) concept of *viral justice*, enough individual actors have to begin taking transformative actions for social justice. It starts out as just a few people working against injustice here and there. Then more and more join in, fighting against the larger body of social injustice, and sooner or later the justice energy generated by their actions takes hold, invading the body of injustice, and it could eventually overtake this system of oppression.

The Meaning of Transformation

The two stages of transformation presented in this chapter are reciprocal processes of change impacting the SAA individuals, SAA groups, and social institutions that they are interacting with. These dynamics of change are often gradual and complex, and they often do not develop in a linear fashion. Further, the big question that we are exploring in this book is whether the cumulative results of these transformative actions have a positive and meaningful impact on the involved entities. In other words, how are we transforming segments of higher education and the

CLS? And perhaps also, we are asking, why are many people in the SAA movement so motivated to enact this change? (Or at least, why do they believe they are so motivated to enact radical changes?)

Many SAA people highlighted examples of efforts to influence change in multiple environments (e.g., the correctional system, universities, supportive groups) or levels of society (e.g., society, institutions, networks of people, individuals). Their scholarvist-informed initiatives include such things as completely tearing down the prison system and replacing it with various alternatives, bringing college programs into prisons, increasing the presence of SAA members in higher education, and creating scholarship programs and resource centers for system-contacted people.

The roots of motivation for transformative change are diverse. An example is that many SAAs members' perceptions of oppression in the carceral system consequently motivated their actions and work to transform the system and bring about decarceration. Among the majority of participants, there was strong negative sentiment against the correctional system and mass incarceration. Many had been subjected to bias while imprisoned and/or while under the supervision of the carceral system (i.e., probation, parole). There was a range of strong sentiment expressed toward the carceral apparatus. Some people pointed out varying examples of oppression from very direct to quite subtle, while others pointed more generally to the systemic inequalities that the CLS perpetuated. Those who did not describe experiencing bias or oppression while under the supervision of the CLS seemed to describe rather uneventful journeys through corrections. Of those who had already been through the CLS (had served sentences for previous convictions), the initial shock of system contact may already have been absorbed.

It must also be noted that generally, the study participants from outside of the U.S., who served sentences for their convictions in the U.K. and Australia, did not report bias while incarcerated. They experienced a great deal more educational and social support during and after their justice system contact. Yet many people stated that while being in prison in and of itself was not a good experience (as they often had internalized trauma during incarceration) from most perspectives, their mandatory direct system contact did have the forced latent effect of giving them time to reflect on their previous realities. Consequently, that phenomenon (being dislodged from a previous destructive life course) created a situation in which they had time to refocus their lives, even though this process occurred within the traumatizing confines of a total institution. For SAA members, positive transformative outcomes are often described as mixed, as they are often coupled with the lifelong damaging impacts of incarceration.

The Time Is Right for Shifting into a Transformative Space

The people who would come to comprise the SAA movement were forged from a myriad of conflicting dynamics, including the pains of incarceration, the oppression of the CLS, the ability to navigate prison culture, overcoming substance use disorders, learning to adapt and survive in hostile environments, and reintegrating back into society after prison. Yet as I described earlier in this chapter, before meeting networks of supportive scholars with similar backgrounds, my accumulated insider perspectives and knowledge gained during and after prison seemed like useless dead weight to me. To reiterate, "I walked out feeling like a jaded, beaten-down man, a scared individual dragging a wasted life with me." But the SAA movement's resources and cooperative energy, comprising the collective knowledge storehouses within our networks, shifted that "dead weight" into construction materials for transformative initiatives.

One potential explanation for the SAA movement's ability to access more transformative spaces and resources is greater acceptance of the movement within the current social, cultural, and political climate of youth demographics. Many of us also have stepped into the current SAA movement during a unique cultural era in which the younger generations of Gen Y (millennials) and Gen Z are disillusioned by many of the unfulfilled promises of their social institutions and leaders and are far more politically and socially left leaning, less supportive of capitalism, radically humanistic, and more progressive in their views (Lipsitz, 2022; Parker et al., 2019) than the previous Gen X and Boomer generations. We are in the era of the failed recovery of the 2008 recession and derailed attempts of the Occupy Wall Street movement to stand up to an elite power structure that disproportionately possesses the vast (and rapidly growing) majority of wealth, while to most Americans, the "American dream" is little more than an inaccessible pipe dream. Some have compared the younger New Left generations of the present to those in the protest era of the 1960s (Lipsitz, 2022). The recent SAA movement has roughly developed within the same timeframe of this more progressive and left-leaning shift in the younger generations. Among the millions of system-contacted people created by the fallout of mass incarceration (Shannon et al., 2017) who have returned to society, those who engaged with higher education (many of whom populate the SAA movement) did so within a more liberal and tolerant academic population of students that was more open to prosocial policies for the common good.

Thus, when discussing when we engaged with the SAA movement, many SAAs described an environment in which the cumulative knowledge, wisdom, and traumatic experiences we had accumulated through our life struggles and system contact were now recognized as having meaning and value. We had created the capacity to potentially impact personal and prosocial change that could benefit the system contacted. In a sense, we had transitioned out of a space of vulnerability to a place of strength and agency in which prosocial change seemed possible.

SAA Activist-Scholars Driving Transformation

Our fight for system transformation and equality for the carcerally impacted population is not composed of perfect victories and idealistic platitudes, but of continuing struggle. An example of this ongoing battle involves a March 2022 incident with a chapter of the Underground Scholars at the University of California–Santa Barbara, in which the entire membership of this group, which was active in advocacy work, applied to and was denied admittance into the UCSB sociology graduate program (Moody, 2022). The students involved in this specific incident have spoken out publicly against UCSB, stating that they have been excluded from this space because of their system-contacted backgrounds and activist work speaking out about discrimination against system-affected people.

In another example of SAA struggle from over twenty years ago that demonstrates how long we have been fighting for justice in higher education, a fellow SAA colleague was being considered for tenure at a major midwestern university and had fully and unequivocally met the requirements. They had a strong record of professional and scholarly performance and were expected to receive tenure. Yet in one of the final meetings of their tenure review committee, one of the committee members suddenly and unexpectedly presented the tenure committee with the SAA member's long past legal conviction records, information that was already known to the university, in an attempt to deny them tenure. Thus, instead of a smooth tenure process, this faculty member was placed in the stressful position of professional precarity. Following this, several of their fellow SAA peers came to support them, and the university was informed that a lawsuit on the basis of discrimination would be filed if this faculty member's tenure was denied due to their legal conviction. It was only after this entire process took place that the faculty member was finally awarded tenure. Even when it seems that SAA members' career futures are secure, they are sometimes forced into advocacy work in order to advance their careers and to support their fellow SAA peers, before they can even begin to step into the ring of SAA organizing and activist scholarship work.

While the words of the people in this book present hope for our population's expanded presence in higher education, the realities are still stark. Fewer than one in twenty FI people obtain a bachelor's degree (Couloute, 2018), while they exist in a system in which job requirements are becoming more and more rigorous. This is in addition to issues such as 27 percent unemployment for the carcerally impacted segment of the population. These statistics are even more bleak for those of the lowest levels of education and for People of Color. There is still an enormous amount of work to be done, as we create change within higher education and the carceral system.

The SAA walks many paths to transformation. As defined throughout this text, I apply an inclusive definition of activist-scholars as system-affected people within higher education taking various actions to advocate for and support social justice measures designed to help others affected by the CLS. The impacts of their broad-ranging actions could eventually lead to further systemic and institutional changes within higher education, the CLS, and potentially wider humanistic endeavors in society. Their diverse efforts, informed by lived experiences within the legal system, may not always be directly framed around transformative action, but they can still result in transformative impact.

CHAPTER 5

The Academic and Public Voice

Writing in the SAA Movement

I begin this chapter with a more recent intention that has developed in my writing. The struggle is to humanize/personalize my lived experiences, which has been part of the journey of writing this book, and to humanize the lived experiences of others. I arrived at this juncture through years of struggle, exploration, and some good old-fashioned serendipity.

Graduate school and the wider field of academia trained me to be an analytical, cold, and "objective" writer, which often removes humanness from scholarship. Yet as I progressed further as a scholar, my work focused more and more on interacting with oppressed people. In my research, I have had many shared life experiences with those I work with. Thus I treat my scholarship more as a collaboration with people who are system contacted, and this situation demands that I humanize my perspectives when describing their lives. Otherwise, the rich personal impact of their stories is lost in cold, abstract academic language. The people in this book who trusted me enough to sit in an interview and share their lives with me deserve a writing style that captures their essence in high resolution. Within the insider-informed research that I practice, anything less than that disrespects the integrity of their narratives. Yet I am often asked: What is the value of writing about these narratives, how does it help other people who are system contacted, and society? I answer these questions in this chapter, using our voices and stories.

Writing has always been a struggle for me. I struggled to learn academic writing, to compose as a scholar. Then after years of practice, I became acclimated to the style. Yet for many of us as SAA scholars, pure academic writing is just one of several forms of work we engage in. For example, within the confines of this book, I use many writing styles, such as storytelling through personal anecdotes, qualitative analysis, and building narratives through the sharing and interpretation of lived experiences. To you the reader, I would be lying if I said that writing in these many forms came easily for me. I have participated in this process while experiencing several different emotional states, often digging through memories and sections of my past that can be painful or traumatic to think about. Through this process, I was often attempting to find an essence or central phenomenon to tie together the meaning of lived experience in criminology and explore how to help other people who are system contacted.

But a conflict I often ran into when writing is that there is a lot of difference within the experiences and worldviews of people who are system impacted. So pinpointing an "essence" was elusive. It is difficult to concisely define the value/potential of the insider perspective for both the people in the SAA movement and society. Does it have a positive or negative impact on people that are system contacted who choose to use it? Should those of us in the SAA movement use it in our writing?[1]

Some of my scholarship is partially autoethnographic, a research methodology that critics pejoratively label as navel gazing. I argue that it is much more than that—it provides the raw materials to build new insights and concepts that can function to help other people who are system contacted, to guide them toward opportunities and equality. It has the potential to inform policymakers and community activists alike. The dynamic influence of ever-evolving educational growth developing alongside my reentry journey, now twenty years in the making, informs all of the writing I engage in, whether analysis, theorization, journaling, or various research methodologies.

Through my scholarship, I am constantly building, polishing, and improving upon a definition of myself as impacted, molded, and influenced by the seismic effect that incarceration had on my life. As my writing process evolved, how I viewed my lived-experience self also shifted. As I moved from the shock of incarceration, in which I saw blatant racial and class inequalities, into a new world of higher learning, I went through a period of intense intellectual enthusiasm. I could barely contain my thoughts and ideas on paper. Yet initially they were very disjointed, directionless, and unconnected. I tended to stray into wormholes of thought, just writing about whatever struck my fancy. While this type of writing can be very rewarding, it was not serving me very well from a scholarly perspective. While I was eagerly gaining an academic knowledge base in my graduate courses, I still lacked focus and follow-through in my composition of papers.

Eventually I became burned out on the writing process, after a couple of years of frustration with failed attempts at publication, and my enthusiasm for learning and scholarship production stagnated. I settled into depression (many people in the SAA movement carry long-standing trauma and struggles with them) and the day-to-day tedium of an academic career that was losing steam. Yet I gradually became more familiar with broader work that other people in the SAA movement were doing, and they encouraged me to get involved. I became active in SAA group participation, and I started to believe that I could be a part of building something that could actually help people who were system contacted. Armed with this belief, I was motivated to work on building up my writing abilities. I got to work, writing nearly every day, organizing collaborative research projects, and editing and revising the writing of others. Through constant practice, this gradually improved my writing, keeping me enthused and engaged. This is a skill set that all system-contacted people interested in being scholars could learn if provided with the opportunity through educational support and resources.

Through my struggles with long-standing issues, including recovery from incarceration and addiction, I began to think about how I could use these insights to build pathways for others. Yes, while this may sound like a cliché, perhaps some of this process was a form of therapy for me, a journey to better understand myself, and I am not ashamed to admit that. Thus, from this period of growth new creativity of thought was unlocked, flowing outward into my academic work, including scholarship, journalistic papers, and thought pieces. I began to see how the influence of lived experience permeated all facets of my life, in complicated ways. I realize that not all of these influences were positive and empowering, sometimes manifesting as irrational fears and trauma.[2] At other points, in more beneficial terms, I could use my insider knowledge to help construct solutions to problems or mentor others.

When thinking about my writing and the wider circles of writing within the SAA movement, I use the word *process* to present writing as a never-ending journey of development.[3] There is no final destination for me to arrive at. I am continually realizing self-discoveries of conceptual understanding along my path. These shifts and changes are influenced by a variety of motivators, some predictable and others more random. For example, factors of influence have included research interactions with other system-contacted people, major and minor life occurrences, reading an impactful book, and the presence or absence of distractions.

As I expand the number of scholars and activists in my professional network who are system impacted, I am also learning from them. I gain insights from their unique lived experiences and while sharing mine with like others. This exchange of knowledge pushed my writing in new directions. Through working with and learning from others in the SAA movement, I know that there are many different theoretical frameworks and philosophies used to understand carceral experiences. This provides a continually evolving (and hopefully improving) lens that I can use to interpret my academic perceptions. For example, I have met many members of the newer generation of the SAA movement who grew up experiencing intersectional oppression, racism, and exclusion in the twenty-first century. They have lived through the 2008 recession, opiate epidemics, ever-growing discrepancies in wealth between the ultrarich and the extreme poor, and the shift away from the tough-on-crime era of the 1980s and 1990s against the backdrop of the hypermodern chaos. All of this in the midst of the rise of MAGA nationalism and Christo-fascism, and round-the-clock sensationalism played out on social media. These views have molded many of us into radical and critical activist-scholars. Meeting this demographic has breathed new life into me, and that has drastically altered the direction and motivation of my writing.

Similarly, both as a scholar and a human being, the new events I encounter continually reshape the relationship I have with my carceral life experiences. This has occurred in different formats. for example, experiencing an episode of the recurring symptoms of prison trauma can jolt my thought process in different directions, or it can be something as simple as attending an intriguing lecture or reading a new book. I describe this as being similar to running the update function on a computer. I eliminate concepts that no longer function, refresh perceptions, and add new work-arounds to solve social problems. Thus, one of the first places these shifts in perception manifest is in my scholarly writing.

In the past five to six years, I have met a large number of more heavily engaged activist-scholars, who have a more revolutionary and radical worldview of the CLS.[4] Many of them have directly experienced racial and class oppression. They do not believe in merely changing the system; they believe in transforming the system, rebuilding it from the ground up. Meeting them jolted me back into action from my previous state of burnout. I had spent prior years feeling that I was fighting a losing battle to transform the system. I had given up hope. But the energy of meeting motivated people tossed me back into the ring, and I became involved with social justice groups that engage in direct community action. From here I began to aggressively pursue my criminological writing again, with a renewed sense of purpose.

As other parts of my life flourished and evolved, how I identified with my prison story changed, and this was expressed through my work. My network of support from allies and scholars who are system impacted grew. I also attended lectures and read new research and books within and outside of criminology. I learned a great deal from my interactions with these new people and experiences. I began incorporating a broader spectrum of ideas into concept building in my papers.

Martin (2022), an author with years of recovery from alcoholism, wrote about how her relationship with a long-past addiction no longer had the same meaning after gaining further knowledge and life experiences in sobriety: "Perhaps it is necessary to be a stranger to oneself in order to make room for new lenses through which to filter the world." For many years I had framed myself within my prison experience. I viewed my life dichotomously, as preprison and postprison. A large part of the written works I produced after incarceration were efforts to understand how confinement had impacted me. Through studying the dynamics of this institution, I believed I could perhaps overcome its impact on me. I could then command ownership of my experience, which I thought would give me a sense of control over my stigma. But this only partially worked. While my intellectual grasp of carceral phenomena was greatly expanded, I still struggled with the more human side of incarceration, the pain and trauma that I still carry today. Concurrently, I generated a body of written work that reinforced my conceptual framework and consequently confined/limited me to a reality of abstract facts and theories. As a consequence, I was still grappling with prison's damage to my psyche, mind, social life, and body. I had recurring nightmares of legal persecution, dreaming of standing in a courtroom and being told by an ominous police officer that I was going to spend many decades in prison. I relived my resentment and shame at being ridiculed by correctional officers who sought to dehumanize me at the lowest point in my life. I felt again the anger and shame that I wasn't allowed to attend my grandfather's funeral because I was imprisoned. For me, these are examples of how incarceration has worked its way deep into my psyche. These sentiments and many more have been churning around in my thoughts for decades. Whenever they come to the surface, they affect my emotions. This effect often finds its way into my scholarship.

It was not until I began to work (writing and activism) more closely with other people with system contact within the SAA movement that I began to change. Through the influence of the collective wisdom and support of SAA peers, the old labels stamped on me by social institutions, such as the CLS, grade schools, and counselors, began to lose their strength. I became a stranger to myself in my scholarship, because the old version of self did not define me anymore. Through my written work, I was able to initiate the process of reenvisioning myself.

Yet this was not a panacea or magical and immediate transformation into complete utopia. Changes happened gradually and organically. I am still evolving through my writing. Through collaboration on writing projects with many colleagues, my perceptual spectrum expanded. I learned about more experiences and could access others' greater stores of knowledge. This gave me more tools to see myself as able to embrace my past, as helping capital. As a result of this, I became better equipped to assist in the rebuilding process for others with similar struggles. Incarceration is a part of me that has permanently altered by being yet does not define my actions or existence. It is similar to storage space on a computer hard drive; it is information that can be called forth to bolster scholarship, define concepts, and give direction.

LIVED WORDS: WRITING THAT ILLUMINATES THE UNSEEN CARCERAL WORLD

Initially, I was going to structure this chapter as a simple descriptive analysis of representative examples of SAA scholarship. Yet that would not capture the wider human experience of writing within the SAA movement. It leaves out the transformative potential of writing, in which scholars who are system contacted are changed by their writing, their writing evolves over time, and they can engage with their writing to change society. It is important to demonstrate how system contact interacts with the writing process and how we integrate the humanistic perspective of those impacted by the carceral system into our words. While not all SAA writing focuses directly on the insider perspective of the CLS, this is an area of our literature that we are often associated with.

SAA scholarship and media is a diverse body of work. It contains much qualitative analysis, but also includes critical quantitative analysis (Tietjen, et al. 2018). A few examples of researchers' perspectives can take into account those who have lived through the trauma of prisons, suffered the loss of a parent to incarceration during childhood, or supported transformation of education to be inclusive of people with legal convictions.

SAA activist/critical scholarship can function as a vital transformative mechanism (Aresti et al., 2016; Lynn, 2021; Ortiz, 2024). Stated another way, this is the intersection at which the reciprocal transformative processes of the SAA movement and higher education meet. From this crossroads of scholarship, we can expand our influence to wider spheres of criminal legal practice and public awareness. Our academic work (Abeyta et al., 2021; Anderson et al., 2024; Fox et al., 2023; Kilty & Fayter, 2022; Quach et al., 2022; Smith & Kinzel, 2021), coupled with literary, social, and digital media, is a product of many types of thought, including activist, critical, social justice, and policy development. Our body of writing is one of the primary mediums through which our insights can reach both academia and the criminal legal system. Through the voices of system-affected people, I attempt to show that writing is part of our struggle. Through our words, we can grow and improve ourselves individually. Yet we can also show the world the blunt inhumanity of the carceral system through our pain, trauma, and struggles to navigate social and individual difficulties. All of these factors can be part of the nonlinear journeys of transformation and emancipation that many of us are undertaking.

WRITING OUR MOVEMENT: HUMANIZING SCHOLARS WITH LIVED EXPERIENCE

The breadth of much of the SAA movement is established and communicated through our writing. Writing is produced by people who are system contacted through such channels as personal narratives, autobiographies, research, and scholarship. The recording of our major concepts, social justice actions, and initiatives into written media is filtered through our personal interactions with the carceral system.

SAA members have historically been excluded, ignored, and disregarded in spaces of privilege such as higher education (Ortiz et al., 2022). Thus, a major focus of this book is on how we can amplify our voices, and then how our voices can influence social justice change once they have been acknowledged. While the production of written scholarship and media is a great way to inform others of our ideas, the next issue is how our voices influence our intended audiences. Many of the discussions of writing I had with SAA members emphasized the value of their lived experiences. This insider-informed writing, reinforced in the scholarly rigor of system-affected academics, is a quality of our scholarship that could function to humanize those who are system contacted.

People in our movement have long been the victims of systems of structural violence that function to take away our personhood and replace it with stigmatizing labels both inside and outside of prisons. Society and higher education can also function in the same harmful capacities as the correctional facilities that many SAA members have directly experienced. If SAA people are regarded as intrinsically flawed, they are vulnerable to dehumanization. Further, the scholarly and official public discourse surrounding the carceral system has been (and still is) dominated by statistically focused research (Copes et al., 2020; Jacques, 2014; Tewksbury et al., 2005) that excludes humanity from criminological discussions and replaces it with abstract numbers. Writing informed by human lived experience can bring the insights of real people into the scientific and public discourse of the CLS.

Many recent SAA members believe they are breaking through boundaries and are more equipped to write about standing up to systems of power in the current system. There is respect for the work of earlier members of the movement. Many of the current scholars feel that this is their time, and the time is now. This current proactive stance, which some scholars refer to as a more radical zeitgeist (Lipsitz, 2022), among many recent system-contacted academics can have a contagious effect. This spirit may have the potential to reenergize and refresh the attitudes and mind-sets of previous generations of our population. Yes, I am speaking from a perspective of limited generalizability, using my own writing, research, and lived experiences, but this has been a noticeable phenomenon in segments of the SAA movement.

Cynthia, a student SAA group member, explains how the insider-informed process of writing can better capture her standpoint as part of a minority group:

> It's very easy to talk about or write about women incarcerated, incarcerated ethnic minority women. But when it's written by a middle class, white privileged, white woman, she can't really get into how difficult it is and what these people experience, you know, because it's so so complex, you know, we get into it, we get cultures into it.

As a graduate student, she emphasizes the value that her lived experience possesses. She unlocks the power to add unique insights to her scholarship that might be missed or overlooked by people who have not lived in those positions. Yet Cynthia also draws attention to the damage that can be done when those in privileged positions attempt to "speak for" the oppressed through their own writing. This potentially speaks to how the SAA writing process can be used to address and call out systems of racial and class inequality within the academy.

Edward is an SAA group leader who works in an academic-adjacent field, has graduate-level education, and works in an important nonacademic support role. He emphasizes the use of social media:

> I'm not a professor, but I participate, or I write a lot of the content for social media, I just have a different way. But I also have a, kind of a different way of thinking about things that, that adds that to the mix of the professors because they can get a bit of a group think.

This individual means of digitally written communication is currently used by many SAA members. It has the potential to amplify their voices from a personal perspective that can be widely viewed through social media's ability to reach massive audiences. As a system-contacted activist, Edward's voice brings different perspectives to SAA scholars and scholarship.

Encouragement from Supportive Faculty

Many people in the movement were encouraged to expand their writing by instructors while attending college. As an international system-contacted student, Amber outlines that she is encouraged to publish about research she is conducting with populations who are incarcerated: "I mean, my supervisor keeps on saying we need to publish, you know, based on your info we need, you need to publish based on what you find now with your PhD. So I will be publishing based on those." Amber's work is not directly about her own personal experience, but is focused on the women she was in the correctional system with. She considers them her friends. She is interested in constructing programs to provide better services for women in the system. This provides an example of diversity of perspective in how SAA writing can work to humanize people within the system. Studies by FI people can focus both inward on their own stories and externally on the lives of other imprisoned people. In either capacity, lived experience can provide a more personal and empathetic picture of people in the system.

In another example of support from instructors, SAA members develop more in-depth discussions of insider perspectives through the use of writing genres outside of pure scholarship. Neil, a system-contacted student, explains an interaction he had with a professor about writing literature:, "She started saying to the class if I was in the class, she'd be like, you can write, you're able to write a short story." As a student in a writing program, Neil was interested in presenting the story of system-impacted people through the telling of creative stories, including the use of fiction that was inspired by his life experiences. The humanizing impact of SAA writing also takes place on the other side of the equation, through the support of ally-scholars. Glen, an established university professor and strong ally of system-impacted students, provides an example of this:

> And so the world of books in the world, to the world of thinking is really what and writing really is what turns me . . . sort of flips my switch, and so when the group sort of starts early on, that's, the focus is how do we make sure that you're successful scholars and thinkers, and then, you know, into your sort of career, you know, how do you remain active and critical in your thinking?

Glen helped establish a major SAA group, while at the same time helping build the individual writing skills of its members. As demonstrated here, developing the empathetic and person-centered perspectives of system-contacted people is often filtered through many sources of support before it reaches academia and society. Most SAA people enter academia without formal writing training to use in capturing the unique dynamics of our lives within our work. Yet supportive faculty can often see the potential in our lived experiences, sometimes even when we cannot. Encouragement and mentorship from faculty can lead to cultivation of our experiences from abstraction into powerful stories of human struggle.

INCLUSION IN TRANSFORMATION

SAA writing can be a purposeful exercise in inclusion of others who are system affected, which may also function to strengthen our stances within academic and social circles. This process can function through actions as simple as collaboration with peers and colleagues on research, or by writing policy and legislation that impacts wider groups of people who are FI. The SAA movement's population has had to continually fight for greater inclusion in academia. This endeavor can be framed as part of our struggle against structural inequality in higher education, with our writing acting as a means of drawing us together under our movement's banner.

Ramona, an independent SAA activist, explains how she uses writing to empower people who are system contacted:

> We did several zoom discussions that we then transcribed, and then one person wrote the paper, and we came back for the people . . . who . . . weren't great at writing, and we had verbal comments on the, on the paper and integrated them. So we tried different methodologies by which to make sure that people whose voices otherwise would never be published, get published.

Her work facilitates collaborative writing projects to bring often-unheard people who are system contacted into scholarship, thus expanding the human reach of SAA writing. Yet her work also strives to shift the position of SAA people toward social engagement: "I told you what it is like trying desperately, trying to move us away from being the researched, to being the research." Instead of SAA people interacting with researchers (representing powerful institutions) from a subordinate position of being written about, her work repositions us as researchers and writers who have agency in constructing our own narrative. In addition to working toward centering SAA people within our research, we have important discussions about illuminating marginalized voices in the movement. Joanne, an independent SAA individual and graduate student, discusses women's representation in scholarship: "So when I see men writing these books—that they have sections on female prisons, which they have no impact from female writers. . . . It drives me mad." She strongly advocates including the lived insights of women who are system affected in books about correctional issues, instead of presenting reality from the often male-centric stance of criminal justice. As another example of how SAA members' lived experiences influence their writing styles in the educational setting, Holly, a system-contacted student and professional advocate, explains that academic writing did not come naturally to her: "I write how I speak. I was brought up that way."

She worked with her mentors to learn the scholarly writing process, which she framed as helping her become a better written communicator. Anna, an SAA group member who is system contacted, wants her writing to have meaning, to have real tangible social impact, beyond just racking up publications for an academic résumé:

> I want to write books and publish articles and do that, but I also want to make sure that my stuff means something.
>
> I want to write laws, I want to change policy.

Her focus is on harnessing the power of her lived experience–informed writing for the purposes of social change. Yet her motivation to focus her scholarship on transforming an oppressive system was not serendipitous. As Anna learned more about the climate of academic criminology, she realized that the system contacted were subjected to mass inequalities within the institution, stating, "They're writing about us. And they're getting awards and other divisions are writing about us. And then when we write about us, we don't get the same recognition, and to me, that's just, I mean, that's just oppression." Such oppression is seated within the scholarship of academia. Consequently, she began to direct her work toward legitimating the academic writing of system-contacted people within criminological research and scholarship. Thus, her written scholarship became a powerful conduit for calling out such institutional inequalities.

Diego, a system-contacted faculty member, points out other ways that writing can be used to help people who are incarcerated: "We have workshops, on writing, just writing, we have workshops on writing to people that are incarcerated, giving them hope, say like, you know what, we're here for you." He organizes with others to encourage and teach writing as a means of reaching people who are incarcerated and bringing them into systems of support. This demonstrates one of the many different ways that writing can be used create bridges of outreach between system-contacted people. Tera, an independent SAA individual and system-contacted student activist, further demonstrates building connections: "I write lots of academic stuff. I do lots of academic work with students, with other academics, lots of them are involved in prison research and health-care research in prisons, which I have a kind of input in to speak the language."

Her insider perspective allows her to more smoothly build rapport with the people who are incarcerated. Tera works to pull people together (both system-contacted and justice-free populations) through research and writing projects she is involved with. Through this process, the input of populations who are system contacted can achieve greater exposure, interacting with wider social spheres and contexts.

Pete, an active SAA group member and instructor from the U.K., describes working with people who are system contacted in different contexts:

> We call them inside and outside students; we don't call them prisoners, and our students they're all now students, right, so yeah, so the other two long-term, more data to prison projects they're writing academic papers. Man

> that's amazing, so publishing in the JPP [*Journal of Prisoners on Prisons*], there's a paper in there from our inside and outside students.

His actions within an academically focused SAA program bring together students who are on different sides of the prison walls. This collaborative scholarship often grapples with carceral issues that impact both currently and FI members of the SAA population. This has the potential to illuminate unseen nuances of the contrast between inside and outside that are amplified through system contact. This scholarship tells the story of the many often unseen facets of system-impacted people. Our population is diverse in our experiences and in our reintegrative journeys from the carceral system to society. We acknowledge through our body of writing that even within SAA organizations, there are vast differences of experience and perspective that can open the doors to more inclusive discourse within our movement.

THE STRUGGLE OF FINDING OURSELVES IN OUR WRITING

The SAA writing process can be a struggle to find ourselves within our work. As SAA people progress along our academic journeys, our writing often evolves alongside our learning, education, and shifting perceptions of ourselves. For those with direct system contact, how we interpret our direct contact may shift over time, as we gain more knowledge about how our experiences were influenced by various social forces, such as structures of inequality and oppression. Finding one's self within the SAA experience may be as simple as getting a good read on one's social status within society and understanding one's interactions with external social forces such as race, class, and gender inequality and the more complex dynamics of intersectionality. Or this may be a more personal journey of deep introspective struggle, as we try to understand how the traumas and harms of system contact have affected us.

Tomás, an active SAA group student member with system contact, explains how he interacts with his higher education writing through his lived experiences:

> In school, you become a scholar. At school, you are writing papers, you're writing in your fashion, your statement, either by the theories . . . provided within, you're also thinking in a different, I think different lens—important. We come from what we have; we see things in a completely different lens.

He highlights going through a process of perceptual and intellectual change within higher education. On this journey his writing evolved, and the way he viewed the world also shifted.

Alex, an established system-contacted professor and strong writer, frames how he perceives SAA scholars progressing in their scholarship:

> So then you meet all that, and you don't write about it, and you write about maybe tangential things. You do real research, where it's like, you know, and then once you establish this is my situation, and you get tenure, then you're like, Fuck everyone else. Right? I wrote my book. It's all beautiful research. Like, I don't want to hear about it anymore. Right? Now, I'm going to go back potentially to writing more activist pieces using my background in the piece. It's about status, right? I mean, once you get to a certain place, right, it's like, oh, people say whatever the fuck they want. Feels like that a little bit. Yeah, we can kind of go back to how we started.

He describes a return to our real selves, after showing the establishment of academia that we can produce more formal academic work. At this stage, he describes encountering a sense of freedom, in which SAAs can potentially open up and be more honest about their insider-informed perceptions in their work.

When asked if he was open about his past system contact, Edward says of college writing courses: "I mean, I would write about it. I think some of my creative nonfiction classes potentially, I brought some, some of my past history up." He used these classes as an opportunity to explore his lived experiences in a creative capacity. The journey of attempting to find ourselves within our writing is just that, a journey. It is rarely straight and simple, and could be even described as meandering and convoluted.

Anna provides an example of her writing journey:

> I wrote this long report and unlike, here's everybody who has been released from a correctional facility since 1985. And here's why we need to lower sentencing like, like the maximums. And when we got in the room and did this big presentation, they're like, well, that's nice, but like, we like the prosecutors, they're like, we want to be able to threaten people with longer sentences so that they plead to like shorter sentences, and I was like, fuck this.

Her suggestions were focused on system transformation. When a state correctional employer rejected her work in favor of traumatizing policies, it reinforced who she was and what she stood for.

Our reactions to how others process the meaning and intention of our writing can play an impactful role in how we develop our values as authors. Marie, a system-affected faculty member, discusses how reactions to the writing of her fellow SAA peers influenced her: "I think my personal struggles were doable, but I definitely saw a lot of other, you know, intense struggles [that] my grad student friends wrote on." This demonstrates how we can influence each other in powerful ways within the SAA movement.

Our experiences, uncovered through writing, may congeal into a more potent collective voice and perhaps clearer pictures of ourselves as system-contacted scholars. The self of academics with lived experience is not a static object but a fluid and subjective definition. We are constantly redefining our definitions of self as our various pathways through the CLS and higher education interact with social statuses and constructs that shape us. In this book, inequality and privilege have powerful impacts on this process. Some SAA members would argue that system-contacted people are saddled with additional obstacles and hurdles due to the issues of inequality that commonly impact carcerally contacted populations. This may add to difficulties that SAA people have in working their way through their journeys toward self-discovery, while also increasing the breadth of issues explored in our writing repertoires. Some may say that the expanded breadth of issues that we explore due to our additional struggles is somehow beneficial because it increases our potential scope of scholarly and prosocial impacts. Yet the long-known damage of carceral contact, including greater likelihood of exposure to trauma and social inequality, is carried by many people in the SAA movement. Thus, while writing may function as a therapeutic activity for some, for many of us, our life struggles continue. But our writing can help bring awareness to society and provide fuel for transformative action.

WHAT WE TAKE HOME FROM INCARCERATION: GRAPPLING WITH LONG-TERM CARCERAL TRAUMA

In another important vein of SAA writing, discovering the value and potential of lived experiences can be motivated by working through our carceral traumas within scholarship. In her book about being a trauma-responsive instructor in correctional environments, Em Daniels (2021) stated: "If we are full of unaddressed rage and pain and shame, we will transmit that dirty pain to our students, continuing cycles of trauma and oppression" (p. 98). Similarly, scholars who are system affected can transmit the carceral trauma that many of us carry from prison through their writing. The writing process may help SAA members be more mindful of how trauma impacts our lives. This could allow us to access our insider perspectives, which are often connected to trauma, in a nontoxic manner (Daniels, 2021). This can productively bring lived-experience knowledge into our work, to build co-learning environments of trust with students and like others who are system contacted.

In another incident of grappling with trauma through writing, Madeline, a graduate student and SAA group member, talks about a conversation she had with her professor:

> I told her, and she said, you know, and the reason I told her was I asked her if I could write a paper about it, about my identity as being FI, and how the fact that I had to carry my prison ID with me all the time, because I was still on paper. How that was a constant reminder of that trauma. And she said, hell yeah, you need to write about this.

Madeline had found higher education, yet that did not magically solve all of her problems. As many in the SAA movement reveal, it is common to carry a heavy load of carceral and precarceral trauma with us. Our work can be a means of framing and promoting critical awareness of this often unseen issue. Tera blogs on the topic of trauma: "And I write a lot on a blog of mine about [how] language labels are systemic violence, state tactics to make sure that we're excluded, and also the harms of people who adopt those labels to themselves." Her writing addresses how the power of the state subjects those in the system to oppressive forces, such as the systemic violence of the criminal label. When the state and society accept the meaning of the "criminal" or "convict" stereotype, these stigmatizing labels are more likely to stick. Struggling with past pain and hardships is a common issue among SAA members. Writing about trauma can have many different purposes, such as to work through our pain or to help others understand and sort through their own traumas.

THE TIME IS NOW: THE NEW GENERATION OF ACTIVIST-SCHOLARS

There is a new generation of activist-scholars building energy in the SAA movement. Many members have expressed a genuine enthusiasm and love for writing. They have discovered enjoyment in creating their own scholarship, but also express that there is a timeliness in their work—that their work is needed and necessary. There is a sense among many SAA members of working under the motivation of a cultural mandate.

Sue, an active SAA group member and junior faculty member at a university, embodies much of this spirit of empowerment and enthusiasm contained within the movement. She exclaims, "I want to write a book!" Excitedly, she points out her level of engagement:

> My actual genuine love for, like, reading, writing, like, when the opposition is fucking hard, man, like, Monday through Friday, and all right, but you got to write for, you know, thirty minutes or whatever, like, just to get the shit done. Like, this is like a life-long, like, you know, publish, perish, whatever, like, it's real. It's very real, but I fuckin love it.

She stresses that her learning and writing is a serious lifelong commitment, and she has a strong dedication to her work and fervently believes in what she is doing. Neil, a founding SAA group leader, graduate student, and accomplished author, shares this strength of spirit and dedication to work. He describes his dedication to writing, which developed while he was still incarcerated: "But the people inside were like they saw my vision for writing and they saw my work ethic for writing. Yeah, I'd write for four hours every day."

Tenacity was a trait shared by many SAAs. Shaun, a system-contacted SAA group member and graduate student, makes a point that his writing skills came through continuous practice: "My writing is pretty decent now. But it just took me practicing." He had to learn some of the tools of higher education through strong mentorship:

> And she was like, you need to get a master's degree and you could write a thesis, and I was like, what the fuck's a thesis? And she was like, it's a small book. And I was like, that shit's fucking stupid, I can barely write 250-word paragraphs right now. And she's like, I'm going to help you to, don't worry about it.

Through the help of supportive faculty, Shaun was able to strengthen his scholarly writing skills. He diligently put in the work and is progressing toward completion of his graduate program.

Isaac, an international SAA group member and activist, frames his commitment to writing:

> I continued, my book is more or less a journal of week to week, day to day and my four years in prison or my six years in prison. . . . [A]nd then when I get, I just continued on as a blog. So what am I saying? So a lot of the questions that they're asking me, a lot of stuff are [*sic*] actually on my blog as well, because I just continued writing that sort of daily or weekly thing of what was going on as they [*sic*] happened. I stopped, right. Not whenever my samples finished. So done the six years in the book, which was published. And then I've done the six years as a blog that I just finished.

He is heavily involved in advocating for system transformation for people who are FI and uses multiple forms of discourse to express his work within his writing, including books and blogs.

Alisa, a dedicated member of the CC SAA group, brings the "time is now" energy of SAA to her focus on writing, enthusiastically exclaiming: "I'm gonna write a book on the women of convict criminology, because I think right now is a really good time to go for it." Her focus is on telling the story of women who are system contacted within the SAA movement, from their unique perspectives. She strives to support other women in her group.

Carl, a student and SAA group thought leader, when speaking about the value of lived experience, points to the timeliness of new ideas: "Something's got to give, and you know, if the purely academic standpoint, if the throwing the textbook at the problem isn't going to fix it, then maybe it's time to write a new textbook." He points to a broken system and argues that new ways of thinking and problem solving are needed beyond the traditional scholarship that has been used so far. Further, like many other SAA people, he sees that people with system contact can play an active role in transforming the justice system.

"YOU NEED TO WRITE ABOUT THIS!"

Our writing is a conduit through which we can address many transformative and liberatory actions. Many in the SAA movement believe that they can effect greater social change than just cranking out cold data analysis in "high-impact factor" journals for the sake of obtaining academic prestige and research grants.

SAA writing can translate the abstract bureaucracy of the criminal legal institution into the intricate and complicated experiences of the actual people within it. It does not function on its own, as described in Weber's (1958) conceptualizations of bureaucracy. As I tell students, the CLS is actually made up of real living, breathing, feeling people, not abstract prisons, handcuffs, and courts. Scholars with direct system contact have been in the system, often experiencing trauma and oppression in the process. Many choose to write firsthand about what they have seen, or at least to inform their scholarship with their lived insights.

Many members of the SAA movement view their insider-informed writing as possessing both individually and socially transformative potential. Having been exposed to the inequalities and oppression of the CLS, they feel an urgency to get something done, not just write prestige articles. Real people are suffering in the system all the time. Thus, SAAs often focus on action-based research. There is a preference for scholarship that has greater potential to bring about change.

The Writing Process: An Endless Journey of Transformation

As I mentioned before, I describe writing as a *process* to present it as a never-ending journey of development. While this may sound too abstract, I frame the SAA writing journey this way to encompass all of the variability it contains. While our members encounter writing from many different levels of experience, education, and standpoints, many people with system contact come from disadvantaged backgrounds, with lower-than-average levels of formal education. They have to overcome steep learning curves in order to master scholarly writing forms. Also, scholarly writing captures only one facet of writing, from the standardized academic perspective. There are many other types of writing under the umbrella of the SAA movement, in which writing follows many different trajectories. Before we become involved in this movement, system-contacted people come from all kinds of skill levels regarding written composition. Some of us (the minority) already have advanced levels of formal education, while many of us, in alignment with FI demographics, come from lower-than-average levels of education.

Thus, strong writing is often a skill many of us learn during contact with formal education and further through the SAA movement. We learn writing skills through college courses, collaborative projects, and mentorship with skilled writers. Once again, not all of us learn purely academic writing skills, as literary and journalistic forms of writing are also part of the SAA repertoire. Writing with other system-contacted activist-scholars is a useful way to develop our abilities and expand our lived-experience perspectives past our own. We gain access to a knowledge storehouse of people who have directly interacted with the CLS through many individual frames of reference. They could be compared to a living library of reference materials, which we as SAAs translate into the written word.

Within the movement, fostering a supportive writing environment can manifest in several ways. While many SAAs attempt to work as lone wolves, others, myself included, have taken advantage of a community that welcomes cooperation. Some SAA groups and individuals have also put forth the effort to build writing support groups and workshops, providing resources to our peers. This effort can be focused on the many areas involved with SAA writing, such as scholarly publication, peer review, revising, and editing.

In SAA groups, opportunities for scholarly publication were frequently organized by more experienced members. Early in my SAA contact, I was a student learning the basics of writing while also putting out some of my first clumsy attempts at scholarly writing. There was still a lot for me to learn, and patient mentors were there when I developed to the point that I was ready to learn. A graduate school faculty member came forward and took a chance on me, including me in a paper that became my first peer-reviewed publication. This provided me with a powerful sense of confidence that I could be an academic writer. Now I work with mentees, and we influence each other reciprocally, as we share knowledge and writing styles with one another.

Yet this not a perfectly repeating cycle of transferal and influence of writing abilities and ideas between mentor and mentees. Our written composition might seem to evolve in chaotic directions, yet it is also likely influenced by larger dynamics such as ever-shifting cultural, social, and professional norms, coupled with shifts in prison populations and criminal legal policies. This is in conjunction with the skills and practice we acquire through higher education.

Writing Engaging with Action

Another unique component of SAA writing is its connectedness to the movement's prosocial initiatives (or those adjacent to the movement), both as a catalyst and an outcome of our own social justice projects. While it is common for academic disciplines to produce written scholarship, often such work is unconnected to the direct actions of those in that specific discipline. This proactive stance attached to our writing can function to motivate greater SAA-affiliated social change.

Writing and initiatives may impact one another reciprocally within our movement, as we are continually engaged in both activities. For example, thinking about writing-into-action, a paper about the impacts of labels in system-impacted populations may spur students and faculty to formally encourage their universities to change their policies, encouraging more human-first language usage. In contrast, in action-into-writing, a prison censoring the books of those it incarcerates may motivate writing papers on why censoring is dangerous and harmful to incarcerated populations, or why access to literature and sources of knowledge by SAA populations is necessary and beneficial.

Our writing is connected to our past actions in regard to framing and analyzing situations and traumas that we have lived through. The impacts of past actions, such as how we processed the various forms of system contact, are connected to our future actions, such as engagement with higher education. SAA writing is a means to connect us to our complex pasts and to generate our futures.

Owning Our Stories

The potential for change can also be unlocked by taking ownership of our lived-experience narratives. Through writing SAA scholarship, we can center ourselves as producers of knowledge, operating from a position of strength, instead of being subordinated by an elitist "academic" gaze. To frame this sentiment, I reiterate what Ramona states (earlier in this chapter) when discussing collaborative writing projects she organizes for SAA people: "From being the researched, to being the research." We write about ourselves, instead of others writing about us. Consequently, we tell our own stories.

This is a means of emancipating our narratives. Our stories vary greatly, including stances that are heavily informed by academic and scholarly thinking, perspectives of those fresh out of penitentiary cellblocks, and thought pieces on individual carceral experiences. Yet we want to be free to write our stories from our own stances. Such freedoms may seem trivial to the uncritical observer, but we perceive that it is especially important to the SAA population, who have been subjected to forced confinement in harsh prisons, where dehumanizing conditions subjected them to daily trauma. The unnecessary state regime of punishment pressures people in the system to accept oppressive social control. For SAA members, writing through our experiences can be a means of both realistically and symbolically resisting and emancipating ourselves from such systemic violence.

Use of Writing to Unify System-Affected People

The words of SAA people could also potentially serve as an instrument of unification. As more and more scholars who are system contacted publish various forms of written discourse, our imprint on social awareness has the opportunity to expand. As our writing includes the more traditional scholarship of peer-reviewed journals; substantial works such as books and journalism; and more modern forms of high-impact writing such as digital social media and blogs, we now have multiple channels to broadcast our message. Wider audiences of SAA people can see our words and gain awareness of the movement. Additionally, there are more powerful ways to network and connect through social media outlets, with additional outlets constantly under development. Within the online realm, multiple forms of media can be accessed simultaneously, such as SAA articles, video recordings of lived-experience scholars and activist groups, and podcasts featuring people involved in the movement.

Groups of SAA people have established growing networks and read each other's studies, blogs, media posts, and research. As multiple SAA groups exist online now, groups cross-promote each other's ideas. Through social media pages, we can see the strength of our diversity and also experience our similarities. When we see the breadth of our voices in writing, presented in public venues (virtual and in print), we can experience each other as more approachable and human. We see that we are out there, advocating for change.

Untraditional Traditional Scholarship

SAA members have produced a sizable library of peer-reviewed articles, considered the gold standard of traditional scholarly work. Yet within this genre, our works are often not considered to be "conventional." Some may argue that this has to do more with our methodologies, which can include the often-criticized autoethnography, than with our writing. Yet it's our written words that form the backbone of what our readership sees. We write in an academic discipline that has relied on the words of towering experts from elite institutions, far removed from the grinding hardships and oppression that the majority of those in the CLS encounter every day. Our work is close to the grinding boots-on-the-ground reality of the streets. We are the hardships and oppression that we study. They define us and bleed through into our scholarship.

Our Secret Weapon: The Power of the Autoethnography

It is no secret that the authors of the SAA movement have harnessed the utility of autoethnography (Chang, 2016; Earle, 2021) as a means to center the importance of their lived experiences. For the SAA researcher and author, this method of research offers a unique means to construct systems of meaning and identity (Choi, 2016) from their unique carceral experiences. Further, autoethnography allows the SAA researcher to critically explore their subjective interpretations of their reality (Duncan, 2004), then contrast these perceptions with the conventional presentations of their reality that they have learned and read about in criminology textbooks. This allows for a liberating frame of analysis, in that it unlocks resources that we possess within, as a hard-earned block of qualitative data that belongs solely to the SAA author. This book presents the valuable autoethnographic work of SAA members, which should not be staged as secondary to statistical analysis or as mere background support for the more "legitimate" works of quantitative research (Jewkes, 2012), but should be seen as a necessary form of analysis that stands on its own. Jewkes (2012) described how autoethnographic work allows the carceral researcher to capture the legitimate importance of their own feelings and emotions, which would otherwise be lost in an attempt to be "objective." In our SAA writing, we can capture a more honest research experience, rich with feelings and interesting human subjectivity, while at the same time maintaining methodological and theoretical rigor.

Books

System-contacted and SAA-affiliated authors have made many inroads into the world of books. Books, a more substantial writing commitment, can be both scholarly and for general readership. A purely SAA-group-focused academic book is *Convict Criminology* by Jeffrey Ian Ross and Stephen Richards (2023). Another scholarly book, written by system-contacted author Dan Murphy (2012), is *Corrections and Posttraumatic Stress Symptoms*. An autobiography and commentary on the federal prison system from a general-readership perspective is Piper Kerman's (2010) *Orange Is the New Black*. In an autobiography for non-academic audiences, Dr. Stanley Andrisse (2021) discussed his journey from incarceration to higher education: *From Prison Cells to PhD: It Is Never Too Late to Do Good*. In comparison to articles and social media posts, the lengthy volumes of books provide a powerful means for people with carceral experiences to fully define and expand upon their lived-experience knowledge. This can provide a valuable way of substantiating the social footprint of the SAA movement.

Journalism

Another area of system-affected writing is journalism. There have been too many journalistic pieces written about carcerally impacted people to list here, yet we are beginning to write our own journalism. Of course not all FI journalists are associated with the SAA movement. While this book generally focuses more on the academic and activist sides of writing, the area of journalistic writing is too important to exclude from this discussion. It provides another example of a written media platform in which people who are system contacted are becoming more open in voicing their lived-experience views.

Keri Blakinger, a journalist for the Marshall Project, is open about her system-impacted background. Her book, *Corrections in Ink* (2022) was released to national critical acclaim. This memoir highlighted her experiences working as a journalist who actively advocated for the rights of incarcerated people. Several journalists who are either currently or FI also publish through the Prison Journalism Project.[5] This program trains incarcerated people to become impactful journalists and even publishes its own journal, *PJPxInside*. Many of its writers have gone on to win prestigious journalistic awards.

Digital Media, Including Social Media and Blogs

On digital media, SAA members have accessed new ways to discuss social justice and promote their initiatives, missions, activism, and scholarship. Social media sites such as X (formerly Twitter), Instagram, and Facebook have been used to organize events and SAA group actions and generate promotion for SAA groups and individual members.

We have built a diverse means of communicating about our lived experiences in addition to the bedrock publishing of academic books and articles by scholars within the SAA ranks. This matters from the perspective of the types of audiences we reach. While traditional scholarship generally reaches scholars and researchers, our many forms of content production on social media can exponentially expand our thoughts to more general demographics outside of higher education. This increased reach ranges from the public to activists and organizations that can potentially provide us with funding and resources.

For example, newer groups such as the non-university-affiliated FICGN was organized through social media, using Facebook to successfully attract a large following. FICGN has subsequently branched out to other platforms such as X and Instagram. Many other organizations, such as CC, the DCC, Underground Scholars, and Rising Scholars are also on social media, using the power of this medium as a means to communicate with many audiences. For example, Jeffrey Ian Ross, a CC scholar, SAA group member, and widely published author, uses blogs on social media to discuss wide-ranging topics. A recent example of his blog writing is "Should criminologists speak to the media" (Ross, 2024). Another example of the use of blogs in the SAA movement is the blog page for the Berkeley Underground Scholars SAA group, used to promote news and activities of this organization (Underground Scholars News, 2022). Through digital media, collaboration between and within SAA groups has become much more possible. Groups such as DCC and FICGN have cross-promoted each other's events.

Wrap-Up

There is a lot of variation within our writing, so much so that attempting to capture SAA work within an organized framework might seem like a futile task. However, I argue that it is quite possible to express the spirit of our genre by being mindful of our spectrum of inclusive content. We acknowledge such things as our dissimilarities in writing style, stark contrasts of worldview, and incremental nuances of style.

To illustrate, some books have grappled with deep theoretical discussions of SAA concepts (Earle, 2016), while others are inspirational autobiographies (Andrisse, 2021). Other works, such as Davis's (2003) *Are Prisons Obsolete*, have taken strong critical stances against the prison system, in comparison to the peer-reviewed article "The Emotional Geography of Prison Life" (Crewe et al., 2014), which took a nuanced look at emotional experiences of people incarcerated in the prison system. These works highlight the contrast of scope of our writing, from broad questioning of the existence of the entire prison system all the way to exploring how incarcerated people navigate spaces of emotion. When comparing research methodologies, an article by Beasley and Xiao (2023) used advanced quantitative methods of analysis to examine ethnic bias in hiring practices of people who are FI. Yet in another SAA-affiliated article, Boppre et al. (2022) used rigorous qualitative methods including interviews and focus groups to explore the obstacles families face when attempting to visit their imprisoned relatives. In another vein of discussion, practitioner-focused SAA members such as Murillo (2021), in "The Possibility Report: From Prison to College Degrees in California," have written reports on the possibilities that education holds for system-contacted people.

Spirit of SAA Writing

So a defining quality of our writing is breadth in scope. Much is folded into the discourse that defines our ever-growing and -evolving movement. This gives us the capacity to absorb the many diverse experiences of people with system contact, which can provide for greater SAA acceptance and inclusivity and the ability to broadcast a wider message to society. Another dynamic prevalent in SAA work is the possibility to reach deeper into the often unseen and unknown human nuances (by people without system contact) of the CLS. This may allow our writing to access more detailed levels of systemic and human comprehension. This may include accessing further realms of awareness and analysis when exploring concepts surrounding the human component of carceral experiences. This potential for expanded vision could provide further insights into human emotions in total institutions, spiritual impacts of prison, acclimation to new environments, how we process pain, nuances of carceral subcultures, and how people ingest and cope with traumatic experiences.

We can talk directly about the influence of carceral experiences that we were personally engaged with and also provide more nuanced stances that inform justice concepts with lived experience. This ability adds a genuine character to our writing, shaping our concepts through the forge of harsh social realities, including oppression, trauma, inequality, and loss. This flavor of written scholarship is often difficult for conventional prosystem academics to stomach. It is perceived as less than, as biased, as contaminated by our experiences. Our lives are the very experiences and phenomena that they are attempting to define as they lay their own claims to expertise and ownership of our knowledge.

Of course, increased reach does not guarantee the quality of the messages that we project. Yet the varied nature of our work has the potential to speak to people in more ways. Considering the long-standing, ingrained nature of bias against system-affected people, reaching more audiences (through more media channels) may increase the possibility of moving the dial on societal awareness and empathy toward our plight.

CHAPTER 6

Retroflexive Transformation

Finding a Place and Creating Space

Sharing lived experience in the classroom is a two-way street; we can generate transformative action. An academic colleague of mine, speaking to a prospective student, emphasized the range of lived experiences that the various professors in our criminal justice department possess: "The faculty in our department have experience and expertise in many areas of criminal justice." My experiences were included in that list, valued as a legitimate form of knowledge. I work in an academic department that is aware of and supportive of my lived-experience background. While there is currently not a study that can provide the percentage of criminal justice departments that would be supportive of including a system-contacted faculty member, I am certainly aware that we are not welcome in all institutions. Yet I want to describe what acceptance looks like in some institutions that are open to system-contacted faculty, and what that means to me.

I have been a faculty member in two universities, one in the Midwest and my current institution in the Pacific Northwest. Being accepted by my department colleagues as an open system-impacted academic does provide a feeling of inclusion and empowerment. I do not have to hide my identity and endure a sense of being shamed. While this is a positive situation, I still grapple with my personal perceptions of how I believe others see me, similar to Cooley's concept of the looking-glass self. In my "looking glass," I experience the phenomenon of status fragility (Tietjen & Kavish, 2021). Throughout my life course, I have been socialized to view people with criminal convictions as untrustworthy, to be looked down upon, and as a group of people whom it is acceptable to publicly shame. This is accompanied by a nagging fear that my career and reputation are continually at risk, that if I make the smallest mistake, I will not be given the benefit of the doubt.

Consequently, regardless of the amount of acceptance and critical perspective I may gain in reality, it is difficult for me to feel fully secure from an emotional perspective, even though I may have reached some degree of acceptance from an intellectual stance. Thus, I am still intermittently wracked with doubts even in empathetic and progressive environments. For SAA members, even our acceptance can be a complicated rollercoaster of psychological peaks and valleys. We are often internally grappling with our own personal difficulties, including traumatic pasts and social-structural inequalities that follow us into the often elite culture of greater academia.

The most powerful sense of acceptance that I have encountered was in the classroom. The feelings of doubt and anxiety about how I am perceived by society and my academic coworkers were assuaged when I was instructing. Students in the academic courses I teach in the fields of criminology, sociology, and criminal justice have been very accepting of my lived experiences. Many are interested to know more about topics such as what it was really like in prison, asking me to describe the process of being transported by passenger jets by the Federal Bureau of Prisons (no, it was not like the movie *Con Air*) and what it was like to be processed through the courts. Their minds were open to learning through sharing of insider perspectives, and several students expressed gratitude that someone would take the time to explain the unglamorous and gritty realities of the system to them.

Further, I emphasized that the sharing of lived experiences was encouraged and highly valued in my classroom by both students and instructors and thus a reciprocal process. Then an interesting thing happened. Students began sharing their struggles with me, both in and after class. They told me about the issues and problems that had made them who they were and that they had survived. I do not mean that this was in the "teacher-as-counselor" type of dynamic. I discerned that they were sharing with me because in the space that we made in the educational environment, they knew that their experiences were valued and given purpose and meaning. Based on the critical knowledge acquired in class, both the students and the instructor saw that their experiences had the potential to help solve social problems and bring about solutions to issues within their very own communities. This reconstructed the classroom into a locus for generating transformative change in both society and the CLS.

In an insider-supportive classroom, a sense of empowerment and hope can exist that empowers both the students and the instructors (myself). In this setting, students begin applying the critical thought and humanistic concepts we have learned in course activities directly to their own lives. For example, one of my students in an upper-level course used social-structural definitions of class oppression to explain their own experiences with growing up in poverty. They shared the difficulties and personal struggles their family had endured and continued to endure as a result of lacking financial resources. During such interactions, we as a class have the opportunity to engage in active conversations about how to understand these sensitive social dynamics that are often not discussed.

In another classroom discussion, a student talked about their previous legal convictions and system contact and related it to our lesson topic of rampant economic class inequality in criminal justice institutions. Through this process, our classroom was able to engage in Freirian (2018) style critical pedagogy and question systems of power. As Harm and Bell (2021) explained, bringing lived experience perspectives into the classroom setting expands a more comprehensive understanding of the inequalities and oppression that exist within the legal system. For students, this also demonstrates how to apply the abstract academic concepts from their readings to the realities of actual system-contacted people.

Over the years, as my students have felt empowered and continued to share their valuable insights, my teaching methods have continued to evolve and learn, fueled by lived-experience dialogue. Reciprocally, students' learning processes can continue to evolve within classrooms that embrace liberatory pedagogy informed by openness to lived-experience perspectives. This breaks down to a very organic human process, in which the student and the instructor seek to understand the lives of people caught in the legal system. We also seek to explore knowledge about the everyday struggles and difficulties of people with system contact.

"The legal system is made up of people." I frequently repeat this statement in the classroom, for the sake of both students and myself, lest we forget our humanity in the fast-paced hyperreality of sensationalized news, social media misinformation, and political propaganda that we are continually bombarded with in the twenty-first century. By making this statement I attempt to accomplish the important step of moving beyond abstractions of the system that are presented in textbooks and much of mainstream media to see how the system destroys the people forgotten behind the walls and fences.

INTRODUCTION

The SAA movement provides a means of assisting in the transformation of the broken, punitive CLS through the work of SAAs. Remember, Cressey's (1955) concept of retroflexive reformation, presented in chapter 1, states that FI people working to assist and help other struggling FI people succeed also realize positive benefits from their actions, exhibiting greater psychological well-being and reduced likelihood of relapsing into criminal behaviors and criminogenic attitudes. Taking the retroflexive reformation idea one step further, I propose that the people comprising the SAA movement are engaging in retroflexive transformations. We are involved in an attempt to deconstruct oppressive systems and to disengage from the traumatic and harmful impacts those systems have had on us. Further, many in this growing SAA campaign are seeking to change the system and our places in society into something intrinsically different, to achieve a situation that resembles equal rights and liberation for system-contacted people everywhere.

THE VALUE OF OUR LIVED EXPERIENCES

Studying populations of which we are a member is engaging in *insider research* (Dwyer & Buckle, 2009; Kanuha, 2000). While this is prima facie important, the SAA movement's struggle reaches further to issues of representation and exposure. For many years, if not decades, the voices of carcerally impacted people were not recognized in the academic study of crime and criminal justice. Yet in recent years our voices and academic footprint have grown, expanding to the point that it is now difficult to ignore us. This phenomenon was likely correlated with the corresponding progressive and rehabilitative shifts in criminal legal policies and practices in the U.S. and even in the U.K., and perhaps SAA work has played some part in that systemic change. SAA members have demonstrated that their lived experiences have value. The inclusion of their perceptions can illuminate dynamics that would otherwise be disregarded or unnoticed by researchers and academics who have not had exposure to prison and postprison situations.

Viewing the world through a system-contacted lens is a self-defining endeavor for many SAA members. It's a perspective that many SAAs view as the essence of their scholarship and perception of justice. A system-affected person in a high-status position as a university professor talking to students and fellow academics about their carceral experiences can carry a great weight. This approach connects a human being to the cold and abstract prison concept, and they are presented with the human face of incarceration. Not only that, but the process of legitimating the perspectives of SAA people can begin to take place when the wider academy and students are shown rigorous scholarship filtered through individual lived experience.[1]

The writing of SAAs can bring the human empathetic experience into criminology and also connect the theoretical to the personal. Using previous carceral life experiences to frame the building of SAA-rooted concepts to inform policies and social actions can bring forth a form of praxis. For example, the system-contacted written work of John Irwin (1972, 1980, 1987, 2005) informed the emergence of subsequent SAA organizations such as Project Rebound (which Irwin founded) and CC.

SAA MEMBERS ARE BOTH THE TEACHERS AND THE SUBJECTS OF THEIR OWN LESSONS

A large portion of the SAA movement's impact very likely occurs within the classrooms of system-contacted instructors. This is where the insights of carceral lived experiences are shared with learners, often students or members of the public at presentations. This can act as a direct process of humanization, adding the human experience to the educational discourse on criminal legal issues. Understanding that there is a person with feelings and similar life struggles in that cellblock—a member of someone's family, a mother, a brother—can reframe how students perceive the abstract concept of the penitentiary. Students and audiences (including public, practitioner, and academic) being informed by these perspectives could lead to the development of policies and programs that engage (are aware of, embrace) these more human dynamics and needs in ways that program development without exposure to carceral lived experiences could not see or perceive.

Disclosure Dilemma

SAA members who instruct classes in colleges and universities take different approaches to how they interact with their lived experiences in the classroom. The choice of how to project our insider knowledge to students involves many contextual factors. For instance, it can be based on the results of previous attempts at this process. Some SAA members might fear that their audience would not receive their message well, even though opening up about our pasts in an impactful manner that emphasizes our experiences as strengths is often received with applause and strong support. Another point to consider about disclosing is whether providing our insider perspectives would somehow strengthen or improve the lesson we are trying to teach. How we frame our insider knowledge is also important. We can present such information in many different ways, such as conveying knowledge specific to a particular situation, describing events that only happened to ourselves, or offering supplemental insights that we do not personally claim (we are just providing supporting information not attached to ourselves).

Disclosure as a Means of Reaching Students

Another important point to consider in an SAA person's classroom is how sharing of insider perspective impacts students. A lot could potentially be at stake here. This is where the SAA movement has the power to change the public's perception of system-contacted people, to break through harmful stereotypes. Openly presenting students with human-centered depictions of the realities of incarceration and the CLS can give them a whole new way to view the realities of "justice." For students who may have family who were, or who were themselves, system affected, such openness from an SAA instructor may provide a sense of acceptance, empowerment, safety, and awareness. Such measures may function in a transformative capacity, possessing the ability to nudge the dial of social perceptions further toward awareness and acceptance of people who are system contacted.

Moving to the level of educational impact, reframing the academic gaze toward viewing prisoners and the incarcerated as real people instead of invisible numbers in abstract and distant institutions could radically change how justice policies and programs are constructed. This process starts with educating college students about the SAA vantage point. They are society's future voters, professionals, and legal system practitioners. To shift the future trajectory of CLS policy toward prosocial policies, it could be helpful to use SAA perspectives to refocus student perceptions of prisons on viewing people in prisons empathetically and on finding ways to decarcerate in place of the standard practice of failed punitive justice measures.

Additionally, in the U.S. many college students sitting in classrooms are themselves system affected. Thus, a lived-experience-informed instructional platform could activate and further validate their lived experiences, helping to empower new cohorts of lived-experience scholars. As seen in the previous chapters of this book, the SAA population, when able to couple the power of education with its lived potential, has demonstrated the capability to enact powerful systemic changes.

Adding to the Conversation but Not Taking Over the Narrative

Taking a closer look at how the SAA instructor uses insider perspectives in the classroom, it is important to state that many system-contacted faculty carefully emphasize that their lives are not the central focus of their courses. Yet their perspectives can add useful contexts to their lessons in a supplemental or instrumental capacity. Certain SAA instructors choose not to disclose their lived experiences to students, explaining that they feel that doing so exposes them to society's biased judgments toward carcerally impacted people. As framed in Tietjen and Kavish's (2021) discussion of status fragility, many SAA members spend their careers in a professional space of additional fears and anxieties about the stability of their positions in academia. Yet whether they choose to openly discuss their personal lived experiences or not, directly contacted instructors have personally experienced carceral and criminal legal environments, and they walk into their classrooms with this unique knowledge.

DISPERSIVE TRANSFORMATIVE IMPACT OF THE SAA MOVEMENT

The diverse group of people speaking the words of this book are building bodies of experience and knowledge. While many scholars correctly argue that social movements start from the people on the streets, in the prisons, and in their communities, this work provides an example of what happens when people from the prisons and streets find their way to engagement with higher education. The SAA movement creates a unique type of individual, the activist-scholar who has *been there*. This is to say that lived-experience people with formal academic contact are somehow superior as activists, but to emphasize that we can add unique strengths to the movement toward equality for FI and criminally convicted groups and should be included at the table.

For example, many members of the SAA movement, having lived with structural oppression throughout their lives, are familiar with how systemic inequality works. They can see it from two perspectives: as trained critical scholars and as a personal experience. This multifaceted knowledge that couples life experiences with critical scholarship skills can provide the insights needed to deconstruct oppressive systems such as the CLS and institutionalized biases against the system contacted in higher education and society.

SAA people represented in this book have described being involved in their communities, with their system-contacted peers, with other activist groups, and with their educational institutions. The SAA message transmits through many channels, such as direct interactions with people, written scholarship, and virtually through the use of social media platforms. Beyond these important representations of SAA social interaction, there is perhaps a more important outcome: the growth of acceptance of the experiences of system-contacted people. We are increasingly welcomed into many spaces, to talk to society, and many people are eagerly listening to and internalizing our message of equality and empowerment for those with system contact. This holds the potential to create opportunities and generate progress.

We Are the Transformation: Getting Involved in Equality at All Levels

The ground-level actions of the SAA movement on the streets and in neighborhoods takes many forms in regard to level of direct engagement with ever more diverse system-contacted populations. Some SAA people choose to work specifically with people who are FI, while others join actions that are broader in social scope but still improve opportunities for SAAs in general. From the perspective of standpoints of engagement, some of us choose to work in our own neighborhoods, advocating for those we grew up with. Aligning with broader social movements, the inclusion of voices that have traditionally been socially marginalized has further empowered and amplified the voices of system-contacted people who have already been involved in building many SAA organizations. An example of the power of this phenomenon is the actions of

SAA women members, who while only comprising around 7 percent of the global prison population (Fair & Walmsley, 2022), represent 43 percent of the purposeful sample in this book! Their work has shown up in scholarly presentations and activist work of system-contacted women in scholarvism spaces around the world (Bozkurt et al., 2020; Bozkurt, 2023; Misra, 2022; Vianello, 2020). While the scope of this book does include discussions of inclusivity and equality, further research about the powerful and foundational presence of women in the SAA movement needs to be done. I pose that SAAs current and future work will increasingly drive the transformative potential of the SAA movement to bring justice to marginalized and previously ignored populations.

The broader SAA work in wider social movements is not always recognized as the specific advocacy work of system-contacted people, yet all of our work can have powerful impacts. We often get involved in general social justice initiatives and blend into the crowd when working with community groups and in our professions. Yet the impacts of our actions can still function to benefit the lives of FI people attempting to reintegrate into society and further increase equality for all. For example, I have spent years working with local equal justice and progressive action groups in my current community on a multitude of issues ranging from advocating for more rehabilitative programs for youth, to racial equality, to LGTBQ rights, to protesting the construction of even more jails and correctional facilities. I have drawn on my lived experience in committee and boardroom discussions to advocate for the hiring of lived-experience people.

From the perspective of demographics and socioeconomic status, the SAA movement is represented internationally. I cautiously propose that there may be greater SAA motivation and membership in regions with greater contrasts of social inequality present, such as regions where there is immense poverty in the immediate presence of elite wealth and unreasonable costs of living (e.g., the East and West Coasts of the U.S.). I frame this statement carefully, because there does need to be some level of progressive social support and economic infrastructure available, including institutions of higher education to provide the educational component of our structure. For example, in the U.S., support for humanistic programs and resources that provide support for populations facing structural inequalities varies greatly in individual states. SAA people in more well-resourced states with more progressive state governments may have greater chances of both overcoming structural barriers and successfully enacting pro-SAA policy.

These examples and the many examples of lived-experience actions by SAA members provided throughout this book are provided to demonstrate that we are this group. We are the movement in its most organic state. Whether we are accomplishing great deeds or stumbling through the many difficulties and struggles that people with system contact often face, this is part of the movement. This process includes the raw realities of mass incarceration and its traumatic aftermaths, which we bring with us as we attempt to reintegrate ourselves into society by using higher education and activist scholarship. It is often a messy and difficult process.

ADDING A MISSING PIECE TO THE PUZZLE

The work of SAA members can frame the knowledge of people who have faced discrimination and been shut out of the discourses of criminological scholarship and policy building. This is a missing component that could support creating effective humanistic transformation within the CLS. As I have stated several times in this book, members of our movement engage in research, activism, and policy construction, and we are continually referring to how SAA literature and insights provide missing components and illuminate unseen components of conventional prosocial research and policy formation. So, the next logical step is to define these unseen dynamics that are generally absent from status quo criminal justice narratives. The information that lived-experience scholars may illuminate can be framed and defined from many different perspectives, for example, the intellectually abstract and, alternatively, more organic or gritty exposure to individual incidents. These frames of perception can function to simply assist in telling a story, help to construct complex theoretical models to explain academic/social concepts, or address how to tackle issues of bias and inequality within society and the carceral system.

In order to have a rigorous discussion about the nature of lived data based in experiential knowledge, it is important to parse out the unique qualities that may differentiate this information from conventional data. The nature and content of lived experience can often make it difficult to quantify or measure, as the nature of these events is dealing with incidents and perceptions that SAA members encountered before they were formally academics or had interacted with higher education. Further, we, as the scholars, may have been physically, socially, or psychologically damaged or altered by the content we discuss in our research. The often-damaging consequences of contact with the system could alter how we interpret and study criminological phenomena. For example, many SAA members, including me, discussed how experiencing oppression and structural violence (Weigert, 2010) in corrections led us to question mainstream academia's acceptance of the prosystem, oppressive practices and policies that traumatized us. For example, textbook descriptions of processes, practices, and conditions in various types of carceral facilities often contradicted the experiences of many system-contacted students and academics. Attempting to analyze the magnitude of how much discrepancy there is between descriptions of prison from the perspectives of the FI and those of conventional scholars is outside the scope of this book. Be that as it may, our perceptions of the culture and environments of the carceral world can and have been used to critique and question status quo criminology's grasp of carceral realities. This brings in research dynamics that scholars who have not been exposed to such realities may disregard, not want to accept, or not be able to comprehend.

Further, our lived experiences have the potential to empathetically and emotionally connect us to how justice-contacted people interact with the system when considering how we develop research and policy. It must also be noted that some of our most impactful research (Murphy, 2012; Oliver, 2007) may also stem from the more damaging individual consequences of legal contact, such as being the victims of traumatization and violence in the system. Directly contacted SAA members with educational credentials in criminological and legal policy, theory, and practices can add these perspectives to discussions and design of solutions to reentry barriers. A viable program that is designed around the difficulties actually encountered by a reentering person may add potential for life-course success. Our combined academic- and lived-knowledge streams can provide more thoughtful and comprehensive assessments and solutions to problems that apply to people who are incarcerated, FI, or impacted by other forms of system contact.

SAA work can also add useful insider-focused perspectives to more comprehensively understand the realities of returning home after incarceration and its human and social impacts. Coming home from jail or prison is a difficult process to fully grasp from the humanistic stance without having lived through it in some capacity. While the general public can certainly read about the reentry concept in a journal article or criminal justice textbook, the frustration of not being able to find a place to live, being turned down by employers, struggling to survive on the streets, and enduring the looks of public disapproval impacts system-contacted people on multiple levels. These are emotionally charged life experiences that also affect SAA members at the structural level, in regard to economic disadvantage, diminished career opportunities, mental health struggles, and exposure to social biases and discrimination.

REJECT THE HEGEMONY OF INSTITUTIONAL WORLDVIEWS

While this is not a major theme of this book, it is worth noting that SAA people are aware of and resist the hegemony of institutional worldviews. One such worldview described to me was the process of shame-motivated reentry perpetuated by the correctional system. To frame this issue, I highlight the noteworthy insights of Ramona, a system-contacted, independent SAA individual (from the U.K.). She discusses the pitfalls faced by system-affected people attempting to overcome stigmatization through the acceptance of prosystem values:

> So, you see a lot of people with lived experience who through the stigmatization seek validation, and once they, and then they want to work in the system, want to become quasi-probation officers or prison officers, and you know, because of that deep shame, it's like, if you feel accepted in that system, then somehow that's expunged as a sort of a, an issue that you need to deal with, right, and synthesize into who you are. So I tried to do, so I teach on courses about guilt and shame, I teach on courses about synthesizing the past into the now to build to the future. How do you become more integrated as a person? And how do you also refute vulnerability as an identity? Because the narrative of the system is about those of us who make it through, it's always about our redemption narratives, isn't it? It's about our hero's journey through and the gist of it is what we're actually doing is endorsing the system by playing into that redemption narrative. So yeah, absolutely one of my big mantras is death to the misery memoir.

As a graduate degree–holding advocate and mentor, Ramona teaches methods of empowerment to carcerally impacted people. Working outside of the legal system as an advocate (she perceives that working within the legal system was not the best way she could help justice-involved people), she teaches system-affected people how to think and act in ways that expand their prosocial potential. In her work she has found that many people with direct lived experience would seek out employment in fields aligned with the legal system and subsequently limit their transformative potential. She emphasizes that aligning with the values of a broken legal system in an attempt to attain societal acceptance only serves to project the falsehood that the prison system is somehow benefiting the incarcerated. Further, Ramona explains that seeking the system's approval relegates the actor to a submissive role in the system. Thus, system-affected people are diminishing the power that they possess to bring about meaningful change in the carceral structure. Institutionally based values and practices, such as placing all of the onus for criminal actions on the individual's "free will" while completely ignoring the massive social-structural issues of intersectional inequalities and oppression (e.g., racism, classism, gender discrimination, ageism, ableism), do not serve system-contacted populations and can lead to the further perpetuation of such harmful practices.

A Call to Action

To accept the correctional system's narratives of shame and incorrectly internalize (and verbalize) that it was the system itself that somehow led FI people to positively change their lives sends society the message that we are endorsing the legal system's traumatizing methods. In resistance to this system of harm, I would like to call for resisting the expectations of shame-motivated reentry, through rejection of norms and values based in the harmful and oppressive institutional practices of the CLS. This is a call to society, SAA allies, and the SAA movement itself. To answer this call is to refute the manufactured vulnerability that institutions such as the CLS impose on system-contacted people. This process often serves to further perpetuate the narrow-sighted narratives that society should disregard the heavily researched social-structural explanations for oppression and systems of inequality (Handler & Hasenfeld, 2006; Smith, 2012) and place all of the blame for social ills on the backs of disadvantaged individuals. All of this benefits elite systems of power that prosper by extracting wealth, capital, and resources from those on the lower rungs of the socioeconomic ladder. But this system only continues to function as long as the victims of legal system oppression continue to accept the narratives of moral failing, character flaws, and individual self-will as the explanation for why they are under the control of the CLS.

The SAA movement can help interrupt this harmful framework of punitive-centered indoctrination. For example, through our many methods of research, often informed in some capacity by insider perspectives, system-contacted people are able to shine a uniquely educated light on the many falsehoods of systemic inequality in state legal institutions. A new process of real justice is in order that can transform the broken processes of the punitively centered legal system. It is vital that we effectively organize, and that these projects be carried out strategically to maximize impact.

It is essential that a permanent roadway of access to opportunities for higher education is established for system-contacted people. Through the long-term advocacy work of university-affiliated SAA groups, who are working to build rigorous and organized programs within institutions of education, a process of destigmatization and social equality can begin to take place. This is also a call to the institutions of higher education that have access to vast resources to take part in advocating for SAA people. Through collaborative efforts between system-contacted people and colleges, SAA people can access the support and credentials needed to find their way to positions of influence that can impact policy in legal and academic institutions.

Many SAA members quoted in this book are engaged in leadership-focused endeavors and see the value of accessing positions that allow us to take part in dictating policies instead of having them be dictated at us.

Another step to reframing our narratives outside of the shame-based model is building expansive community justice initiatives created by the SAA movement. This includes activists, program directors, scholars, and stakeholders of many types and from multiple SAA groups working together. When society and the institutions therein see that our actions and voices are not in alignment with the stereotypes and labels created to disempower us, then a new story of empowerment and group agency is written. We have already endured incarceration and the legal system's traumas, and we now use both carceral lived experiences and the knowledge and skills we've gained from higher education to engage in humanistic transformation of the oppressive systems that previously attempted to label and control our lives.

An important part of the SAA mission also needs to focus on transforming how the state implements higher education programs in justice and criminal legal processes. Because educational efforts play a leading role in reducing rates of return to the legal system, they are vital to reversing the damage caused by mass incarceration and to expanding prison abolition. In other words, such efforts can help reduce prison populations and the need for incarceration, further perpetuating the process of Mathiesen's (1974, 2008) negative reforms. This can be accomplished by encouraging major universities and colleges to bring high-quality, rigorous educational programs into the CLS. Such programs present improved and/or more effective alternatives to current system programs through educational opportunities that reduce the traffic traveling through the revolving door back into prisons (eliminating the need for prisons by addressing the social factors that create them).

The process can be expedited by providing incentivization for educational institutions, such as state-supported subsidies for providing services to incarcerated and FI populations. For example, the 2023 reintroduction in the U.S., through the FAFSA Simplification Act, of Pell Grant accessibility for incarcerated populations involved in prison education programs (Weissman, 2023) is a good way to encourage universities to reinvest in correctional program development. Further measures that could also be greatly expanded upon across the country are the plans to convert certain sections of correctional facilities, such as San Quentin Prison in California, into college campuses. The California legislature recently approved funding for Governor Gavin Newsom's prison project to convert a section of San Quentin Prison into a college campus (Shafer, 2023).

USING OUR STRENGTHS! INTEGRATION OF OUR BACKGROUNDS INTO THE PRESENT, TO SPEAK TRUTH TO POWER

A dynamic that I believe is a vital strength of the SAA movement is our capacity to bring our pasts into the present as form of human capital (Coleman, 1988). Instead of hiding behind our pasts in continual shame and further perpetuating, accepting, and internalizing society's and the legal system's attempts to stigmatize and oppress us, many SAA members have begun to embrace our past legal encounters as part of us (Brown, 1991). This is not to state that we are proudly endorsing our convictions or legal system contact. We have formally completed our legally required sanctions and are forced to personally endure the collateral consequences of our actions throughout the duration of our lives. Yet the SAA movement does not consider this situation to be acceptable or equitable. Consequently, we are using our past experiences as building materials (Brown, 1991; Ebaugh, 1988) to help construct pathways, programs, and resources to create equality and opportunities for current and future system-contacted people.

Through this process of building structures of support, we use our past lived experiences as instruments for helping others, instead of seeing them as baggage to be shamefully hidden away or discarded. In this transformative process, we repurpose stigmatized identities that society often views as worthless, such as "convicted felon," into an object of value.

An important narrative to emphasize here is that we, the system-contacted people, not the CLS, have been motivating and engineering our own successes and opportunities. As many SAA people who shared their experiences for this book noted, they often sought out and interacted with mentorship and peer support within higher education and society to help facilitate this process.

A Life of Truth: We Saw the Truth, and Now We Speak the Truth

Some SAA members speak their truths about institutions of power without fear of consequences, directly to such entities, even at risk of rejection or facing sanctions. Yet it must be noted that scholars who have system contact in the reality of our current milieu are very much aware of the stigmatized status placed on those with legal convictions. Thus, many are cautious about the consequences of fearlessly speaking from an individual perspective. From the SAA group perspective, truth-focused research and heuristic actions (those that speak to systems of power) function to amplify our voices, consequently generating a mass fearless effect through strength in numbers. Through this empowered speech, we can force criminal justice and state institutions of power to grapple with these truths and engage in self-examination, even if only briefly.

The process of such fearless speaking of truth to power is described by Michel Foucault as *parrhesia*; "the ethical and public responsibility of the philosopher was to 'speak truth to power'" (Farquharson, 2008, p. 24). In this discussion I shift the focus from philosophers to justice-impacted criminology scholars as I present Foucault's (1983) explanation of *parrhesia*, or fearless speaking of truth. System-contacted scholars and academics engage in a form of truth ownership.

Here is an example of the process of parrhesia works. Foucault described a parrhesia-focused interaction between two historical figures in ancient Greece. The ancient Greek philosopher Diogenes confronted the king, Alexander the Great (Foucault, 1983, p. 133), who represented the largest empire the world had ever known at that time (arguably one of the most powerful figures alive during that era), with many harsh truths, at great risk to himself. (Diogenes's remarks were very blunt, bordering on insulting.) Yet Diogenes has the courage to speak frankly to Alexander and force Alexander to confront his own internal defects. Similarly, lived-experience academics' truth spoken persistently to institutions of power have the potential to compel such institutions to realize/confront their own defects and/or transform unjust policies and practices.

Another facet of how parrhesia-based activity enables FI scholars to speak truth to power is through developing the ability and desire to fearlessly extend the reach of their voices. For example, Tamboukou (2012) pointed out that parrhesia generates and encourages active engagement of scholars beyond writing journal articles and statistical analysis, and injects them into the public sphere. Tamboukou (2012), when discussing the trend in academia toward inaction, stated, "We are not short of analyses or theories; what we are short of is action, the mere gesture of reiteraring Bartleby's simple response: 'I would rather not' (Melville, 1853/2014)" (p. 862). By engaging in the practice of parrhesia, carcerally impacted scholars can speak truth to power and expose hidden/unrealized problems that exist in carceral systems at the macro and micro levels of analysis.

I end this book by proclaiming that system-contacted academics can generate more comprehensively informed truths through the process of parrhesia. Further, I explain that SAA parrhesiastes, through their actions, can bring about prosocial changes/impacts in systems of authority that perpetuate inequality and oppression. While I am arguing that it is the ethical and moral duty of SAAs to speak their lived-experience truths fearlessly to systems/institutions of power, I also assert that this process does not require us to engage in self-disclosure of our criminal legal backgrounds. SAA members are accessing and expressing the truths of their lived experiences whether they have publicly disclosed their past or not. As repeated throughout this book, the motivations for disclosure or nondisclosure of a past felony conviction among SAAs are myriad, and the opinions and worldviews of members of this group are varied and complex (Newbold & Ross, 2013). Some of us choose complete disclosure of our backgrounds in all social spheres (i.e., professional, scholarly, and personal), while some choose complete nondisclosure, and others choose some combination thereof (i.e., open in scholarship, yet not in the classroom, and not to their faculty peers). The fearless speaking of truth can place those who engage in full disclosure in a very publicly exposed position, which may give them a great deal of social visibility (e.g., in media, on social media, at conference presentations, and at their academic institutions), yet because of their high profile, they will also be more vulnerable to retaliation from the authority structures/powerful individuals they are speaking to. Yet those who partially disclose or choose not to reveal their backgrounds also engage in speaking powerful, fearless truths. For example, they substantiate their scholarship, instructional techniques, and professional presentations by accessing the cache of insider perspectives they have accumulated from their criminal justice lived experiences. The possession of inside knowledge of the justice system, aligned with classic criminological academic training, can create scholars who are more versatile. Scholars with the ability to perceive concepts differently illuminate systems of oppression that others may not recognize, propose creative solutions from the vantage point of the oppressed and voiceless, and recognize previously unknown perspectives.

Becoming a proficient SAA radical truth teller is accomplished through the practice of speaking fearless truth using personal insights coupled with rigorous scholarship within the academic process. Luxon (2008) expanded on the process of becoming a fearless truth teller: "As individuals improve their ability to manipulate their curiosity, they learn to forestall immediate reactions and instead to maintain a steady attitude towards themselves, to attend to changes and reactions, and to sift through a raft of information—some sensory, some analytic—before drawing a conclusion" (p. 387). Thus, the justice-contacted scholar learns the process of practicing critical literacy, being steady in practices of seeking truth, and sifting through multiple types of information from multiple sources in order to arrive at more robust truths.

In order to emphasize that it is the moral and ethical obligation of lived-experience academics to fearlessly speak truth to power, I add the concept of living a life of truth, "conjoined to the 'true life,' one without dissemblance or compromise, indifferent to the past or the future, this art of truth-telling yields a certain style, a beautiful life whose traces can be an object of admiration for others" (Flynn, 1985, p. 538). The SAA arrives at such a "truth life" through an amalgamation of carceral lived experience with the parrhesia aspects of their scholarship. It must be noted that there may be variation in how their life of truth manifests. Of course, I am not implying that they must be capable of continually focusing on speaking fearless truths, nor am I stating that they take an oath to commit to a ceaseless and noble vision of the voiceless and oppressed incarcerated masses in order to practice true parrhesia. SAA members will adhere to their own adaptation of truth life. But I do suggest that the truth life (framed by permanently life-altering lived experiences in the legal system) generated by SAAs is produced in conjunction with the outcomes of their published rigorous scholarship, professional presentations, and the insights they can purvey to their students within their university classrooms.

Given these points, FI scholars are placed in a complex relationship with the truths they have access to. To illustrate, the critical SAA members' relationship to truth is paradoxical because their viewpoints often stand in opposition to the punitive systems of power they exist within. Thus a question for further discussion: Can SAAs truly separate their truths from the *regimes of truth* that Foucault argues are forged within the very systems of power that SAAs operate within? The SAA movement may speak fearless truths to multiple sources of power, such as their own universities, state/federal legal systems, and the larger state/federal government. The individual segments of truth that SAAs experienced in the CLS are part and product of larger regimes of truth produced by constantly shifting political, economic, cultural, and social dynamics. While in correctional facilities or on parole or probation, we were subjected to systems of power; consequently, our truths originate from systems of oppression and marginalization. In addition, further complicating the SAA movement's relationship to the regimes of truth are the professions of its members. When SAAs leave incarceration and reenter society, we gain positions in the sphere of academia, one of the institutions of power per Foucault's (1977b) definition of truth. For lived-experience scholars to choose to speak fearlessly against the very organizations (i.e., universities, research institutes, and academic societies) that they are affiliated with is to place themselves in a precarious position (the danger component of parrhesia), especially when they rely on the support (i.e., tenure, graduate assistantships, research resources, or income) of these academic institutions and organizations. Yet amplified messages of fearless truth are being produced through unified persistent scholarship and the university classroom instruction efforts of ever-increasing numbers of SAA members. When the SAA truth message reaches a critical mass, populating the meeting agendas of influential progressive justice advocates and policy action committees, the carceral institutions of power (governmental power) will be forced to take notice, and the potential for change will be activated.

I have argued that SAA knowledge of the inside of correctional processes and institutions has immense value when framed and presented appropriately. As the destructive force of American mass incarceration (the primary criminal justice practice) grinds on, increasing numbers of returning people and the invaluable truths they bring with them are finding their way to critically focused segments of social science disciplines such as criminology, sociology, and criminal justice. Capturing the ability to legitimately own and fearlessly speak SAAs' truths to systems of power is vitally important to the process of illuminating oppressive dynamics within the correctional world that are not captured and/or presented by other sources. The fearless truths of those of us who have lived inside the machine illustrate the need for transformation of the incarceration-addicted justice system from a socially destructive force into a restorative mechanism of prosocial change.

APPENDIX A

Terminology

ACQUAINTANCE CONTACTED Refers to individuals who do not have a criminal conviction yet may have friends, family, and/or loved ones who have been formerly incarcerated or system involved. (Referred to as *system impacted* by the Underground Scholars SAA group.)

CARCERALLY IMPACTED Refers to the full breadth of people who have been affected by the criminal legal system. (*System affected* is used in the same manner.)

CONVICTION ONLY Refers to individuals who were convicted of a criminal charge defined by legal code yet were not incarcerated. They may have incurred other legal sanctions such as probation, community corrections, or fines. (Referred to as *system involved* by the Underground Scholars SAA group in the University of California system)

DIRECT SYSTEM CONTACT Refers to having experienced formal legal sanctions within the criminal legal system, such as incarceration, probation, community corrections, and restitution, as a result of a criminal conviction.

FORMERLY INCARCERATED (FI) Refers to individuals who have been convicted of a criminal charge defined by legal code and sentenced to incarceration in a correctional facility.

INDEPENDENT SAA INDIVIDUALS Refers to independent actors who are not affiliated with any specific SAA group. They often publish research and media about or informed by their respective criminal justice experiences and/or criminal legal systems (if located outside the U.S.). Such individuals can also be involved with professional and nonprofit organizations (non-SAA organizations) and both activist and critical scholarship.

INDIRECT SYSTEM CONTACT Refers to informal contact with the criminal legal system, such as the incarceration or formal legal sanctioning of a family member, loved one, or friend.

JUSTICE FREE Refers to people without a criminal conviction and without criminal legal system contact at the felony or misdemeanor level. (Referred to as *non-cons* by Convict Criminology in the U.K.)

SAA GROUP Refers to the respective organized networks of activist and critical scholars.

SAA MOVEMENT Refers to the entirety of impact and actions of the cumulative SAA population (groups and independent individuals). The cumulative actions of multiple organized groups of justice-involved individuals in academic roles, working toward justice and equality focused on societal change for fellow system-affected people.

SAA POPULATION Refers to the group of people who fall under the SAA definition, including SAA group members and independent SAA individuals.

SYSTEM-AFFECTED ACADEMIC (SAA) Refers to a person who has been affected by the criminal legal system and is involved in academia (faculty, scholar, college instructor, student, graduate student). The adjective *affected*, meaning, "acted upon; influenced," was not chosen for convenience, but out of a sense of the breadth of variation in experiences and interpretations that carcerally impacted individuals describe, in regard to how the criminal legal system interacts with their lives. The SAA member may have been formerly incarcerated, been convicted of a crime but not incarcerated, have served time in jail or prison, or be acquaintance contacted (have family members or loved ones who have been or are incarcerated). As an adjective is used to describe the entire population (SAA population), respective organized groups (SAA group), or collective movement (SAA movement).

APPENDIX B

Research Methodology

STUDY PARTICIPANTS: SEMISTRUCTURED IN-DEPTH INTERVIEWS

Due to the geographically dispersed nature of this relatively small population and the global COVID pandemic that was occurring during the major portion of the data collection phase, this study used a qualitative method approach of semistructured in-depth interviews (Creswell & Clark, 2017; Williams & Heikes, 1993), conducted through virtual conferencing software. Within the course of this research project forty-six interviews were conducted, ranging from forty-five minutes to three hours in length. The interviews used open-ended questions that were later transcribed and coded according to recurring themes within the dialogue. Through the use of the transcripts of qualitative semistructured in-depth interviews with system affected academic (SAA) individuals and members of SAA organizations and groups, a thematic analysis examined their motivations for organizing, guiding principles, primary directives, production of various forms of activist scholarship, and the focus of future advocacy and research directions.

Participants and Sampling Techniques

Participants were recruited through snowball methods, meaning that participants passed on study information to others they thought might be interested in participating. Snowball sampling is also referred to as the convenience sampling technique. Because of the relatively rare and geographically widely dispersed nature of this population, many of the participants in this study could not be reached using standard random sampling techniques. A convenience sample of forty-six people with higher education credentials (or currently pursuing educational credentials) from SAA groups in social justice, criminology, and criminal justice–related fields was acquired through group member contacts.

All those who agreed to participate in this study took part in a onetime in-person interview. Interviews were held at a location of the participant's choosing, yet due to the geographically dispersed nature of this population and the study taking place during the COVID-19 epidemic, most interviews were held via digital conferencing venues such as Zoom. All interviews were audio recorded, and all recordings were erased following transcription.

Coding and Data Analysis

While conducting qualitative research, large amounts of data were created, including hundreds of pages of interview transcripts. When analyzing in-depth interviews in the first phase of the study (Caughey, 2006; Creswell 2007; Strauss and Corbin, 1998), the material was analyzed in order to find recurrent themes and/or prevalent ideas faced by ex-offenders engaged in postgraduate education. The qualitative data was arranged in an orderly fashion in chronological order. This interview data was then "open coded" according to recurrence within the transcriptions using the Comment function in a Word document format. To open code I wrote memos and inserted Comments in the Word document, looking for general important concepts. In the next phase, referred to as "focused coding," I examined the text for important categories of information and concurrent concepts or themes. I used Excel files to track and record recurrent themes. These themes were then organized into a table, which contains the most prevalent themes found throughout the interview data, which allowed me to categorize the data in an orderly fashion.

In regard to my in-depth interviews data analysis procedure, I used the grounded theory procedures laid out by Creswell (2007, pp. 156–57).

- Data managing (create and organize files for data)
- Reading, memo-ing (read through text, make marginal notes, form initial codes)
- Describing (describe open coding categories)
- Classifying (select one open coding category for the central phenomenon in process)
- Interpreting (engage in selective coding and interrelate the categories to develop "story" or propositions)

AUTOETHNOGRAPHY/LIFE NARRATIVES/ PERSONAL ANECDOTES

At the beginning of each chapter of this book, I include a personal anecdote of lived experiences relevant to the topics and themes of the chapter. Because of my training as an academic sociologist and criminologist, some of this discussion contains autoethnographic language and perhaps some analysis. However, I strove to keep these anecdotal sections as personal and story-like as I could, to purvey the humanness of the SAA phenomenon. This book is part research and part our stories, our narratives that define this movement, and there is a unique sense of empowerment in that quality.

Notes

INTRODUCTION

1. *Inmate* is an institutional term used by the Federal Bureau of Prisons (n.d.).

2. See appendix A for definitions of terms used in the text.

3. See appendix B for methodological details of this study.

4. Donald Cressey began to mentor the student John Irwin, who had recently been released from prison, at UCLA. They went on to coauthor one of the very first theorizations (Irwin & Cressey, 1962) of an incarcerated person's identity written by an SAA author.

5. Refer to appendix B for further information about this study's research methodology.

6. Refer to appendix B for further information about the SAA participants and inclusion criteria for this study.

7. See https://callink.berkeley.edu/organization/usi.

8. Telephone conversation with Dr. James Binnall, faculty academic adviser for Rising Scholars CSULB, September 1, 2020. There is a Rising Scholars CSULB Facebook page at www.facebook.com/rising.scholars.csulb/.

9. See https://risingscholarsnetwork.org/.

10. Not all SAA groups are attached to specific institutions of higher learning, and not all SAA people are part of a group, yet all of these individuals have interacted with academic establishments. Among organized SAA groups, there is variance. Some groups are tied to specific institutions, while other groups are regional, national, or international in membership coverage, and thus their members are tied to their own universities or academic institutions across different states or even different continents.

11. Their activist and critical stances toward justice issues place the scholars in this book at odds with their more traditional/establishment-centered colleagues and may negatively impact their careers through status fragility (Tietjen & Kavish, 2021), which may potentially stymie SAA movement progress. For a comprehensive discussion of status fragility, see Tietjen and Kavish (2021).

1. FINDING OUT THAT THE DOOR IS OPEN

1. The disregard of evidence-based criminological and criminal justice practices and policies in favor of publicly and/or politically popular policies and practices (often one and the same) is especially problematic in the U.S. Other countries (i.e., the U.K., Australia) that are featured in the scope of this book's argument are generally more open to embracing evidence-based criminal justice practices.

2. The foundational theories of the SAA movement are new criminology, cultural criminology, Thomas Mathiesen's perspectives on prison abolition and positive and negative reforms, peacemaking criminology, John Irwin on extreme overuse of incarceration in the U.S., and feminist standpoint theory.

3. Prior to the postincarceration collateral consequences that negatively impact learning for intersection-ally oppressed communities, many correctional institutions also limit access to educational materials while people are still incarcerated. I am referring to the practice (by prison administration) of banning certain books and censoring prison library reading lists (Conrad, 2012; Doyle, 2013; Monobe et al., 2021). Books especially susceptible to censorship by prison officials include those by authors of color (whereas in certain prisons, books about white supremacy [Dholakia, 2022] have been allowed to stay in libraries), that speak about revolutionary topics, and that discuss critical theories, as well as any book that prison officials may deem to be a "security risk" according to their nearly unlimited subjective judgment.

4. At the 2019 ASC Conference hosted in San Francisco, CA, Assistant Professor Dan Kavish organized the first quantitative CC panel.

5. I took part in several Zoom videoconferencing and phone conversations throughout 2020, with multiple members of CC, Underground Scholars, Rising Scholars, and FICGN.

6. In the media-sensationalized story that involved Willie Horton, politics became involved with the CLS. In 1988 an incarcerated African American man in Massachusetts, Willie Horton, was released on a weekend furlough and committed a violent crime. This occurred during a presidential election year, and the Republican nominee, George H. W. Bush, used this event against his Democratic opponent, the governor of Massachusetts, Michael Dukakis. A series of national television commercials funded by the Bush campaign implied that Dukakis was weak on crime. This worked perfectly for Bush Sr. and destroyed Dukakis's presidential campaign (he was polling far better than Bush before these commercials). The commercials showed Horton's black-and-white mugshot, while using ominous, racially coded language (Hurwitz & Peffley, 2005) and strong racist stereotypes of the criminalized Black man, presenting Horton as a dangerous "convict" to be feared.

7. It must be noted that there will be nuanced differences in respective SAA branches, based on factors such as varying affiliations with educational institutions, geographic location, years of operation, and discrepancies in organizational structures. Yet the organic focus on activist scholarship, mentorship, and support for fellow SAAs and acting as agents of humanistic criminal justice transformation is generally found in varying degrees throughout the SAA population.

8. Faculty choosing to critique their employers as part of activist-based research may place their personal career advancement at risk.

2. THE JOURNEY OF HIGHER EDUCATION

1. While Pell Grants have once again become available to some incarcerated people through recent federal legislation, during the period when I was incarcerated, in the early 2000s, self-funding was generally one of the few means through which people confined in prison could access college courses. It must be noted that the largely disproportionate representation of people from the lower rungs of the socioeconomic ladder within corrections places the majority of incarcerated people at a disadvantage in regard to securing the necessary funds to pay for often-expensive college-level courses. Also, there are college programs located within certain prisons that provide some financial assistance for indigent incarcerated people. But these programs are sporadic, institutional coverage is limited, and they are not available in most correctional facilities.

3. BUILDING A PRISON-TO-SCHOOL PIPELINE

1. Including academic conferences and universities, and via more modern venues such as online social media platforms (e.g., Facebook and X, formerly Twitter).

5. THE ACADEMIC AND PUBLIC VOICE

1. Some may not see themselves as part of the movement and choose not to use their lived experiences.

2. I also attempted to reflect these contrasts in my writing.

3. Many of us have followed different pathways. For example, some began to compose books and articles while still incarcerated, while others started writing when they reentered society and began college.

4. Many are from oppressed minority groups.

5. See https://prisonjournalismproject.org.

6. RETROFLEXIVE TRANSFORMATION

1. Legitimating SAA perspectives in regard to shifting biased public and justice system sentiments toward acceptance. I certainly do not mean to imply that our sentiments were initially illegitimate. They have always been legitimate, yet were disregarded and/or marginalized.

References

Abbott, J. H. (1982). *In the belly of the beast.* Vintage.

Abeyta, M. (2022). Academic pathways for formerly incarcerated students. *Journal Committed to Social Change on Race and Ethnicity (JCSCORE), 8*(1), 37–49.

Abeyta, M., Torres, A., Hernandez, J. L., & Duran, O. (2021). Rising scholars: A case study of two community colleges serving formerly incarcerated and system-impacted students. *Journal of Applied Research in the Community College, 28*(1), 99–109.

Acker, S. (2000). In/out/side: Positioning the researcher in feminist qualitative research. *Resources for Feminist Research, 28*(1–2), 189–210.

Adler, P., & Adler, P. (1987). *Membership roles in field research.* Newbury Park, CA: Sage.

Ajunwa I., & Onwuachi-Willig, A. (2018). Combating discrimination against the formerly incarcerated in the labor market. *Northwest University Law Review, 112*(6), 1385–1416.

Alexander, M. (2010). *The new Jim Crow: Mass incarceration in the age of colorblindness.* New Press.

Alinsky, S. (1946). *Reveille for radicals.* University of Chicago Press.

Alonso, J. (2023, August 30). Measuring higher ed's benefits beyond earnings. *Inside Higher Ed.* https://www.insidehighered.com/news/students/careers/2023/08/30/study-shows-higher-ed-linked-kinder-healthier-citizens?utm_source=Inside+Higher+Ed&utm_campaign=45bbff9ce7-DNU_2021_COPY_02&utm_medium=email&utm_term=0_1fcbc04421-45bbff9ce7-197400649&mc_cid=

Alper, M., Durose, M. R., & Markman, J. (2018). *2018 update on prisoner recidivism: A 9-year follow-up period (2005–2014)*. US Department of Justice, Office of Justice Programs, Bureau of Justice Statistics.

Alvarado, L. M. (2020). *The invisible wall: A study of formerly incarcerated community college students and stigma* [Unpublished doctoral dissertation]. California State University, Fullerton.

Anderson, A., Fox, R., Jones, P., Joseph, R., Witherell, W., & Adams, A. (2024). Reentry and transition into college life: A study of formerly incarcerated individuals in Southern California. *Journal of Human Behavior in the Social Environment*, 34(2), 256–289. https://www.tandfonline.com/doi/abs/10.1080/10911359.2023.2244019

Andrisse, S. (2021). *From prison cells to PhD: It is never too late to do good*. Post Hill Press.

Andrisse, S., Billings, K., Xue, P., & Wu, S. (2018). Insulin signaling displayed a differential tissue-specific response to low-dose dihydrotestosterone in female mice. *American Journal of Physiology-Endocrinology and Metabolism*, 314(4), E353–E365.

Antojado, D. (2023) "Nothing about us without us": Analyzing the potential contributions of lived experience to penological pedagogy. *Journal of Criminal Justice Education*, 1–18. https://doi.org/10.1080/10511253.2023.2275101

Aptheker, B. (1975). *The morning breaks: The trial of Angela Davis*. International Publishers.

Arditti, J. A. (2002). Doing family research at the jail: Reflections of a prison widow. *The Qualitative Report*, 7(4), 1–16.

Aresti, A., & Darke, S. (2016). Practicing convict criminology: Lessons learned from British academic activism. *Critical Criminology*, 24(4), 533–547.

Aresti, A., Darke, S. & Earle, R. (2012, August 1). Developing critical insider perspectives on prison. *InsideTime*.

Aresti, A., Darke, S., & Manlow, D. (2016). Bridging the gap: Giving public voice to prisoners and former prisoners through research activism. *Prison Service Journal*, 224, 3–13.

Arrigo, B. A., & Bersot, H. Y. (2016). Revolutionizing academic activism: Transpraxis, critical pedagogy, and justice for a people yet to be. *Critical Criminology*, 24(4), 549–564.

Asselin, M. E. (2003). Insider research: Issues to consider when doing qualitative research in your own setting. *Journal for Nurses in Staff Development*, 19(2), 99–103.

Baca Zinn, M. (1979). Field research in minority communities: Ethical, methodological and political observations by an insider." *Social Problems*, 27(2), 209–219.

Ball, S. J. (2012). Performativity, commodification and commitment: An I-spy guide to the neoliberal university. *British Journal of Educational Studies*, 60(1), 17–28.

Baranyi, G., Cassidy, M., Fazel, S., Priebe, S., & Mundt, A. P. (2018). Prevalence of posttraumatic stress disorder in prisoners. *Epidemiologic Reviews*, 40(1), 134–145.

Battle C. L., Zlotnick C., Najavits L. M., Gutierrez, M., & Winsor, C. (2003). Posttraumatic stress disorder and substance use disorder among incarcerated women. In P. Ouimette and P. J. Brown (Eds.), *Trauma and substance abuse: Causes, consequences, and treatment of comorbid disorders* (pp. 209–225). American Psychological Association.

Beasley, C. R., & Jason, L. A. (2015). Engagement & disengagement in mutual-help addiction recovery housing: A test of affective events theory. *American Journal of Community Psychology*, *55*(3–4), 347–358.

Beasley, C. R., & Xiao, Y. J. (2023, January 17). Incarceration history and ethnic bias in hiring perceptions: An experimental test of intersectional bias & psychological mechanisms. *PLOS One*, *18*(1): e0280397. https://doi.org/10.1371/journal.pone.0280397; https://journals.plos.org/plosone/article?id=10.1371%2Fjournal.pone.0280397&fbclid=IwAR2jVubUJmzwdlcXGC1U-5Rs5ltaNmw1q2vFeQfiOeLiHxjou17qe3O2ODI#references

Beattie, I. R. (2018). Sociological perspectives on first-generation college students. In B. Schneider (Ed.), *Handbook of the sociology of education in the 21st century* (pp. 171–191). Springer International Publishing.

Beckwith, K. (1996). Lancashire women against pit closures: Women's standing in a men's movement. *Signs: Journal of Women in Culture and Society*, *21*(4), 1034–1068.

Benjamin, R. (2022). *Viral justice: How we grow the world we want.* Princeton University Press.

Bentley, D. (1998). *English criminal justice in the nineteenth century.* Hambledon Press.

Berger, D. (2014). *Captive nation: Black prison organizing in the civil rights era.* UNC Press Books.

Berger, D. (2013). Social movements and mass incarceration: What is to be done? *Souls: A Critical Journal of Black Politics, Culture, and Society*, *15*(1–2), 3–18.

Berila, B. (2015). *Integrating mindfulness into anti-oppression pedagogy: Social justice in higher education.* Routledge.

Berkeley Underground Scholars. (n.d.). *Building a prison-to-university pipeline through recruitment, retention and advocacy.* https://undergroundscholars.berkeley.edu/

Bevington, D., & Dixon, C. (2005). Movement-relevant theory: Rethinking social movement scholarship and activism. *Social Movement Studies*, *4*(3), 185–208.

Binnall, J. M. (2018). Summonsing criminal desistance: Convicted felons' perspectives on jury service. *Law & Social Inquiry*, *43*(1), 4–27.

Binnall, J. M. (2021a, October 14). Carceral wisdom. *Inquest: A Decarceral Brainstorm.* https://inquest.org/carceral-wisdom/

Binnall, J. M. (2021b). *Twenty million angry men: The case for including convicted felons in our jury system.* University of California Press.

Binnall, J. M., Scott-Hayward, C., Petersen, N., & Gonzalez, R. M. (2022). Taking roll: College students' views of their formerly incarcerated classmates. *Journal of Criminal Justice Education*, *33*(3), 347–367. https://doi.org/10.1080/10511253.2021.1962932

Bint Faisal, A., Dean, M., Demirtas, M., Dharmarajah, S., Hinde, D., Mathias, M., Milner, G., Raynor, R., Muzzaker, S. Stanford, A., & Taylor, G. (2018). Insider perspectives in higher education within the British prison system. *Journal of Prisoners on Prisons*, 27(2), 75–90.

Blakinger, K. (2022). *Corrections in ink: A memoir*. St. Martin's Press.

Bloom, T., & Bradshaw, G. A. (2021). Inside of a prison: How a culture of punishment prevents rehabilitation. *Peace and Conflict: Journal of Peace Psychology*. Advance online publication. https://doi.org/10.1037/pac0000572

Boppre B., DeHart D., & Shapiro C. J. (2022). "The prison system doesn't make it comfortable to visit": Prison visitation from the perspectives of people incarcerated and family members. *Criminal Justice and Behavior*. Advance online publication. https://doi.org/10.1177/00938548221094823

Borkman, T. (2008). The twelve-step recovery model of AA: A voluntary mutual help association. In L. Kaskutas & M. Galanter (Eds.), *Recent developments in alcoholism* (Vol. 18, pp. 9–35). New York: Springer.

Bosworth, M. (2004). Review of the book *Convict criminology*, by J. I. Ross & S. C. Richards, Eds. *British Journal of Criminology*, 44(6), 998–990. https://doi.org/10.1093/bjc/azh089

Bowling, B. (2006). A brief history of criminology. *Criminal Justice Matters*, 65(1): 12–13.

Bozick, R., Steele, J., Davis, L., & Turner, S. (2018). Does providing inmates with education improve post release outcomes? A meta-analysis of correctional education programs in the United States. *Journal of Experimental Criminology*, 14(3), 389–428.

Bozkurt, S. S. (2023). *A woman's liberation*. Michael Terence Publishing.

Bozkurt, S. S., Merico, M., Aresti, A., & Darke, S. (2020). Crossing borders, pushing boundaries and privileging 'marginalised' voices: Surviving motherhood and prison. In *Convict criminology for the future* (pp. 21–34). New York: Routledge.

Brisman, A. (2004). Double whammy: Collateral consequences of conviction and imprisonment for sustainable communities and the environment. *William & Mary Environmental Law & Policy Review*, 28(2), 423–475.

Brisman, A. (2007). Toward a more elaborate typology of environmental values: Liberalizing criminal disenfranchisement laws and policies. *New England Journal on Criminal & Civil Confinement*, 33(2), 283–457.

Broido, E. M., & Reason, R. D. (2005). The development of social justice attitudes and actions: An overview of current understandings. *New Directions for Student Services*, 110, 17.

Brown, J. D. (1991). The professional ex-: An alternative for exiting the deviant career. *Sociological Quarterly*, 32(2), 219–230.

Cancian, F. M. (1992). Feminist science: Methodologies that challenge inequality. *Gender & Society*, 6(4), 623–642. https://doi.org/10.1177/089124392006004006

Carlton, G. (2022. May 11). Student activism in college: A history of campus protests. *Best Colleges*. https://www.bestcolleges.com/blog/history-student-activism-in-college/

Caughey, John L. 2006. *Negotiating cultures & identities: Life history issues, methods, and readings*. University of Nebraska Press.

Chang, H. (2016). *Autoethnography as method* (Vol. 1). Routledge.

Choi, J. (2016). *Creating a multivocal self: Autoethnography as method*. Routledge.

Christensen, A. D., & Jensen, S. Q. (2012). Doing intersectional analysis: Methodological implications for qualitative research. *NORA—Nordic Journal of Feminist and Gender Research*, 20(2), 109–125.

Clear, T. (2008). The effects of high imprisonment rates on communities. *Crime and Justice*, 37(1), 97–132.

Clemmer, D. (1940). *The prison community*. Christopher Publishing House.

Cohen, L., & Spinak, J. (2018). Busting the "juvenile super-predator" myth. In *Rights, Race, and Reform* (pp. 269–284). Routledge.

Coleman, James S. 1988. Social capital in the creation of human capital. *The American Journal of Sociology*, 94, 95–120.

Collier, L. (2014). Incarceration nation: The United States leads the world in incarceration; A new report explores why—and offers recommendations for fixing the system. *Monitor on Psychology*, 45,(9). https://www.apa.org/monitor/2014/10/incarceration#:~:text=In%20addition%2C%20imprisonment%20can%20create,or%20schizophrenia%2C%20the%20report%20finds

Collins, P. H. (2000). *Black feminist thought: Knowledge, consciousness, and the politics of empowerment* (2nd ed.). Routledge.

Connell, R. (2019). *The good university: What universities actually do and why it's time for radical change*. Zed Books.

Conrad, S. (2012). Collection development and circulation policies in prison libraries: An exploratory survey of librarians in US correctional institutions. *The Library Quarterly*, 82(4), 407–427.

Copenhaver, A., Edwards-Willey, T. L., & Byers, B. D. (2007). Journeys in social stigma: The lives of formerly incarcerated felons in higher education. *Journal of Correctional Education*, 58(3), 268–283.

Copes, H., Beaton, B., Ayeni, D., Dabney, D., & Tewksbury, R. (2020). A content analysis of qualitative research published in top criminology and criminal justice journals from 2010 to 2019. *American Journal of Criminal Justice*, 45(6), 1060–1079.

Cornwall, G. (2023, February 6). "Revolutionary" housing: How colleges aim to support formerly incarcerated students. *The Nation*. https://hechingerreport.org/revolutionary-housing-colleges-aim-to-support-a-growing-number-of-formerly-incarcerated-students/#:~:text=Less%20than%204%20percent%20of%20people%20released%20from%20prison%20ever,to%20obtain%20a%20postsecondary%20credential

Couloute, L. (2018, October). *Getting back on course: Educational exclusion and attainment among formerly incarcerated people*. Prison Policy Initiative. https://www.prisonpolicy.org/reports/education.html

Crenshaw, K. 1991. Mapping the margins: Intersectionality, identity politics, and violence against women of color. *Stanford Law Review*, 43(6):1241–1279.

Crenshaw, K. 2017. *On intersectionality: The essential writings of Kimberlé Crenshaw.* New Press.
Cressey, D. R. (1955). Changing criminals: The application of the theory of differential association. *American Journal of Sociology, 61*(2), 116–120.
Creswell, J. W., & Clark, V. L. P. (2017). *Designing and conducting mixed methods research.* Sage Publications.
Creswell, J. W., & Poth, C. N. (2016). *Qualitative inquiry and research design: Choosing among five approaches.* Sage.
Crewe, B., Warr, J., Bennett, P., & Smith, A. (2014). The emotional geography of prison life. *Theoretical Criminology, 18*(1), 56–74.
Cross, K. P. (1981). *Adults as learners: Increasing participation and facilitating learning.* Jossey-Bass.
Custer, B. D. (2018). Applying to university with criminal convictions: A comparative study of admissions policies in the United States and United Kingdom. *Journal of Higher Education Policy and Management*, 40(3), 239–255.
Custer, B. D., Malkin, M. L., & Castillo, G. (2020). Criminal justice system-impacted faculty: Motivations, barriers, and successes on the academic job market. *Journal of Education Human Resources, 38*(2), 336–364.
Daniels, E. (2021). *Building a trauma-responsive educational practice: Lessons from a corrections classroom.* Routledge.
Davis A. Y. (2003). *Are prisons obsolete?* Seven Stories Press.
Davis, A. Y., & Rodriguez, D. (2000). The challenge of prison abolition: A conversation. *Social Justice*, 27(3), 212–218.
Davis, C. H., III, Harris, J. C., Stokes, S., & Harper, S. R. (2019). But is it Activist? Interpretive criteria for activist scholarship in higher education. *The Review of Higher Education*, 42(5), 85–108.
Davis, L. M., Bozick, R., Steele, J. L., Saunders, J., & Miles, J. N. V. (2013). *Evaluating the effectiveness of correctional education: A meta-analysis of programs that provide education to incarcerated adults.* RAND Corporation.
Delgado, R., & Stefancic, J. (2007). Critical race theory and criminal justice. *Humanity & Society, 31*(2–3), 133–145.
Denver, M., Pickett, J. T., & Bushway, S. D. (2017). The language of stigmatization and the mark of violence: Experimental evidence on the social construction and use of criminal record stigma. *Criminology, 55*(3), 664–690.
Desmond, M., & Emirbayer, M. (2009). What is racial domination?. *Du Bois Review: Social Science Research on Race*, 6(2), 335–355.
DeVeaux, M. (2013). The trauma of the incarceration experience. *Harvard Civil Rights-Civil Liberties Law Review*, 48(1), 257–77.
Dholakia, N. (2022, April 4). *The cruel practice of banning books behind bars.* The Vera Institute. Link: https://www.vera.org/news/the-cruel-practice-of-banning-books-behind-bars
Dholakia, N. (2023, June 21). *How college in prison is changing lives.* The Vera Institute. https://www.vera.org/news/how-college-in-prison-changes-lives
Dietsche, L. A., & Kilmer, A. (2024). Poetic inquiry criminology: Opportunities for imaginative scholarship, healing, and transformative justice. In *Handbook on prisons and jails* (pp. 422–432). Routledge.

Division of Convict Criminology. (n.d.). American Society of Criminology. https://concrim.org/

Doyle, B. C. (2013). Incarceration and the "Freedom to Read": How prison libraries function as instruments of state power. *Genders* (58). link.gale.com/apps/doc/A356353844/AONE?u=anon~6c948269&sid=googleScholar&xid=347cb576

Du Bois, W. E. B. (1953). *The souls of Black folk*. The Blue Heron Press.

Duncan, M. (2004). Autoethnography: Critical appreciation of an emerging art. *International Journal of Qualitative Methods*, 3(4), 28–39.

Duru, J. (2004). The Central Park Five and the Scottsboro Boys, and the myth of the bestial Black man. *Cardozo Law Review*, 25(1315), 1–41. https://digitalcommons.wcl.american.edu/cgi/viewcontent.cgi?article=2556&context=facsch_lawrev

Dwyer, S. C., & Buckle, J. L. (2009). The space between: On being an Insider-Outsider in qualitative research. *International Journal of Qualitative Methods*. 8(1), 54–63.

Earle, R. (2014). Insider and out: Making sense of a prison experience and a research experience. *Qualitative Inquiry*, 20(4), 429–438.

Earle, R. (2018). Convict criminology in England: Developments and dilemmas. *The British Journal of Criminology*, 58(6), 1499–1516.

Earle, Rod. (2016). *Convict criminology: Inside and out*. Policy Press.

Earle, Rod. (2021). Exploring narrative, convictions and autoethnography as a convict criminologist. *Tijdschrift over Cultuur & Criminaliteit* [*Journal of Culture and Crime*], 2020(3), 80–96.

Ebaugh, H. R. F. 1988. *Becoming an ex: The process of role exit*. University of Chicago Press.

Ekunwe, I. O., & Jones, R. S. (Eds). (2011). *Global perspectives on re-entry*. University of Tampere Press.

Elliott, W., & Lewis, M. K. (2015). *The real college debt crisis: How student borrowing threatens financial well-being and erodes the American dream*. Praeger.

Emirbayer, M., & Desmond, M. (2015). *The racial order*. University of Chicago Press.

Ewald, A., & Uggen, C. (2012). The collateral effects of imprisonment on prisoners, families, and communities. In J. Petersilia and K. Reitz (Eds.), *The Oxford handbook on sentencing and corrections* (pp. 83–103). Oxford University Press.

Fair, H., & Walmsley, R. (2022). *World female imprisonment list*. ICPR.chrome-extension://efaidnbmnnnibpcajpcglclefindmkaj/https://www.prisonstudies.org/sites/default/files/resources/downloads/world_female_imprisonment_list_5th_edition.pdf

Farquharson, A. (2008). The impossible prison. *British Society of Criminology Newsletter* (62), 22–25.

Federal Bureau of Prisons (FBOP). (n.d.). *Federal inmates*. https://www.bop.gov/inmates/

Ferree, M. M. (2002). *Shaping abortion discourse: Democracy and the public sphere in Germany and the United States*. Cambridge University Press.

Ferrell, J. (1999). Cultural criminology. *Annual Review of Sociology*, 25(1), 395–418.

Ferrell, J., Hayward, K., Morrison, W., & Presdee, M. (Eds.). (2016). *Cultural criminology unleashed.* Routledge.

Ferrell, J., Hayward, K., & Young, J. (2015). *Cultural criminology: An invitation.* Sage.

First Step Act, S. 3747, 115th Cong. (2018). https://www.govtrack.us/congress/bills/115/s3747

Flynn, S. I. (2011). Types of social movements. In *Sociology reference guide: Theories of social movements* (pp. 100–101). Salem Press.

Flynn, T. (1985). Truth and subjectivation in the later Foucault. *The Journal of Philosophy*, 82(10), 531–540.

Formerly Incarcerated College Graduates Network (FICGN). (2024). *Welcome to the largest network of college educated previously incarcerated individuals in the world.* https://ficgn.org/

Formerly Incarcerated College Graduates Network (FICGN). (n.d.). *Home* [Facebook page]. Retrieved February 13, 2024, from https://www.facebook.com/FICGN/

Forsyth, D. R. (2019). *Group dynamics* (7th ed.). Wadsworth.

Foster, M. (1997). *Black teachers on teaching.* New Press.

Foucault, M. (1977a). *Discipline and punish: The birth of the prison.* Vintage Books.

Foucault, M. (1977b). *Truth and power, power/knowledge: Selected interviews & other writings 1972–1977* (C. Gordon, Ed.). Pantheon Books.

Foucault, M. (1983). *Discourse and truth: The problematization of parrhesia; six lectures given by Michel Foucault at the University of California at Berkeley.* (Also published in 2001 under the title Fearless speech by Semiotexte)

Fox, R., Rodriguez, J., Joseph, R., & Anderson, A. (2023). Career building among formerly incarcerated college graduates. *Journal of Career Development*, 50(6), 1189–1205. https://doi.org/10.1177/08948453231170211

Freire, P. (2018). *Pedagogy of the oppressed.* Bloomsbury.

From Prison Cells to PhD. (n.d.). *Mission and vision.* https://www.fromprisoncellstophd.org/mission-and-vision.html

Fry, R., & Cilluffo, A. (2019, May 22). *A rising share of undergraduates are from poor families, especially at less selective colleges.* Pew Research Center. https://www.pewresearch.org/social-trends/2019/05/22/a-rising-share-of-undergraduates-arefrom-poor-families-especially-at-less-selective-colleges/.

Furlong, A., & Cartmel, F. (2009). *Higher education and social justice.* McGraw-Hill Education.

Galtung, J. (1969). Violence, peace and peace research. *Journal of Peace Research*, 6(3), 167–191.

Garland, D. (2002). *The culture of control.* University of Chicago Press.

Gelsthorpe, L., & Sharpe, G. (2005). Criminological research: Typologies versus hierarchies. *Justice Matters*, 62(1), 8–43.

Gewin, V. (2019, November 12). Moving from prison to a PhD. *Nature.* https://www.nature.com/articles/d41586-019-03370-1

Gilmore, R. W. (2009). Race, prisons and war: Scenes from the history of US violence. *Socialist Register, 45*, 73–87.

Gilmore, R. W. (2022). *Abolition geography: Essays towards liberation*. Verso.

Goffman, E. (1959). *The presentation of self in everyday life*. Doubleday.

Goffman, E. (1961). *Asylums: Essays on the social situation of mental patients and other inmates*. Anchor Books.

Goffman, E. (1963). *Stigma: Notes on the management of spoiled identity*. Prentice Hall.

González, N., Moll, L. C., & Amanti, C. (Eds.). (2006). *Funds of knowledge: Theorizing practices in households, communities, and classrooms*. Lawrence Earlbaum Associates.

Grimaldi, E. (2012). Neoliberalism and the marginalisation of social justice: The making of an education policy to combat social exclusion. *International Journal of Inclusive Education, 16*(11), 1131–1154.

Gramlich, J. (2020). *What the data says (and doesn't say) about crime in the U.S.* Pew Research Center. https://www.pewresearch.org/fact-tank/2019/10/17/facts-about-crime-in-the-u-s/

Gray, A. C. (2018). Communities behind bars: A review of mass incarceration and the coercive mobility hypothesis. *New Visions for Public Affairs, 10*(1), 19–29.

Green, C. M. (2018). *Against criminalization and pathology: The making of a Black achievement praxis*. City University of New York.

Haiven, M. (2014a). *Crises of imagination, crises of power: Capitalism, creativity and the commons*. Zed Books.

Haiven, M. (2014b). The ivory cage and the ghosts of academe: Labor and struggle in the edu-factory. *Truthout*. http://www.truth-out.org/news/item/23391-the-ivory-cage-and-the-ghosts-of-academe-labor-and-struggle-in-the-edu-factor

Hale, C. R. (2001). What is activist research? *Social Science Research Council*, 2(1–2), 13–15.

Hale, C. R. (2008). *Engaging contradictions: Theory, politics, and methods of activist scholarship*. University of California Press.

Halkovic, A., & Greene, A. C. (2015). Bearing stigma, carrying gifts: What colleges can learn from students with incarceration experience. *The Urban Review*, 47(4), 759–782.

Hall, L. L. (2015). Correctional education and recidivism: Toward a tool for reduction. *Journal of Correctional Education (1974–), 66*(2), 4–29.

Hamm, M. S. (1997). The offender self-help movement as correctional treatment. In P. Van Voorhis, M. Braswell, & D. Lester (Eds.), *Correctional counseling and rehabilitation* (4th ed., pp. 211–224). Anderson Publishing.

Handler, J. F., & Hasenfeld, Y. (2006). *Blame welfare, ignore poverty and inequality*. Cambridge University Press.

Haney, C. (2008). The consequences of prison life: Notes on the new psychology of prison effects. In D. Canter & R. Zukauskiene (Eds.), *Psychology and law* (pp. 143–165). Ashgate.

Haney, Craig. 2003. The psychological impact of incarceration: Implications for postprison adjustment. In J. Travis & M. Waul (Eds.), *Prisoners once removed: The impact of incarceration and reentry on children, families, and communities* (pp. 33–66). The Urban Institute.

Haraway, D. (1988). Situated knowledges: The science question in feminism and the privilege of partial perspective. *Feminist Studies*, 14(3), 575–599.

Harding, S. (2004). *The feminist standpoint theory reader: Intellectual and political controversies*. Routledge.

Hare, W. (1979). *Open-mindedness and education*. McGill-Queen's University Press.

Harkavy, I. (2006). The role of universities in advancing citizenship and social justice in the 21st century. *Education, Citizenship and Social Justice*, 1(1), 5–37.

Harm, A. L., & Bell, C. (2021). Teaching beyond the textbook: Integrating formerly incarcerated individuals into criminal justice learning environments. *Journal of Criminal Justice Education*, 32(1), 126–142.

Hartsock, N. (1983). The feminist standpoint: Toward a specifically feminist historical materialism. In *Money, sex and power: Towards a feminist historical materialism* (pp. 231–251). Longman.

Hernandez, J. L. (2019). *You are about to witness the strength of street knowledge: How formerly incarcerated Latinx/a/o students transfer their knowledge acquired through their lived experiences to find success in higher education and build resiliency*. California State University, Long Beach.

Herzing, R., & Piché, J. (2024). *How to abolish prisons*. Haymarket Books.

Hillyard, P., Sim, J., Tombs, S., & Whyte, D. (2004). Leaving a "stain upon the silence": Contemporary criminology and the politics of dissent. *British Journal of Criminology*, 44(3), 369–390.

Hochstetler, A., Murphy, D. S., & Simons, R. L. (2004). Damaged goods: Exploring predictors of distress in prison inmates. *Crime & Delinquency*, 50(3), 436–457.

Honeywell, D. (2021). The research experience from an insider perspective. In M. Maycock, R. Meek, & J. Woodall (Eds.), *Issues and innovations in prison health research*. Palgrave Macmillan. https://doi.org/10.1007/978-3-030-46401-1_5

Horowitz, V., & Uggen, C. (2018). Consistency and compensation in mercy: Commutation in the era of mass incarceration. *Social Forces*, 97(3), 1205–1230.

House, J. S. (1981). *Work stress and social support*. Addison-Wesley.

Hurwitz, J., & Peffley, M. (2005). Playing the race card in the post–Willie Horton era: The impact of racialized code words on support for punitive crime policy. *Public Opinion Quarterly*, 69(1), 99–112.

Huskies Post Prison Pathways. (n.d.). University of Tacoma, Washington. https://www.tacoma.uw.edu/hp3

Ikpe, I. B. (2015). The decline of the humanities and the decline of society. *Theoria*, 62(1), 50–66.

Irwin, J. (1972). The prison experience: The convict world. In *Correctional Institutions*. Lippincott.

Irwin, J. (1980). *Prisons in turmoil*. Little, Brown.

Irwin, J. (1987). *The felon*. University of California Press.

Irwin, J. (2005). *The warehouse prison: Disposal of the new dangerous class.* Roxbury Publishing.

Irwin, J., & Austin, J. (1994). *It's about time: America's imprisonment binge.* Wadsworth Publishing.

Irwin, J., & Cressey, D. R. (1962). Thieves, convicts and the inmate culture. *Social Problems, 10*(2), 142–155.

Jackson, B., & Reynolds, J. (2013), The price of opportunity: Race, student loan debt, and college achievement. *Sociological Inquiry, 83*(3), 335–368.

Jackson, G. (1970). *Soledad brother.* Bantam.

Jackson, G. (1972). *Blood in my eye.* Random House.

Jacques, S. (2014). The quantitative–qualitative divide in criminology: A theory of ideas' importance, attractiveness, and publication. *Theoretical Criminology, 18*(3), 317–334.

James, J., & Gordon, E. T. (2008). Activist scholars or radical subjects. In C. R. Hale (Eds.), *Engaging contradictions: Theory, politics, and methods of activist scholarship* (pp. 367–373). University of California Press.

James, N. (2014). *Offender reentry: Correctional statistics, reintegration into the community, and recidivism.* Congressional Research Service.

Jason, Z. (2018, Fall). Student activism 2.0: A look back at the history of student activism and whether today's protesters are making a difference. *Harvard Ed Magazine*, 20–27.

Jensen, S. Q. (2011). Othering, identity formation and agency. *Qualitative Studies, 2*(2), 63–78.

Jewkes, Y. (2012). Autoethnography and emotion as intellectual resources: Doing prison research differently. *Qualitative Inquiry, 18*(1), 63–75.

Jewkes, Y., & Letherby, G. (2001). Insiders and outsiders: Complex issues of identification, difference and distance in social research. *Auto/Biography Studies, 16*(2), 41–50.

Johnson, R. M., Alvarado, R. E., & Rosinger, K. O. (2021). What's the "problem" of considering criminal history in college admissions? A critical analysis of "Ban the Box" policies in Louisiana and Maryland. *The Journal of Higher Education, 92*(5),704–734.

Jones, A. (2018, December). Correctional control 2018: Incarceration and supervision by state. In *Prison Policy Initiative.* https://www. prisonpolicy.org/reports/

Jones, D. R. (2015). When the fallout of a criminal conviction goes too far: challenging collateral consequences. *Stanford Journal of Civil Rights & Civil Liberties, 11*(2), 237–268.

Jones, E. R. (1995). The failure of the "get tough" crime policy: Symposium, Violent Crime Control and Law Enforcement Act of 1994. *University of Dayton Law Review, 20*(2), 803–808.

Jones, R. S., Ross, J. I., Richards, S. C., & Murphy, D. S. (2009). The first dime: A decade of Convict Criminology. *The Prison Journal, 89*(2), 151–171.

Kaba, M. (2020, October 30). So you're thinking about becoming an abolitionist. *Level*,https://level.medium.com/so-youre-thinking-about-becoming-an-abolitionista436f8e31894.

Kalica, E. (2018). Convict criminology and abolitionism: Looking towards a horizon without prisons. *Journal of Prisoners on Prisons, 27*(2), 91–107.

Kallman, M. E. (2020). "Living more through knowing more": College education in prison classrooms. *Adult Education Quarterly*, 70(4), 321–339.

Kanuha, V. K. (2000). "Being" native versus "going native": Conducting social work research as an insider. *Social Work*, 45(5), 439–447.

Karabel, J. (2006). *The chosen: The hidden history of admission and exclusion at Harvard, Yale and Princeton*. First Mariner Books.

Kavish, D. R., Mullins, C. W., & Soto, D. A. (2016). Interactionist labeling: Formal and informal labeling's effects on juvenile delinquency. *Crime & Delinquency*, 62(10), 1313–1336.

Kerman, P. (2010). *Orange is the new black: My year in a women's prison*. Spiegel & Grau.

Kilty, J. M., & Fayter, R. (2022). Trigger warnings, feeling rules and other lessons from the inside: The emotional labour of qualitative prison research. In *Qualitative Research in Criminology: Cutting-Edge Methods* (pp. 107–123). Springer International Publishing.

King, M. L., Jr. (1992). Letter from Birmingham jail. *UC Davis Law Review*, 26, 835–851.

Kleck, G., Tark, J., & Bellows, J. J. (2006). What methods are most frequently used in research in criminology and criminal justice? *Journal of Criminal Justice*, 34(2), 147–152.

Knoester, M., & Au, W. (2017). Standardized testing and school segregation: Like tinder for fire? *Race Ethnicity and Education*, 20(1), 1–14.

Knopp, F. H., Boward, B., Morris, M., & Schnapper, M. B. (1976). *Instead of prisons: A handbook for abolitionists*. Prison Research Education Action Project.

Kropotkin, P. (1913). Prisons: Universities of Crime. *Mother Earth*, 8(8), 1–3.

Lageson, S. E. (2020). *Digital punishment: Privacy, stigma, and the harms of data-driven criminal justice*. Oxford University Press.

Larsen, M., & Piché, J. (2012). A challenge from and a challenge to convict criminology. *Journal of Prisoners on Prisons*, 21(1–2), 199–202.

LeBel, T. P. (2007). An examination of the impact of formerly incarcerated persons helping others. *Journal of Offender Rehabilitation*, 46(1–2), 1–24.

LeBel, T. P. (2009). Formerly incarcerated persons use of advocacy/activism as a coping orientation in the reintegration process. In B. Veysey, J. Christian, & D. J. Martinez (Eds.), *How offenders transform their lives* (pp. 165–187). Willan.

LeBel, T. P. (2012). Invisible stripes? Formerly incarcerated persons' perceptions of stigma. *Deviant Behavior*, 33(2), 89–107.

LeBel, T. P., Richie, M., & Maruna, S. (2015). Helping others as a response to reconcile a criminal past: The role of the wounded healer in prisoner reentry programs. *Criminal Justice and Behavior*, 42(1), 108–120.

Leitz, L. (2014). *Fighting for peace: Veterans and military families in the anti–Iraq war movement*. University of Minnesota Press.

Leitz, L. A. (2009). *Identities in conflict: Veterans and military family members in the anti-Iraq war movement* (Publication No. AAT 3371656) [Doctoral dissertation, University of California, Santa Barbara]. ProQuest Digital Dissertations.

Lennox, C., & Yıldız, Y. Y. (2020). Activist scholarship in human rights. *The International Journal of Human Rights*, 24(1), 4–27.

Lerner, M. J., & Montada, L. (1998). An overview: Advances in belief in a just world theory and methods. In L. Montada & M. J. Lerner (Eds.), *Responses to victimizations and belief in a just world* (pp. 1–7). Plenum.

Levinas, E. (1987). *Time and the other*. Duquesne University Press.

Liem, M., & Kunst, M. J. J. (2013). Is there a recognizable post-incarceration syndrome among released "lifers"? *International Journal of Law and Psychiatry*, 36(3–4), 333–337.

Lilly, R. J. (2009). Book review of Prison, Inc: A convict exposes life inside a private prison. *Criminal Justice Review*, 34(3), 460–463.

Lipsitz, R. (2022). *The rise of a new Left: How young radicals are shaping the future of American politics*. Verso Books.

Love, M. C., Roberts, J., & Klingele, C. M. (2013). *Collateral consequences of criminal convictions: Law, policy and practice*. Thomas West.

Loyd J. M. (2015). Carceral citizenship in an age of global apartheid. *Occasion*, 8, 1–15.

Luhtakallio, E. (2019). Group formation, styles, and grammars of commonality in local activism. *The British Journal of Sociology*, 70(4), 1159–1178.

Luxon, N. (2008). Ethics and subjectivity: Practices of self-governance in the late lectures of Michel Foucault. *Political Theory*, 36(3), 377–402.

Lynch, M. J. (2000). The power of oppression: Understanding the history of criminology as a science of oppression. *Critical Criminology*, 9(1), 144–152.

Lynn, V. (2021). Prison autobiographical narratives: Making sense of personal and social (racial) transformation. *Crime, Media, Culture*, 17(1), 65–84.

MacFarquhar, L. (2016, December 12). Building a school-to-prison pipeline. *The New Yorker*. https://www.newyorker.com/magazine/2016/12/12/the-ex-con-scholars-of-berkeley

Maghan, J. (2004). Ex-con professors [Review of the book *Convict criminology*, by J. I. Ross]. https://www.amazon.com/gp/customer-reviews/RUAHIVL1A1C38/ref=cm_cr_arp_d_viewpnt?ie=UTF8&ASIN=0534574335#RUAHIVL1A1C38

Manger, T., Eikeland, O. J., & Asbjørnsen, A. (2019). Why do not more prisoners participate in adult education? An analysis of barriers to education in Norwegian prisons. *International Review of Education*, 65(5), 711–733.

Martin, S. (2022, October 25). *Seeking a new story: On sobriety and the stories we tell about ourselves*. Literary Hub. https://lithub.com/seeking-a-new-story-on-sobriety-and-the-stories-we-tell-about-ourselves/

Martinson, R. (1974). What works?—Questions and answers about prison reform. *Public Interest*, 35(2), 22–54.

Maruna, S. (2001). *Making good: How ex-convicts reform and rebuild their lives*. American Psychological Association.

Maruna, S. (2017). Desistance as a social movement. *Irish Probation Journal*, 14, 5–20.

Maruna, S., & King, A. (2009). Once a criminal, always a criminal? "Redeemability" and the psychology of punitive public attitudes. *European Journal of Criminal Policy and Research*, 15(1–2), 7–24.

Marx, K. (1978). Theses on Feuerbach. In R. C. Tucker (Ed.), *The Marx–Engels reader* (2nd ed., pp. 143–145). Norton. (Original work published 1845)

Mathiesen, T. (1974) *The politics of abolition,* London: Martin Robertson.

Mathiesen, T. (2008). The abolitionist stance. *Journal of Prisoners on Prisons,* 17(2), 58–63.

Mauer, M., & Chesney-Lind, M. (Eds.). (2002). *Invisible punishment: The collateral consequences of mass imprisonment.* New Press.

McCann, W., Kowalski, M. A., Hemmens, C., & Stohr, M. K. (2021). An analysis of certificates of rehabilitation in the United States. *Corrections, 6*(1), 18–44.

McCorkel, J., & DeFina, R. (2019). Beyond recidivism: Identifying the liberatory possibilities of prison higher education. *Critical Education, 10*(7), 1–17.

McIntosh, P. (1989). White privilege: Unpacking the invisible knapsack. In M. McGoldrick (Ed.), *Re-visioning family therapy: Race, culture, and gender in clinical practice* (pp. 147–152). Guilford.

Melville, H. (2014) *Bartleby the scrivener: A story of Wall Street.* HarperCollins. (Original work published 1853)

Meyer, D. S., & Bourdon, K. (2020). Social movements and standing in the American gun debate. *Emory Law Journal, 69*(5), 919–1010.

Miller, R. J. (2021). *Halfway home: Race, punishment, and the afterlife of mass incarceration.* Little, Crown.

Miller, R. J., & Alexander, A. (2016). The price of carceral citizenship: Punishment, surveillance, and social welfare policy in an age of carceral expansion. *Michigan Journal of Race & Law,* 21(2), 291–314.

Miller, R. J., & Stuart, F. (2017). Carceral citizenship: Race, rights and responsibility in the age of mass supervision. *Theoretical Criminology,* 21(4), 532–548.

Mills, C. W. (1956). *The power elite.* Oxford University Press.

Mills, C. W. (1978). *The sociological imagination.* Penguin.

Misra, O. (2022, July 9). Underground Scholars: New grounds for change. *The UCSD Guardian.* https://ucsdguardian.org/2022/01/09/underground-scholars-new-grounds-for-change/

Mobley, A. (2003). Convict criminology: The two-legged data dilemma. In J. I. Ross & S. C. Richards (Eds.), *Convict criminology* (pp. 209–226). Wadsworth.

Moll, L. C., Amanti, C., Neff, D., & Gonzalez, N. (1992). Funds of knowledge for teaching: Using a qualitative approach to connect homes and classrooms. *Theory into Practice,* 31(2), 132–141.

Monobe, D., Bushman, B., & McCall, S. (2021). Collaboration among prison libraries, public, and academic libraries and the impact of censorship. In *Exploring the roles and practices of libraries in prisons: International perspectives* (pp. 105–117). Emerald Publishing.

Moody, J. (2022, March, 10). Formerly incarcerated students struggle to shed their past. *Inside Higher Ed.* https://www.insidehighered.com/news/2022/03/10/challenges-persist-formerly-incarcerated-students

Morash, M., Adams, E. A., Goodson, M. V., & Cobbina, J. E. (2020). Prison experiences and identity in women's life stories: Implications for reentry. In *Beyond Recidivism* (pp. 151–171). New York University Press.

Morris, R. (2000). *Stories of transformative justice.* Canadian Scholars' Press.

Motta, M. (2018). The dynamics and political implications of anti-intellectualism in the United States. *American Politics Research*, 46(3), 465–498.

Muir, E. (1981). *Civic ritual in renaissance Venice.* Princeton University Press.

Mukamal, D., Silbert, R. & Taylor, R. M. (2015, February). *Degrees of freedom: Expanding college opportunities for currently and formerly incarcerated Californians.* Stanford Criminal Justice Center and Chief Justice Earl Warren Institute on Law and Social Policy. https://www.law.berkeley.edu/files/DegreesofFreedom2015_FullReport.pdf

Murillo, D. (2021). *The possibility report: From prison to college degrees in California.* Campaign for College Opportunity. https://eric.ed.gov/?id=ED613716

Murphy, D. (2012). *Corrections and post-traumatic stress symptoms.* Carolina Academic Press.

Murphy, D. S. (2004). *Pre-prison, prison, post-prison: Post traumatic stress symptoms.* [Doctoral dissertation, Iowa State University]. Retrospective These and Dissertations. https://lib.dr.iastate.edu/cgi/viewcontent.cgi?article=1805&context=rtd

Murray, J. (2005). The effects of imprisonment on families and children of prisoners. In A. Liebling & S. Maruna (Eds.), *The effects of imprisonment* (pp. 442–492). Willan.

Naegler, L. (2022). Resistance and the radical imagination: A reflection on the role of the critical criminologist in social movements. *Critical Criminology*, 30(2), 225–235.

Negri, A., & Hardt, M. (2000). *Empire.* Harvard University Press.

NeSmith, R. C. (2015). Tough on crime or tough luck for the incarcerated? Exploring the adverse psychological impacts of mandatory minimum sentencing and pushing for action. *Law & Psychology Review*, 39, 253–266.

Newbold, G., & Ross, J. I. (2013). Convict criminology at the crossroads: Research note. *The Prison Journal*, 93(1), 4–10.

Newbold, G., Ross, J. I., Jones, R. S., Richards, R. C., & Lenza, M. (2014). Prison research from the inside: The role of convict autoethnography. *Qualitative Inquiry*, 20(4), 439–448.

Newfield, C. (2011). *Unmaking the public university: The forty-year assault on the middle class.* Harvard University Press.

Nietzsche, F. W. (1961). *Thus spoke Zarathustra* (R. J. Hollingdale, Ed., Trans.). Penguin.

Nietzsche, F. W. (1966). *Beyond good and evil: Prelude to a philosophy of the future* (W. Kaufmann, Trans.). Vintage.

Nuriddin-Little, A. H. (2020). *The forgotten voices: African American male adult learners and their experiences in higher education* [Unpublished Doctoral dissertation]. Rowan University.

Nyland, J. (2023, August 23). Winning strategy: Bringing educational opportunities to prisoners. *Financial Review.*https://www.afr.com/work-and-careers

/education/winning-strategy-bringing-education-opportunities-to-prisoners-20230810-p5dvfd

Okeke, C., & La Vigne, N. G. (2018, November 29). Restoring humanity: Changing the way we talk about people touched by the criminal justice system. *Urban Wire: Crime and Justice*. https://www.urban.org/urban-wire/restoring-humanity-changing-way-we-talk-about-people-touched-criminal-justice-system

Oliver, B. E. (2007). Three steps to reducing child molestation by adolescents. *Child Abuse & Neglect*, *31*(7), 683–689.

Ortiz, J. (2024). Beyond the ivory tower: The need for collective activism in convict criminology. *Journal of Prisoners on Prisons*, *33*(1), 76–86.

Ortiz, J. M., Cox, A., Kavish, D. R., & Tietjen, G. (2022). Let the convicts speak: A critical conversation of the ongoing language debate in convict criminology. *Criminal Justice Studies*, *35*(3), 255–273. https://doi.org/10.1080/1478601X.2022.2066661

Ortiz, J. M., & Jackey, H. (2019). The system is not broken, it is intentional: The prisoner reentry industry as deliberate structural violence. *The Prison Journal*, *99*(4), 484–503.

Parker, K., Graf, N., & Igielnik, R. (2019). *Generation Z looks a lot like millennials on key social and political issues*. Pew Research Center's Social & Demographic Trends Project. https://policycommons.net/artifacts/616984/generation-z-looks-a-lot-like-millennials-on-key-social-and-political-issues/1597711/.

Patel, V. (2015). Humanities Ph.D. enrollments shrink as programs cut back. *The Chronicle of Higher Education*, *62*(4), A10.

Pepinsky, H. (2013). Peacemaking criminology. *Critical Criminology*, *21*(3), 319–339.

Pepinsky, H. E., & Quinney, R. (Eds.). (1991). *Criminology as peacemaking* (Vol. 659). Indiana University Press.

Peters, M. A. (2019). Anti-intellectualism is a virus. *Educational Philosophy and Theory*, *51*(4), 357–363.

Pettit, B., & Gutierrez, C. (2018). Mass incarceration and racial inequality. *American Journal of Economics and Sociology*, *77*(3–4), 1153–1182.

Pinard, M. (2006). An integrated perspective on the collateral consequences of criminal convictions and reentry issues faced by formerly incarcerated individuals. *Boston University Law Review*, *86*(3), 623–685.

Pinard, M. (2010). Collateral consequences of criminal convictions: Confronting issues of race and dignity. *New York University Law Review*, *85*(2), 457–534.

Prison Journalism Project. (n.d.). Home page. https://prisonjournalismproject.org/.

Project Rebound CSULB. (n.d.). *What is Project Rebound at the Beach?* https://www.csulb.edu/student-affairs/project-rebound

Project Rebound Consortium. (2022, April 7). *Building community: Growing opportunity 2022 annual report*. chrome-extension://efaidnbmnnnibpcajpcglclefindmkaj/https://www.calstate.edu/impact-of-the-csu/government/Advocacy-and-State-Relations/legislativereports1/Project-Rebound-Report-2022.pdf

Pryor, M., & Thompkins, D. E. (2013). The disconnect between education and social opportunity for the formerly incarcerated. *American Journal of Criminal Justice*, *38*(3), 457–479.

Purvis, C., & Devine, J. (2023). Trauma and release from prison: Understanding and navigating trauma responses in the community. In *The Journey from Prison to Community* (pp. 63–84). Routledge.

Quach, K., Cerda-Jara, M., Deverux, R., & Smith, J. (2022). Prison, college, and the labor market: A critical analysis by formerly incarcerated and justice-impacted students. *The ANNALS of the American Academy of Political and Social Science*, *701*(1), 78–97.

Quinney, R. (1970). *The social reality of crime*. Little Brown.

Reich, S. E. (2019). *Beyond the criminal record: An examination of how and why redeemability beliefs and desistance signals matter for employers' willingness to hire a job applicant with a criminal record* [Unpublished doctoral dissertation]. The University of Queensland. University of Queensland eSpace.

Richards, S. C. (2004), Penitentiary dreams: Books will take you anywhere you want to go. *Journal of Prisoners on Prisons*, *13*, 60–73.

Richards, S. C. (2013). The new school of convict criminology thrives and matures. *Critical Criminology: An International Journal*, *21*(3), 375–387.

Richards, S. C., Lenza, M., Newbold, G., Jones, R. S., Murphy, D., & Grigsby, R. (2010). Prison as seen by convict criminologists. In M. Herzog-Evans (Ed.), *Transnational criminology manual* (Vol. 3, pp. 343–360). Wolf Legal Publishers.

Richards, S. C., & Ross, J. I. (2001). Introducing the New School of Convict Criminology. *Social Justice*, *28*(1), 177–190.

Richards, S. C., & Ross, R. I. (2003a, March). Convict perspective on the classification of prisoners. *Criminology & Public Policy*, *2*(2), 243–252.

Richards, S, C., & Ross J. I. (2003b). Ex-convict professors doing prison research. In *The state of corrections: 2002 proceedings ACA annual conferences* (pp. 163–168). American Correctional Association.

Richardson, E. G., & Hemenway, D. (2011). Homicide, suicide, and unintentional firearm fatality: comparing the United States with other high-income countries, 2003. *Journal of Trauma and Acute Care Surgery*, *70*(1), 238–243.

Rickard, D. (2016). *Sex offenders, stigma, and social control*. Rutgers University Press.

Rising Scholars CSULB. (n.d.). *CSULD Rising Scholars: Supporting students affected by the criminal justice system*. Instagram. Retrieved July 7, 2023 from https://www.instagram.com/risingscholarscsulb/?hl=en

Rising Scholars Network. (n.d.). *Serving California's incarcerated and formerly incarcerated community college students*. https://risingscholarsnetwork.org/

Roberts, D. E. (2019). Abolition constitutionalism. *Harvard Law Review*, *133*(1). https://harvardlawreview.org/2019/11/abolition-constitutionalism/

Rodriguez, A. E. (2018, February 27). FIST: Raising awareness for formerly incarcerated students. *Northeastern Illinois University's Independent*. https://neiuindependent.org/9927/features/fist-raising-awareness-for-formerly-incarcerated-students/

Rosales, J., & Walker, T. (2021). *The racist beginnings of standardized testing.* National Education Association. https://www.nea.org/advocating-for-change/new-from-nea/racist-beginnings-standardized-testing

Rosenthal, A., NaPier, E., Warth, P., & Weissman, M. (2015). *Boxed out: Criminal history screening and college application attrition.* Center for Community Alternatives, Inc. http://www.communityalternatives.org/fb/boxed-out.html

Ross, J. I. (2021). Context is everything: Understanding the scholarly, social, and pedagogical origins of Convict Criminology 1. In *Convict Criminology for the Future* (pp. 11–20). Routledge.

Ross, J. I. (2024, January 22). Should criminologists speak to the media. *Jeffery Ian Ross Blog.* https://jeffreyianross.medium.com/should-criminologists-speak-to-the-news-media-72d68590295e

Ross, J. I., & Darke, S. (2018). Interpreting the development and growth of convict criminology in Latin America. *Journal of Prisoners on Prisons,* 27(2), 108–117.

Ross, J. I., Jones, R. S., Lenza, M., & Richards, S. C. (2016). Convict criminology and the struggle for inclusion. *Critical Criminology: An International Journal,* 24(4), 489–501.

Ross, J. I., & Richards, S. C. (2003). *Convict criminology.* Wadsworth Publishing.

Ross, J. I., Richards, S. C., Newbold, G., Jones, R. S., Lenza, M., Murphy, D. S., Hogan, R., & Curry, G. D. (2010). Knocking on the ivory tower's door: The experience of ex-convicts applying for tenure-track university positions." *Journal of Criminal Justice Education,* 22, 267–285.

Ross, J .I., & Vianello, F. (Eds.) (2021). *Convict criminology for the future.* Routledge.

Saleh-Hanna, V., Williams, J. M., & Coyle, M. J. (2022). *Abolish criminology.* Routledge.

Samenow, S. E. (1984). *Inside the criminal mind.* Random House.

Sampson, R. J. (2019). Neighbourhood effects and beyond: Explaining the paradoxes of inequality in the changing American metropolis. *Urban Studies,* 56(1), 3–32.

Sanchez, J., & Tostlebe, J. (Hosts). (2022, January 17). Convict criminology with Grant Tietjen and Jennifer Ortiz (No. 36). [Audio podcast episode]. In *The Criminology Academy.* https://thecriminologyacademy.com/episode-36-ortiz-tietjen/

Schliehe, A., Laursen, J., & Crewe, B. (2022). Loneliness in prison. *European Journal of Criminology,* 19(6), 1595–1614.

Schmid, T., & Jones, R. (1991). Suspended identity: Identity transformation in a maximum security prison. *Symbolic Interaction,* 14(4), 415–432.

Second Chance Act, H.R. 1593, 110th Cong. (2007). https://www.govtrack.us/congress/bills/110/hr1593

Shafer, S. (2023, August 17). Newsom aims to transform San Quentin into a model for prisoner Rehabilitation. *National Public Radio.* https://www.npr.org/2023/08/17/1194349653/newsom-aims-to-transform-san-quentin-into-a-model-for-prisoner-rehabilitation

Shannon, S. K. S., Uggen, C., Schnittker, J., Thompson, M., Wakefield, S., & Massoglia, M. (2017). The growth, scope, and spatial distribution of people with felony records in the United States, 1948–2010. *Demography*, *54*(5), 1795–1818.

Shaw, R. F. (2009). Unorthodox criminologists: Part II, Angela Y. Davis and the prison abolition movement [Special issue]. *Contemporary Justice Review*, *12*(1), 101–104.

Sheehan, S. T. (2012). *Project rebound: The road to successful reintegration* [Unpublished thesis,].San Francisco State University.

Sheldon, R. G. (2008). *Controlling the dangerous classes: A history of criminal justice in America.* Pearson.

Simon, J. (2007). *Governing through crime: How the fear of crime transformed American democracy and created a culture of fear.* Oxford University Press.

Slaughter, S., & Rhoades, G. (2000, April). The neo-liberal university. In *New Labor Forum* (pp. 73–79). Labor Resource Center, Queens College, City University of New York.

Smith, C., Esq. (2013). Nothing about us without us! The failure of the modern juvenile justice system and a call for community-based justice. *Journal of Applied Research on Children: Informing Policy for Children at Risk*, 4(1), Article 11. http://digitalcommons.library.tmc.edu/childrenatrisk/vol4/iss1/11

Smith, D. E. (1987). *The everyday world as problematic: A feminist sociology.* Northeastern University Press.

Smith, J. M. (2012). Maintaining racial inequality through crime control: Mass incarceration and residential segregation. *Contemporary Justice Review*, *15*(4), 469–484.

Smith, J. M. (2021). The formerly incarcerated, advocacy, activism, and community reintegration. *Contemporary Justice Review*, 24(1), 43–63.

Smith, J. M., & Kinzel, A. (2021). Carceral citizenship as strength: Formerly incarcerated activists, civic engagement, and criminal justice transformation. *Critical Criminology*, 29(1), 93–110.

Soto, O. F. (2016). *On the outs: Reentry and the social consequences of coming home* [Unpublished doctoral dissertation]. California State University–San Marcos.

Soto, O. F. (2020). "We will leave the lights on for you": Political education and the push for a revival of radical criminology from a formerly incarcerated Chicano activist-scholar. *Journal of Higher Education Theory and Practice*, 20(16), 119–127.

Spivak, G. C. (1985). The Rani of Sirmur: An essay in reading the archives. *History and Theory*, 24(3), 247–272.

Spivak, G. C. (2023). Can the subaltern speak? In *Imperialism* (pp. 171–219). Routledge.

St. John, W. (2003, August 9). Professors with a past. *New York Times*.

Stabile, S. J. (2016). Othering and the law. *University of St. Thomas Law Journal*, 12(2), 381–410.

Stanley, J. (2020). *How fascism works: The politics of us and them.* Random House Trade Paperbacks.

Strauss, A., & J. Corbin. 1998. *Basics of qualitative research: Grounded theory procedures and techniques.* Sage.

Sudbury, J. (2009). Challenging penal dependency: Activist scholars and the anti-prison movement. In J. Sudbury & M. Okazawa-Rey (Eds.), *Activist scholarship: Antiracism, feminism, and social change* (pp. 17–35). Boulder, CO: Paradigm Publishers.

Sudbury, J. (2015). Challenging penal dependency: Activist scholars and the antiprison movement. In J. Sudbury & M. Okazawa-Rey (Eds.), *Activist scholarship: Antiracism, feminism, and social change* (pp. 17–35). Routledge.

Sudbury, J., & Okazawa-Rey, M. (Eds.). (2009). *Activist scholarship: Antiracism, feminism, and social change*. Boulder, CO: Paradigm Publishers.

Sykes, Gresham (1974). *The society of captives: A study in a maximum security prison*. Princeton University Press. (Original work published 1958)

Tamboukou, M. (2012) Truth telling in Foucault and Arendt: Parrhesia, the pariah and academics in dark times. *Journal of Education Policy*, 27(6), 849–865.

Taylor, I., Walton, P., & Young, J. (1973). *The new criminology: For a social theory of deviance*. Routledge and Kegan Paul.

Taylor, N. (2008, July). *Delivering culturally competent mentoring services to low-income Latino youth*. U.S. Department of Education, Office of Safe and Drug-Free Schools, Mentoring Resource Center. https://educationnorthwest.org/sites/default/files/resources/luz_study.pdf

Taylor, R. M. (2017). Education for autonomy and open-mindedness in diverse societies. *Educational Philosophy and Theory*, 49(14), 1326–1337.

Tewksbury, R. (2009). Qualitative versus quantitative methods: Understanding why qualitative methods are superior for criminology and criminal justice. *Journal of Theoretical and Philosophical Criminology*, 1(1), 38–58.

Tewksbury, R., DeMichele, M. T., & Miller, J. M. (2005). Methodological orientations of articles appearing in criminal justice's top journals: Who publishes what and where. *Journal of Criminal Justice Education*, 16(2), 265–279.

Thompson, H. A. (2017). *Blood in the water: The Attica Prison uprising of 1971 and its legacy*. Vintage Books, Random House.

Tietjen, G. (2013). *Exploring educational pathways: Reintegration of the formerly incarcerated through the academy* [Unpublished doctoral dissertation, University of Nebraska–Lincoln]. Digital Commons.

Tietjen, G. (2019). Convict criminology: Learning from the past, taking on the present, expanding to meet the future. *Critical Criminology*, 27(1), 1–14.

Tietjen, G., Burnett, J., & Jessie, B. O. (2021). Onward and upward: The significance of mentorship for formerly incarcerated students and academics. *Critical Criminology: An International Journal*, 29, 633–647. https://doi.org/10.1007/s10612-020-09507-3

Tietjen, G., Garneau, G., Horowitz, V., & Joie Noel, H. (2018). Showing up: The gendered effects of social engagement on educational participation in United States correctional facilities. *The Prison Journal*, 98(3), 359–381.

Tietjen, G., & Kavish, D. (2021). In the pool without a life jacket: Status fragility and convict criminology in the current criminological era. In J. I. Ross & F. Vianello (Eds.), *Convict criminology for the future* (pp. 66–81). Routledge.

Tietjen, G., Ponder, H., & Garneau, C. (2019, November 15). *Trauma as a predictor of correctional education usage: A mixed methods analysis* [Panel presentation and working paper]. 2019 American Society of Criminology.

Tillman, L. C. (2002). Culturally sensitive research approaches: An African-American perspective. *Educational Researcher*, *31*(9), 3–12.

Transforming, Renewing, Achieving, and Connecting (TRAC). (n.d.). TRAC (Transforming, Renewing, Achieving, and Connecting), A Higher Education in Prison Program. https://www.unomaha.edu/college-of-public-affairs-and-community-service/criminology-and-criminal-justice/undergraduate-programs/trac.php

Travis, J. (2005). *But they all come back: Facing the challenges of prisoner reentry*. The Urban Institute.

Trivedi, C., & Ray, S. M. (2024). Equity, empowerment, and social justice: Social entrepreneurship for formerly incarcerated individuals. *New Horizons in Adult Education and Human Resource Development*, 36(1), 48–64.

Tuckman, B. (1965). Developmental sequence in small groups. *Psychological Bulletin*, 63(6), 384–399.

Uggen, C., & Blahnik, L. (2016). The increasing stickiness of public labels. In J. Shapland, S. Farrall, and A. Bottoms (Eds.), *Global perspectives on desistance*, (pp. 238–259. Routledge.

Uggen, C., Manza, J., & Behrens, A. (2013). "'Less than the average citizen': Stigma, role transition and the civic reintegration of convicted felons." In *After crime and punishment* (pp. 261–293). Willan.

Uggen, C., & Stewart, R. (2014). Piling on: Collateral consequences and community supervision. *Minnesota Law Review*, 99, 1871.

Underground Scholars Initiative. (n.d.). University of California Berkeley. https://callink.berkeley.edu/organization/usi._

Underground Scholars News. (2022, January 12). Newsletter [Blog]. https://undergroundscholars.berkeley.edu/blog/2022/1/12/january-2022-newsletter

Vázquez, I. R. (2018). European and US influences on the 19th century prison reform. In *The Western Codification of Criminal Law* (pp. 413–427). Springer.

Vélez-Ibáñez, C. G., & Greenberg, J. B. (1992). Formation and transformation of funds of knowledge among US-Mexican households. *Anthropology & Education Quarterly*, 23(4), 313–335.

Vianello, F. (2015). Never say never: Against the life sentence, in favor of an unsettled penality. *Sicurezza e scienze sociali*, 2, 79–95.

Vianello, F. (2020). Developing convict criminology: Notes from Italy. In *Convict criminology for the future* (pp. 98–111). Routledge.

Wagner, P. (2014, April 15). Mass incarceration: The whole pie. *Prison Legal News*. https://www.prisonlegalnews.org/news/2014/apr/15/mass-incarceration-the-whole-pie/

Wakefield, S. 2016. Changing the ties that bind. *Criminology & Public Policy*, *15*(2), 543–549.

Walker, M. (2016). Race making in a penal institution. *American Journal of Sociology*, *121*(4), 1051–1078.

Warr, J. (2016). The deprivation of certitude, legitimacy and hope: Foreign national prisoners and the pains of imprisonment. *Criminology & Criminal Justice*, *16*(3), 301–318.

Weber, M. (1958). Characteristics of bureaucracy. in H. Gerth and C. W. Mills (Eds.), *From Max Weber: Essays in sociology* (pp. 196–198). Galaxy Books.

Weigert, K. M. (2010). Structural violence. In G. Fink (Ed.), *Stress of war, conflict and disaster* (pp. 126–133). Elsevier.

Weis, V. V. (2020). It's time! Towards a southern convict criminology 1. In *Convict criminology for the future* (pp. 112–126). Routledge.

Weiss, D. B., & MacKenzie, D. L. (2010). A global perspective on incarceration: How an international focus can help the United States reconsider its incarceration rates. *Victims and Offenders*, *5*(3), 268–282.

Weissman, S. (2023, November 17). Reinstating Pell Grants in prisons moves slowly after 26-year ban. *Inside Higher Ed.* https://www.insidehighered.com/news/governance/state-oversight/2023/11/17/after-26-year-ban-reinstating-pell-prisons-moves-slowly

Western, B., & Pettit, B. (2010). Incarceration & social inequality. *Daedalus*, *139*(3), 8–19.

Wilkerson, I. (2020). *Caste: The origins of our discontents.* Random House.

Williams, C. L., & Heikes, E. J. (1993). The importance of researcher's gender in the in-depth interview: Evidence from two case studies of male nurses. *Gender & Society*, *7*(2), 280–291.

Williams, L. (2018). From ex-convict to student, life on a college campus. *For the media.* https://www.csulb.edu/for-the-media/article/ex-convict-to-student-life-a-college-campus

Williams, T., & Kaplan, T. (2019, August 20). The criminal justice debate has changed drastically: Here's why. *New York Times.* https://www. nytimes.com/2019/08/20/us/politics/criminal-justice-reform-sanders-warren. html

Wincup, E. (2017). *Criminological research: Understanding qualitative methods* (2nd ed.) Sage.

Woodall, D. R. (2020). *Formerly incarcerated activism as transformative intervention: A feminist examination of identity, intersecting oppressions, self, and social change through carceral citizen resistance* [Unpublished doctoral dissertation]. University of Georgia.

Yeager, M. G. (2004). A partial test of life-course theory on a prison release cohort. *Justice Policy Journal*, *1*(3), 1–26.

Young, J. (2002). Critical criminology in the twenty first century: Critique, irony, and the always unfinished. In K. Carrington & R. Hogg (Eds.), *Critical criminology: Issues, debates, challenges* (pp. 251–274). Willan.

Zinn, H. (2014). *Justice in everyday life: The way it really works.* Haymarket.

Index

Founded in 1893,
UNIVERSITY OF CALIFORNIA PRESS
publishes bold, progressive books and journals on topics in the arts, humanities, social sciences, and natural sciences—with a focus on social justice issues—that inspire thought and action among readers worldwide.

The UC PRESS FOUNDATION
raises funds to uphold the press's vital role as an independent, nonprofit publisher, and receives philanthropic support from a wide range of individuals and institutions—and from committed readers like you. To learn more, visit ucpress.edu/supportus.

www.ingramcontent.com/pod-product-compliance
Lightning Source LLC
Chambersburg PA
CBHW020852270326
41928CB00006B/668
* 9 7 8 0 5 2 0 3 9 4 0 8 7 *